POPULAR RECREATIONS
IN ENGLISH SOCIETY
1700–1850

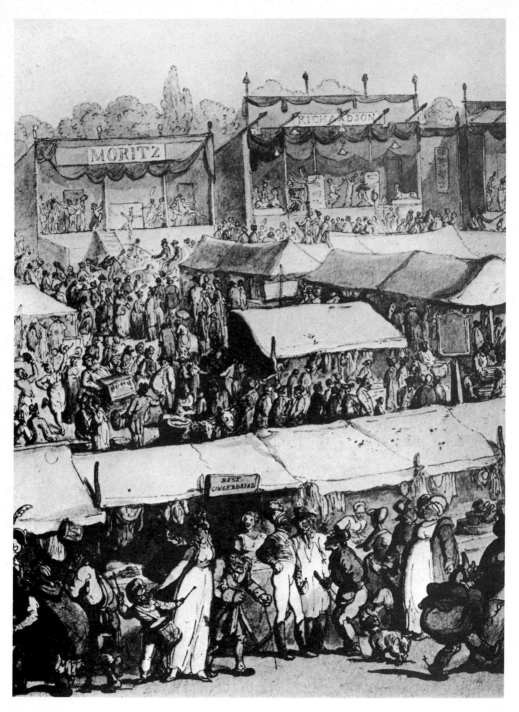

Brook Green Fair by Thomas Rowlandson

POPULAR RECREATIONS IN ENGLISH SOCIETY 1700-1850

Robert W. Malcolmson

Associate Professor of History
Queen's University, Kingston, Ontario

CAMBRIDGE UNIVERSITY PRESS

Cambridge

London   New York   Melbourne

Published by the Syndics of the Cambridge University Press
The Pitt Building, Trumpington Street, Cambridge CB2 1RP
Bentley House, 200 Euston Road, London NW1 2DB
32 East 57th Street, New York, NY 10022, USA
296 Beaconsfield Parade, Middle Park, Melbourne 3206, Australia

Library of Congress catalogue card number: 72–91958

ISBN 0 521 20147 0 hard covers
ISBN 0 521 29595 5 paperback

First published 1973
First paperback edition 1979

First printed in Great Britain by
Western Printing Services Ltd, Bristol
Reprinted in Great Britain by
Kingprint Limited, Richmond, Surrey

I turn, without shrinking, from cloud-borne angels, from prophets, sibyls, and heroic warriors, to an old woman bending over her flower-pot, or eating her solitary dinner, while the noonday light, softened perhaps by a screen of leaves, falls on her mob-cap, and just touches the rim of her spinning-wheel, and her stone jug, and all those cheap common things which are the precious necessaries of life to her – or I turn to that village wedding, kept between four brown walls, where an awkward bridegroom opens the dance with a high-shouldered, broad-faced bride, while elderly and middle-aged friends look on, with very irregular noses and lips, and probably with quart-pots in their hands, but with an expression of unmistakable contentment and goodwill. 'Foh!' says my idealistic friend, 'what vulgar details! What good is there in taking all these pains to give an exact likeness of old women and clowns? What a low phase of life! What clumsy, ugly people!'

George Eliot, *Adam Bede*, Book ıı, chapter xvii

To
my Mother and Father

Contents

Plates

Preface

Two persons have been particularly responsible for arousing and sustaining my interest in the study of English history. My principal debt since beginning this research in 1966 has been to Mr Edward Thompson, under whose supervision an earlier version of this study was presented as a doctoral dissertation at the University of Warwick. He suggested some of the early lines of enquiry, frequently offered advice on source materials, on several occasions suggested further, and fruitful, approaches to the subject, and (in particular) read and criticized my various pieces of writing with great care and penetration. The excellence of this supervision and advice has been a major source of encouragement during the past several years. My other considerable obligation is to Mr John Beattie of the University of Toronto, whose admirable lectures on eighteenth-century England first interested me in this period. I am also indebted to him for numerous personal kindnesses, and for his helpful suggestions concerning the transition of this study from a thesis to a book.

A number of other people have taken the trouble to provide me with valuable references and put at my disposal some of their expert knowledge. Mr John Rule has at various times advised me on Cornish sources; Mr Brian Harrison has been helpful on several occasions, particularly during the early stages of research; and my colleague Mr Paul Christianson kindly read and commented on the first chapter. I am also grateful for the assistance of Mr Christopher Crowder, Mr Eric Dunning, Mr William Keith, Mr Roy Palmer, Mr Rex Russell, Mr Malcolm Thomas, and Mr Barrie Trinder. Thanks are also due to those who allowed me to consult sources in their custody: the officers of the Royal Society for the Prevention of Cruelty to Animals, especially Mr T. Richardson; the Librarian of the Society of Antiquaries of London; the proprietors of the *Stamford Mercury*; and the management of the Essex Chronicle Series Limited and Berrow's Newspapers Limited of Worcester. The staffs of many public institutions courteously facilitated the tasks of research, especially those of the British Museum's Reading Room, Department of Manuscripts, and the Colindale Newspaper Library; the University of London; the Institute of Historical Research; the Public Record Office; the Bodleian Library; the Cambridge University Library; the Northampton Borough Library; and numerous County Record Offices, particularly those of the Bedfordshire and Essex Record Offices. For financial assistance I am indebted to the Canada Council and the Advisory Research Committee of Queen's University. Mrs Beverly Phillips was responsible for the excellent quality of the final typescript. My wife Patricia tactfully provided those services and conveniences which seem to be conventionally expected of wives, and also gave me the benefit of her own training and critical insights as a historian.

The italicization in quotations from primary sources has only been retained when emphasis is clearly required. Otherwise quotations have not been modernized, except in a very few cases on grounds of clarity. Before 1752 the year is always taken to begin on 1 January.

Kingston, Ontario   R.M.
October 1972

Acknowledgements

The author and publisher are grateful to the Record Society of Lancashire and Cheshire for granting permission to reproduce material from *The Great Diurnal of Nicholas Blundell, Vol. 2. 1712–1719*, ed. J. J. Bagley. The transcription of a Crown-copyright record (PRO HO 42/46 128) appears by permission of the Controller of H.M. Stationery Office.

Abbreviations

B.M.	British Museum
B.M. Brand	British Museum copy of John Brand, *Observations on Popular-Antiquities* (142.e.1, 2)
P.R.O.	Public Record Office
R.O.	Record Office
V.C.H.	*Victoria County History*

Introduction

A visitor to England around 1700 could easily spend many months in the country and still remain largely uninformed about the recreations of the common people. All the foreign tourists were gentlemen, and they had (at best) only an incidental interest in popular customs and manners; but there would have been more cause for their ignorance than simple social myopia. For there were few fixed, concrete features in the English setting which could be seen to be obviously connected with recreational activities. The modern tourist unavoidably forms some sort of impression about the people's pastimes and diversions – he cannot fail to notice the playing fields, stadia, bingo halls, television sets, cinemas, and amusement centres – but his eighteenth-century counterpart was less favourably placed. The popular recreations of the day, when they were institutionalized aspects of social life, were normally a part of traditions and customs which left few physical remains after their practice; most sports and pastimes had not yet developed special, full-time locations for their exercise. The popular playgrounds were usually constructed from the materials of everyday life – the market place, the public thoroughfares, the churchyard, an uncultivated close, the open fields. They would not have been immediately recognized by outsiders as places of recreation. The one fixture which the visitor would have readily associated with popular diversions was the public house. But otherwise, though he might have seen a game of quoits by an alehouse, or a crowd being entertained by a harlequin, or several boys playing pitch and toss, he probably would have learned little about those major seasonal festivities which were of the first importance in the recreational life of the common people. He might have taken the opportunity to see one of the well publicized sporting diversions which tended to cut across class lines – perhaps a boxing match, a cock-fight, or a horse race – but his knowledge of most of the seasonal recreations would have depended very much on chance, whether or not he was in a particular locality at the time when a holiday was customarily observed.

The native gentlemen were (at least potentially) in a much more favourable position. The squires and parsons in the countryside had frequent contact with the labouring people in the course of their routine activities. Many of them were intimately involved in the seasonal rhythms of agriculture and the celebrations of the ecclesiastical calendar which together provided the basic framework for recreational customs. There must have been a widespread awareness of these customs, especially the more public events, for most of them could not have passed unnoticed; moreover, the participation of the local gentry was sometimes an essential ingredient of the festivities. The gentry, however, were not students of popular behaviour. Their learning and their enquiries were pursued in the traditional directions, those which supported the distinctive culture of their own class. Most of their observations on popular habits were incidental, often arising out of practical concerns; only a few writers attempted systematic studies.[1] A good deal must have been known about the customs of the people, but the efforts to communicate this knowledge were meagre and generally perfunctory. Contemporaries were not entirely unaware of this lacuna. 'The study of popular antiquities,' observed one writer, 'though the materials for it lie so widely diffused, and indeed seem to obtrude themselves upon every one's attention, in proportion to the extent of his intercourse with the common people, do not appear to have engaged so much of the notice of enquirers into human life and manners as might have been expected.'[2] Writing in 1778 of Northumberland, William Hutchinson remarked on the 'many ancient Customs [which] prevail in this County, the familiarity or outward insignificance of which occasion them to pass without much attention'.[3] Here in fact were probably the main inhibitions: common, unexceptional experiences were not usually considered to be subjects worthy of notice, especially when the experiences were principally those of the common people. In most cases they passed by every year unrecorded, surviving only in the memories of their participants.

For the historian, then, these kinds of popular experience are apt to be elusive. The subjects of his studies were men of little power and formal education, and consequently their lives are only scantily documented. Even after considerable labour among the primary sources, many of his questions remain only partially answered. The difficulties for historical understanding, however, are by no means insurmountable. Although there is no substantial core of primary evidence, there is much scattered, fragmentary, often incidental material, and it is this kind of evidence which provides the major support for our study. Men of education may have seldom paid special attention to the pastimes of the people (unless it was to disparage them), but for various reasons they did not (or could not) altogether avoid mentioning them. Country diarists often noticed the diversions of the villagers they knew and of their servants. Many of the growing number of publications on parish, county, and town antiquities included a few details on the existing state of the locality's amusements. Newspapers sometimes alluded to recreational practices. Relevant references can also be found in the papers bearing on local government. Occasionally short accounts on popular customs were contributed to one

---

[1] There are two important eighteenth-century studies of popular customs, both of which include substantial discussions of recreations: Henry Bourne, *Antiquitates Vulgares; or, the Antiquities of the Common People* (Newcastle, 1725), and John Brand, *Observations on Popular Antiquities* (Newcastle upon Tyne, 1777). The first work to be devoted exclusively to recreations was Joseph Strutt, *Glig-Gamena Angel-Deod; or, the Sports and Pastimes of the People of England* (London, 1801). On these and several of the other early folklorists, see Richard M. Dorson, *The British Folklorists: A History* (Chicago, 1968), chap. 1.

[2] *Monthly Magazine*, v (1798), 273.

[3] William Hutchinson, *A View of Northumberland* (2 vols.; Newcastle, 1778), II, Appendix, p. 3.

of the principal periodicals. And most significantly, when genteel and plebeian interests clashed (as they increasingly did during this period), when the familiarity of popular diversions no longer guaranteed their ready acceptance, the dissatisfactions and disputes which ensued brought them a greater degree of public, and consequently documented, acknowledgement.

The most significant bibliographical feature of this enquiry is the lack of a well-defined body of essential sources. Although popular recreations were certainly organized, most of them were organized within an oral tradition, not an institutional framework which involved the keeping of written records. Consequently, one cannot be directed to appropriate categories of documents in county archives or the Public Record Office. In contrast to most historical studies, then, no primary sources are conspicuously of central importance. On the other hand, an impressive range of material is found to be relevant, or potentially relevant. Since there is no central body of source material, no nucleus to which the less substantial evidence can be related, one is obliged to rely almost entirely on fragments of information, drawn from a large number of scattered sources.

The scope of our study is a direct consequence of these limitations in the sources. Because the sources are so scattered and fragmentary, and so thinly available in local materials, it is necessary to draw one's evidence from all parts of the country in order to be able to offer a reasonably thorough account of recreational life. The returns are most satisfactory if the research net is widely cast; a close study of one or two localities is likely to be less rewarding, especially for the eighteenth century. Local studies, of course, are important, but it is not feasible to investigate the popular recreations of a particular county in detail without at the same time committing oneself to a more general study of local society; one would then become primarily an expert on the locality as a whole rather than a historian with an especial interest in recreations. In the course of intensive local research out-of-the-way evidence which relates to recreations would probably be uncovered, sometimes inadvertently, and this would undoubtedly be a real gain. Recreational themes have been usefully discussed in a recent work on the Cornish miner,[4] and studies of this kind are of considerable value for the historian with an interest in some particular aspect of popular culture. At the moment, unfortunately, such accounts are exceptional, and their information on recreations, if it is to be used to general advantage, must be associated with evidence on similar themes from other regions. An attempt at a full-scale study of popular recreations, then, requires something approaching a national canvass.

This approach has its problems as well as its strengths. Although the perspective may be national, much of the relevant evidence is local, and local materials may be misinterpreted, or not fully exploited, if one has only a sketchy knowledge of the local context. The local historian can sometimes shed added light on a particular incident, and pursue its implications further, because of his knowledge of local traditions and circum-

[4] John G. Rule, 'The Labouring Miner in Cornwall c. 1740–1870: A Study in Social History' (unpubl. Ph.D. thesis, University of Warwick, 1971), pp. 72ff. and 304ff.

stances and the actors involved. On the other hand, the general historian
has the advantage of a comparative perspective: he is able to consider one
custom in relation to other customs, the traditions in one area in the light
of traditions elsewhere; he can focus on the common aspects of social
behaviour, and thus discuss the shared characteristics of football or bull-
baiting, of May Day or the parish feast. He is especially concerned to
understand the regularities of social life, those features of recreations which
recur in a similar form in different localities. Although the diversity of
behaviour, and the importance of regional variations, must be frequently
acknowledged, it is still possible to discern social patterns which were
widely (if not universally) applicable, and movements of social change
which affected many (if not all) parts of the country. This, then, is the
orientation which has shaped the structure of the present enquiry

The meaning of the term 'recreation', about which sociologists have
debated, need not detain us: for a definition we may draw on Samuel
Johnson, who spoke of 'diversion' (the eighteenth-century equivalent of
recreation) as 'Sport; something that unbends the mind by turning it off
from care.'[5]

[5] Samuel Johnson, A *Dictionary of the English Language* (2 vols.; London, 1755).

1

Popular recreations before the eighteenth century

The status of popular recreations in English society has never been completely secure. Moralists and reformers, those least hesitant of writers, have seldom been fully satisfied with the character or consequences of people's pastimes (especially those of the common people), and many of their works are found to include an abundance of allusions to the evils and inconveniences which were thought to be associated with recreational practices. Indeed, the historical records of most periods are much more liberally stocked with evidence concerning the anxieties of the critics of recreations than the sentiments of their supporters. In the Middle Ages, for instance, some sports were charged with distracting men from more useful activities, most notably the practice of archery.[1] Medieval preachers often denounced those festive gatherings which commonly degenerated into occasions of drunkenness, brawling, and indecent revelry; and sporting contests, they knew, were sometimes the cause of riot and bloodshed. Games were frequently played in churchyards, and this was another source of complaint. Moreover, many popular diversions occurred at times when people were expected to be devoting themselves to religious observances. It was often regretted that Sundays and other holy days were apparently valued less for their legitimate functions, worship and participation in the rites of the Church, than for their secular pleasures; such worldly indulgences, it was argued, seriously interfered with the labour of impressing upon the Christian flocks the necessity of piety and religious obedience.[2] During the Tudor and early Stuart periods civil and ecclesiastical courts dealt with the transgressions of Sabbath dancers, dicers, bear-baiters, bowlers, and football players; for the most part these prosecutions were aimed at people who amused themselves during the time of divine service, thereby neglecting their own religious duties and (in many instances) distracting others from worship as well.[3] Civil and ecclesiastical discipline,

---

[1] For examples see Francis P. Magoun, Jr, 'Football in Medieval England and in Middle English Literature', *American Historial Review*, xxxv (1929–30), 37–8, 40, and 42; and Austin L. Poole (ed.), *Medieval England* (2 vols.; Oxford, 1958), ii, 625–6.

[2] See especially G. R. Owst, 'The People's Sunday Amusements in the Preaching of Mediaeval England', *Holborn Review*, N.S., xvii (January 1926), 32–45; and many passing references in two books by the same author, *Preaching in Medieval England* (Cambridge, 1926), and *Literature and Pulpit in Medieval England* (Oxford, 2nd edn, 1961).

[3] F. G. Emmison, *Elizabethan Life: Disorder* (Chelmsford, 1970), pp. 229–30; Dorothy M. Owen, 'Episcopal Visitation Books', *History*, xlix (1964), 185 and 187–8; J. C. Atkinson (ed.), *North Riding Quarter Sessions Records* (3 vols.; London, 1884–5), i, 151, 197, 201; ii, 34, 132; H. H. Copnall, *Nottinghamshire County Records: Notes and Extracts from the Nottinghamshire County Records of the 17th Century* (Nottingham, 1915), pp. 52–3; R. F. B. Hodgkinson, 'Extracts from the Act Books of the Arch-

it is clear, often had to be defended against the counter-morality of popular sports and festivities.

The hostile disposition towards recreational practices which is found in medieval sources continued to be prominent in early modern England. Indeed, during the years between the accession of Elizabeth and the later seventeenth century the question of popular recreation provoked considerable controversy. This, of course, was only one of the many moral and social issues which came under particularly close scrutiny during a period of acute cultural upheaval. The Protestant Reformation, in rejecting so many of the habits and assumptions of the past, stimulated the growth of an outlook which was critical and independent and intensely suspicious of many established traditions; within a relatively short period of time this 'reformist' disposition had developed powerful roots in English society. Reform, once sanctioned and initiated from above, was not easily confined within officially determined channels. Differences arose over how much change was desirable, how far reform should go. Traditions which some reformers found little reason to condemn were judged by others to be prime candidates for a thorough cleansing. Bitter disputes arose over a number of major issues: religious doctrine, liturgical practices, church government, public and personal morality. The legitimacy of widely accepted customs was seriously questioned by some men, and one of the specific concerns which developed within this reforming movement was the manner in which popular recreations were customarily observed.

Much of this dissatisfaction with traditional recreations was generated by the movement of dissident puritanism which had emerged during the reign of Elizabeth. The puritan outlook on established sports and festivities has been often represented.[4] For these 'preciser' sort of people the traditions of popular leisure were objectionable on a number of grounds: they were thought to be profane and licentious – they were occasions of worldly indulgence which tempted men from a godly life; being rooted in pagan and popish practices, they were rich in the sort of ceremony and ritual which poorly suited the Protestant conscience; they frequently involved a desecration of the Sabbath and an interference with the worship of the true believers; they disrupted the peaceable order of society, distracting men from their basic social duties – hard work, thrift, personal restraint, devotion to family, a sober carriage. 'Any exercise', declared Phillip Stubbes, 'which withdraweth us from godliness, either upon the sabaoth or any

deacons of Nottingham', *Transactions of the Thoroton Society*, xxx (1926), 42–6, and xxxi (1927), 142–4; Bedfordshire R.O., A.B.C. 4, pp. 1, 3, 7, 8, 10, 15, 28, 32, 55–7, 61, 64, and 66.

[4] See especially Christopher Hill, *Society and Puritanism in Pre-Revolutionary England* (London, 1964), chap. 5; Thomas G. Barnes, 'County Politics and a Puritan Cause Célèbre: Somerset Churchales, 1633', *Transactions of the Royal Historical Society*, 5th series, IX (1959), 103–22; and Dennis Brailsford, *Sport and Society: Elizabeth to Anne* (London and Toronto, 1969), pp. 127–33. The problem of what is meant by 'puritan' is a matter of some controversy. Since our concern is confined largely to one feature of the early modern period – that is, the relatively rigorous approach to questions of public and personal morality – and since this disposition was normally more pronounced among the puritan believers, it is not necessary to become involved in those larger issues which are relevant to a full understanding of the people called puritans. Dis-

other day else, is wicked, and to be forbidden.'[5] Recreations, said William Perkins, 'must tend also to the glory of God . . . the scope and end of all recreations is, that God may be honoured in and by them'.[6]

The puritan disposition was energetically reformist, opposed to conventional (especially primitive, medieval) practices, earnestly soul-searching, anxious about sin and salvation, firm on the necessity of dutifulness in one's calling; it was almost completely opposed to the inherent temper – the explicit pursuit of pleasure, the levity and boisterousness, the lack of restraint – of the people's customary recreational activities. As one puritan minister exclaimed:

> How perilous is it then to tolerate those prophane pastimes, which open the flood-gates to so much sin and wickedness, as the sad experience of all ages doth testifie? So that if I would debauch a people, and draw them from God and his worship to superstition and Idolatry, I would take this course; I would open this gap to them, they should have *Floralia* and *Saturnalia*, they should have feast upon feast (as 'tis in Popery), they should have wakes to prophane the Lord's day, they should have May-Games, and Christmas-revels, with dancing, drinking, whoring, potting, piping, gaming, till they were made dissolute, and fit to receive any superstition, and easily drawn to bee of any, or of no religion . . . [7]

Similarly, Richard Baxter spoke out against those godless men – 'Voluptous Youths' he called them – 'that run after Wakes, and May-games, and Dancings, and Revellings, and are carried by the Love of sports and pleasure, from the Love of God, and the care of their Salvation, and the Love of Holiness, and the Love of their Callings; and into idleness, riotousness and disobedience to their Superiors'.[8] Although Baxter did not entirely condemn recreation, and even admitted that it might sometimes serve a purpose, he found it necessary to list eighteen common features of recreation which should be regarded as unlawful.[9] Such qualifications, to which most puritan writers would have agreed, went a long way towards undermining the legitimacy of the whole pattern of traditional recreations.

The more zealous Protestant reformers had little patience with the sort of traditionalism which helped to perpetuate those customs which, in their view, were rooted in a popish and heathenish past. A reformed church, they thought, should be thoroughly reformed; all traditional

cussions of these problems may be found in Hill, *Society and Puritanism*, chap. 1; Basil Hall, 'Puritanism: The Problem of Definition', in G. J. Cuming (ed.), *Studies in Church History*, vol. II (London, 1965), pp. 283–96; and C. H. George, 'Puritanism as History and Historiography', *Past & Present*, no. 41 (December 1968), 77–104.

[5] *Phillip Stubbes's Anatomy of the Abuses in England in Shakespere's Youth, A.D. 1583*, ed. Frederick J. Furnivall (2 parts; London, 1877–9), I, 183; cf. Hugh Roberts, *The Day of Hearing* (Oxford, 1600), sig. K, fol. 5r (from a sermon against May games).

[6] *William Perkins, 1558–1602: English Puritanist. His Pioneer Works on Casuistry: 'A Discourse on Conscience' and 'The Whole Treatise of Cases of Conscience'*, ed. Thomas F. Merrill (Nieuwkoop, 1966), p. 222.

[7] Thomas Hall, *Funebria Florae, The Downfall of May-Games* (3rd edn, London, 1661), p. 13.

[8] Richard Baxter, *A Christian Directory* (2nd edn, London, 1678), Book I, p. 390.

[9] *Ibid.* pp. 387–8.

practices should be re-examined in the light of God's commandments as revealed in the Bible. The papists, Christopher Fetherston argued, 'reasoned from customes and antiquitie . . . But wee must not regarde what hath been done in times past, wee muste marke diligently what God hath commaunded us to doe, who was before all times.'[10] The puritan reassessments of established traditions always emphasized the need for change: custom was commonly thought to be associated with the forces of darkness, the realization of God's will on earth assumed significant reform. A tract written around 1581 by Thomas Lovell was appropriately entitled *A Dialogue between Custom and Veritie concerning the use and abuse of Dauncing and Minstrelsie* (London, n.d.); another puritan, Hugh Roberts, rejected arguments based on 'antiquity' and 'custom' as an adequate defence of the continuance of May games.[11] The puritans, in striving for a stricter mode of life, were attempting to wean men from those customary practices which were not clearly warranted by God's law. Fetherston could not condone the usual Sunday sports and diversions: 'I can in no case permit that which God hath not permitted in his law, for if I should adde any thereto, great plagues should be added unto me. I am no pope, I cannot grant men licences to sin.' Although 'dauncing or any other exercise whatsoever, have bin used never so long, or thogh it be used in never so many places: yet if it be contrary to the worde and will of God, and forbidden by the same, it is detestable, and of all men to be eschewed'.[12]

The hostility of puritan reformers towards popular recreations was, to a considerable degree, a logical concomitant to their emphasis on a strict observance of the Sabbath. For puritans the Sabbath was fully the Lord's day, not a day which allowed for any kinds of worldly activities. Attendance at church followed by 'lawful recreations' was not an acceptable compromise. The puritan position was, as on other issues, ethically rigorous and unsympathetic to the traditional, more permissive outlook. It was held, as one historian has said, 'that the whole day should be kept holy and devoted to the public and private exercise of religion; and that this precludes all otherwise lawful recreations and pastimes as well as the work of one's calling, unlawful games and mere idleness'.[13] This, for instance, was the view of William Perkins,[14] as well as many other moralists who were rather less moderate. Contemporary practice, however, was found to be much out of line with the commandments of God; indeed, the prevalence of Sunday sports and festivities was regarded as one of the principal impediments to a holy observance of the Sabbath. As one preacher put it:

> The Lord God hath commaunded . . . that the Sabboth day should
> be kept holy, that the people should cease from labour, to the end

---

[10] Christopher Fetherston, *A Dialogue agaynst light, lewde, and lascivious dauncing* (London, 1582), sig. B, fol. 6r.
[11] Roberts, *Day of Hearing*, sig. K, fols. 5v–6r.
[12] Fetherston, *Dialogue*, sig. B, fol. 4v, and sig. C, fol. 3r.
[13] Patrick Collinson, 'The Beginnings of English Sabbatariansim', in C. W. Dugmore and Charles Duggan (eds.), *Studies in Church History*, vol. I (London, 1964), pp. 207–8.
[14] *William Perkins*, p. 160.

they should heare ye word of God, and give themselves to godly exercises, but custome and sufferance hath brought it to passe that the multitude do most shamefully prophane the Sabboth day, and have altered the very name therof, so as where God calleth it his holy sabaoth, the multitude call it there revelyng day, whiche day is spent in bulbeatings, bearebeatings, bowlings, dicyng, cardyng, daunsynges, drunkennes, and whoredome.[15]

Similarly, Thomas Lovell complained that

the holy Saboth is so unholyly spent, as if it were consecrated to the abhominable idole of fleshly pleasure, rather then to the true service of the almighty God: for if there be any match made for the trial of any mastrie, or meeting for meriment (as they terme it) either between town and town, or neighbour and neighbour, or if there be any keeping ales, either for the maintenance of the Church, or for some that are fallen into decay. When must these be tried or don but upon the Saboth day?[16]

The profanation of the Sabbath and the customs of popular recreation came to be closely associated in the puritan mind.[17] It was not enough for a person simply to present himself at church on Sunday for divine service: he should commit himself to religious rejoicing and the praise of God for the entire day.

Puritan writers also objected to certain recreational practices because of their licentiousness and inducements to sensual indulgence. On this point dancing was held to be particularly dangerous. William Perkins disapproved of the 'wanton gestures' of dancing; 'it is no better', he said, than 'the very bellowes of lust and uncleannesse'.[18] John Northbrooke thought that 'Concupiscence is inflamed (by Dauncing) with the fire of lust and sensualitie.' 'They daunce', he said, 'with disordinate gestures, and with monstrous thumping of the feete, to pleasant soundes, to wanton songues, to dishonest verses. Maidens and matrones are groped and handled with unchaste hands, and kissed and dishonestly embraced: the things, which nature hath hidden, and modestie covered, are then often-times by meanes of lasciviousnesse made naked, and ribauldrie under the colour of pastime is dissembled.' Moreover, as a result of 'this daucing many maidens have beene unmaidened, whereby I may saye, it is the storehouse and nurserie of Bastardie'.[19] Similar opinions were voiced by

---

[15] William Kethe, A Sermon made at Blanford Forum, in the Countie of Dorset (London, 1571), p. 8. Cf. Humphrey Roberts, An earnest Complaint of divers vain, wicked and abused Exercises, practised on the Saboth day (London, 1572), especially sig. D, fols. 1r–6v; John Stockwood, A Sermon Preached at Paules Cross on Barthelmew day, being the 24 of August 1578 (London, n.d.), pp. 50–1 and 132–7; and J. W. Blench, Preaching in England in the late Fifteenth and Sixteenth Centuries (Oxford, 1964), pp. 313–14.

[16] Lovell, Dialogue, fol. 4 (handscript pagination, Huntingdon Library).

[17] M. M. Knappen, Tudor Puritanism: A Chapter in the History of Idealism (2nd edn, Chicago and London, 1965), pp. 442–3.

[18] William Perkins, pp. 46 and 218; cf. Roberts, Day of Hearing, sig. K, fol. 3r, and Stubbes's Anatomy of Abuses, ed. Furnivall, 1, 154–5 and 166.

[19] John Northbrooke, Spiritus est vicarius Christi in terra. A Treatise wherein Dicing, Dauncing, Vaine plaies or Enterludes with other idle pastimes, etc. commonly used on the Sabboth day, are reprooved (London, 1579), fols. 62r, 66v, and 68v.

Thomas Lovell.[20] As for the festivities of May Day, one of Fetherston's objections was that the young men 'doe use commonly to runne into woodes in the night time, amongst maidens, to set bowes, in so muche, as I have hearde of tenne maidens whiche went to set May, and nine of them came home with childe'.[21]

Puritans were also much concerned about the tendency of recreations to lure men from godly activities into an idle and undisciplined way of life. Conscientious labour was a serious responsibility of every truly religious person, and anything which threatened to interfere with this social imperative was regarded with grave suspicion. Industrious employment was a godly as well as a social virture; time was precious and not to be trifled away on unprofitable activities. Idleness, as a corollary, was one of the most serious sins, and puritan writers never tired of enumerating the crimes to which the idle man was prone. Idleness, said Northbrooke, 'is most to be eschued and avoyded of all men, (especially of those that professe the Gospell of Christe) because it is the fountaine and well spring, whereout is drawne a thousande mischiefes: for it is the onely nourisher and mainteiner of all filthinesse, as whoredome, theft, murder, breaking of wedlocke, perjurie, Idolatrie, Poperie, etc. bayne playes, filthy pastimes, and drunkennesse'.[22] Traditional recreations were thought to give great encouragement to the sin of idleness. Those diversions which helped to refresh the mind and body, to prepare them for higher ends, were regarded as worthy and legitimate; but when recreation was enjoyed as an end in itself, it served to divert men's attention from more significant concerns, blunt their sense of holy ideals, and draw them away from the labour of their callings. Northbrooke's view on this question was shared by most puritan writers:

> I do allow of honest, moderate, and good lawful active exercises, for recreation and quickning of our dull mindes. And where you say, that holy dayes (as they are termed) were invented in old time for pastimes, I thinke you say trueth: For the Pope appointed them (and not God in his worde) and that onely to traine up the people in ignorance and idlenesse, whereby halfe of the yeare and more, was overpassed (by their idle holydayes) in loytering and vaine pastimes, etc. in restrayning men from their handie labours and occupations.[23]

Diligent application to one's work could too easily be subverted by recreational indulgence. Dancing, Fetherston argued, was not in fact an acceptable form of refreshment, for 'What heaviness, sleepiness, and sluggishness doth dauncing procure: Howe many mens servauntes being set to woorke, do after their dauncing dayes lie snorting in hedges, because they are so weary that they cannot worke:Whereby their maisters doe reape but small gaynes.'[24]

[20] Lovell, *Dialogue*, fols. 16v, 17r, 23r, and 25r.
[21] Fetherston, *Dialogue*, sig. D, fol. 7v; cf. *Stubbes's Anatomy of Abuses*, I, 149.
[22] Northbrooke, *Treatise*, fol. 16v.
[23] *Ibid.* fols. 11v–12r.
[24] Fetherston, *Dialogue*, sig. B, fol. 1v.

The use (or misuse) of recreation became an issue of high controversy in early Stuart England.[25] Opposing the convictions of the 'preciser' sort of people were the forces of conservatism – the court, Archbishop Laud, the Church hierarchy, aristocratic culture, probably the bulk of the poor. The political implications of this split were reinforced, and tensions were aggravated, as a result of the publication in 1618 of the King's Declaration on Sports and its reissue in an extended form by Charles I in 1633. The royal order, commonly known as the Book of Sports, was a sharp rebuff to puritan sensibilities, which it treated with a marked lack of sympathy. It declared 'that no lawful recreation shall be barred to our good people, which shall not tend to the breach of our aforesaid laws and canons of our Church'. The order sanctioned certain sports on Sundays after divine service and condoned the custom of holding parish feasts. The royal wish was that

> after the end of divine service our good people be not disturbed, letted or discouraged from any lawful recreation, such as dancing, either men or women; archery for men, leaping, vaulting, or any other such harmless recreation, nor from having of May-games, Whitsun-ales, and Morris-dances; and the setting up of May-poles and other sports therewith used: so as the same be had in due and convenient time, without impediment or neglect of divine service.

As for wakes (and this was an addition in the 1633 declaration),

> our express will and pleasure is, that these Feasts, with others, shall be observed, and that our Justices of the Peace, in their several divisions, shall look to it, both that all disorders there may be prevented or punished, and that all neighbourhood and freedom, with manlike and lawful exercises be used: and we further command all Justices of Assize in their several circuits to see that no man do trouble or molest any of our loyal and dutiful people, in or for their lawful recreations, having first done their duty to God, and continuing in obedience to us and our laws.[26]

The declaration was intended by Laud as one tactical move in the strategy to regularize religious practice within the Established Church. His plan, according to one scholar, was that the royal order 'should serve as a precise definition of those Sunday activities acceptable to the duly constituted ecclesiastical authority. Upon this foundation, he could build the structure of uniform practice in such matters throughout the kingdom.'[27]

The puritans were not impressed. Inattentiveness to the need for reform, complacency with regard to decadent customs, were bad enough; but outright, official approbation for such primitive remnants, proclaimed to the godly (and the ungodly) from the pulpits of the nation, was much

---

[25] Brailsford, *Sport and Society*, pp. 99–108; Keith Thomas, *Religion and the Decline of Magic* (London, 1971), pp. 66 and 162; and Christopher Whitfield (ed.), *Robert Dover and the Cotswold Games: Annalia Dubrensia* (London, 1962), pp. 16–18 and 43–4.

[26] 'The King's Majesty's declaration to his subjects concerning lawful sports to be used' is reprinted in S. R. Gardiner, *The Constitutional Documents of the Puritan Revolution 1625–1660* (3rd edn, Oxford, 1906), pp. 99–103. See also L. A. Gowett, *The King's Book of Sports* (London, 1890).

[27] Barnes, 'Somerset Churchales', p. 119.

more than could be tolerated. To many puritans it was a case of sin being licensed from above. The Book of Sports, as Christopher Hill has remarked,

> must have seemed profoundly, satanically wicked to Puritans, and to many of the industrious sort of people, just because [it] . . . appealed to all that was unregenerate, popish and backward-looking in man, to all the bad side (from their point of view) of popular tradition, which it was the function of preaching, discipline and Sabbatarianism slowly and painfully to eradicate . . . But kings and bishops, so far from joining in this civilizing process, were pandering to the very worst instincts of natural man.[28]

The proclamation sharply exacerbated existing sensibilities and reinforced the sceptics' fears, driving some of them into a more extreme position. The social rift was widened: the policy of established authority was revealed for all to see, and it was a policy (so many thought) 'to enfeeble the Church and reconcile it with Rome';[29] the puritan clergymen who declined to read the declaration found their positions in jeopardy – some were censured, others suspended, a few were even deprived of their livings – and tensions were further aggravated.[30] Recreation became an issue which divided men, forcing them to take a stand for either traditionalism or reform; and on the whole, as one historian has observed, 'the industrious saints tended to set themselves apart from both the idle rich' – 'the leisured classes' with their customary notions of pleasure and fashion – 'and the men whom the rich supported', including a large proportion of the poor.[31] Popular culture and godly culture were mutually hostile, and many of the common people chafed under the regime which the 'saints' later imposed. In Maldon, Essex, one such instance of disenchantment was happily recorded (the document is undated but appears to be from the Interregnum):

> John Parker of Maldon chairmaker sworne upon his oath saith that he being in the Company of Wm. Barnes of this Towne Cordwayner in the harvest feild in Lallmahall ground the Last harvest did here the said William Barnes utter these words following (vizt): in former tymes when the Booke of Common prayer was read the people did usually goe out of the church to play at foote ball and to the Alehouse and their continued till they ware drunke and it ware noe matter if they were hanged.[32]

To the puritan conscience this was a voice of unregeneracy, and it was a voice which was especially associated with (as the eighteenth century was to phrase it) the 'profligate multitude'.

[28] Hill, Society and Puritanism, p. 193.
[29] Barnes, 'Somerset Churchales', p. 121.
[30] Ibid. pp. 119–20; Hill, Society and Puritanism, pp. 199–202; and Geoffrey F. Nuttall and Owen Chadwick (eds.), From Uniformity to Unity 1662–1962 (London, 1962), pp. 161n and 164–5.
[31] Michael Walzer, The Revolution of the Saints: A Study in the Origins of Radical Politics (Cambridge, Mass., 1965), p. 211.
[32] Essex R. O., D/B 3/3/149/7.

It is clear, then, that during the century before the Restoration a vigorous movement of reform presented a powerful challenge to the customary practices of popular recreation. But what was the practical impact of this puritan attack? To what extent, if at all, were traditional diversions weakened? Were the puritan reformers at all successful in achieving their objectives, or was their influence strictly limited and ephemeral, without significant and lasting consequences for the conduct of recreational activities?

We must confess that it is easier to raise these questions than to offer very satisfactory answers. Indeed, as long as the recreational culture of the sixteenth and seventeenth centuries, and the character of village life, remain only superficially investigated, it will not be possible to discuss adequately those changes in the experiences of the common people which may have occurred during the period. The evidence which bears on the attitudes of certain vocal groups, especially the puritans, is reasonably well known, but the changing pattern of actual behaviour in town and village has not been closely studied. Our present understanding is, as a result, markedly imperfect. It does seem that churchales had very much declined in significance by the end of the seventeenth century, and many of the saints' days which Catholicism had fostered were abandoned after the Reformation; however, it is just as clear that many customs survived, some of them with vigour. Parish feasts (or wakes) were widely, almost ubiquitously, held during the eighteenth century; many of the principal holidays – Christmas, Shrovetide, Easter, May Day, Whitsuntide – continued to be observed. In all parts of the country fairs served as occasions for festivity and entertainment. The blood sports and athletic exercises which the puritans condemned are frequently mentioned in the sources from later periods. Indeed, the evidence strongly suggests that traditional recreations in the eighteenth century were thriving, deeply rooted, and widely practised. Whether or not they were less prominent than before, and the ways in which they may have altered, are questions which for the moment must remain open.

It is possible, however, to draw attention to some of the circumstances which help to account for the resilience of the traditional practices. Puritanism was always a minority movement, and many of its more rigorous ethical views were uncongenial to the bulk of the population. A large number of people, including many farmers, parsons, and country gentlemen, retained a basic sympathy (or at least tolerance) for the established recreational customs. These were men of moderate or conservative disposition whose moral outlook was relatively worldly and permissive. After the Restoration, with many elements of puritanism discredited and condemned, the strength of these traditionalist convictions in English society was considerably enhanced. Moreover, many men of property were themselves attracted to and involved in the customary recreational practices. They supported cock-fighting with enthusiasm and patronized those athletic sports which readily allowed for gambling; they celebrated some of the major holidays and helped to support certain local festivities which were customary in their own communities. In general they were fairly well disposed towards worldly pleasures 'taken in moderation', and this disposition served to restrain and counteract the influence of puritan reform.[33]

We can also see that English society still (in a sense) 'needed' most of the traditional recreations. In certain respects the puritans were ahead of their times, and this precociousness partly explains their failure to attain some of their social objectives. For not only were puritan attitudes more 'advanced' than those of most of their contemporaries, the general structure of society was still so traditional that fundamental changes in behaviour on a national level simply could not be effected. The fact that society retained its basically agrarian character ensured that the seasonal cycles would continue to shape people's consciousness and, as a result, that those festive intervals which were closely associated with the agricultural calendar – Plough Monday, spring-time celebrations, harvest feasts, autumn fairs – would remain vitally important to most labouring people.[34] Many of the principal festivities were firmly imbedded in the annual cycle of agricultural pursuits – the flux of intense labour and partial relaxation; festive occasions were, in fact, among the most important of those events which punctuated the year's succession of economic activities, complementing the periodic rhythms of 'natural' processes. The outlook of puritanism was too urban in character, too orderly and austere, to be fully acceptable to a pre-industrial society. There was still a widespread need for the sorts of ceremonial values which the traditional recreations embodied and sustained; most of these ceremonies stemmed from an inevitable involvement in the seasonal cycles and a less inevitable (though still significant) commitment to the ecclesiastical calendar, and they were reinforced by the rituals of community and the ties of paternalism. Popular recreations, then, remained socially functional: holidays, for instance, provided psychological counterweights to the burdens of sustained labour – liberties for personal indulgence, excitement and spectacle, temporary distractions from care; they were times of social suspension which freed men from some of the constraints of routine. Indeed, popular recreations offered a variety of satisfactions to many ordinary people in agrarian communities.[35] The puritan challenge was unable to destroy the structure of this conservative consciousness, a consciousness that was rooted in a traditional economy and set of social relations which, though changing, were changing relatively slowly. A really fundamental overhaul of recreational life had to await the more dramatic social and cultural upheavals of the later eighteenth and nineteenth centuries.

[33] For a discussion of these themes, see below, pp. 56–71.
[34] Thomas, *Religion and the Decline of Magic*, p. 71.
[35] For an account of some of these functions, see below, chap. 5.

2

The holiday calendar

In everyday language it is customary to distinguish between the major holidays and special festive occasions, all of which are widely observed, and those routine forms of leisure which occur much more frequently and tend to be taken for granted: a tea break, reading the newspaper, an exchange of pleasantries with a neighbour or a colleague, an evening walk, relaxing in the garden. The same distinction can be applied to the recreational life of pre-industrial England. There was, on the one hand, the holiday calendar, the annual cycle of important festive events; on the other hand, there were the everyday forms of refreshment and diversion: drinking in the alehouse, gossiping among neighbours, telling stories in the evening, playing quoits or pitch and toss. These routine relaxations usually arose out of the normal intervals in the working day; occasionally they were even accompaniments to labour, sweeteners for monotony and fatigue.

There must have been many opportunities for these kinds of everyday recreation. Petty gambling was allowed in many alehouses, and in the spring and summer outdoor diversions were practised after the day's work. By the shoemaker's shop,

> when the winter nights were dark and cold
> The plough boys met, and tales of mirth were told,
> And all the news and scandal of the place
> Was here discussed with comments on each case . . .[1]

Sometimes work and recreation were so closely related that they were almost indistinguishable. Poaching was endemic in many places, and it blended together both profit and pleasure; story-telling might accompany the work of spinners, harvesters, or servants. Weavers sang at their looms, haymakers in the fields. Women gossiped over their sewing. Among some groups of workers one of their members was appointed to read aloud as the others worked. A trip to the market combined business with social pleasures; exchanging news and courtesies with a craftsman or dealer introduced sociability into an economic or service transaction. There were also the frequent though irregular festivities which were associated with the three main events of an individual's life cycle, birth, marriage, and death. Christenings were sometimes attended with small festive gatherings, and marriage feasts must have been common: it was said of running at the quintain, for instance, a sport which survived in Blackthorn, Oxfordshire, that 'there is seldom any public wedding without this diver-

---

[1] J. R. Withers, *Poems Upon Various Subjects* (3 vols.; Cambridge and London, 1856–61), I, 8 (from 'My Native Village').

sion on the common green, with much solemnity and mirth'.[2] An eighteenth-century poem by Edward Chicken, *The Collier's Wedding*, depicts
festivities which were considerably more boisterous than those found in
Thomas Hardy's *Under the Greenwood Tree*. At funerals too the sense of
loss was considerably offset, it would seem, by the abundance of eating and
drinking which frequently marked their celebration.

These forms of diversion will not, however, be receiving detailed attention in our study. This could produce a false impression, for it is likely
that these routine leisure activities and family festivities were, in terms of
the hours involved, more prominent than the large public celebrations
and sporting events. But a bias of this sort is inevitable: everyday leisure
was relatively subdued; it was usually rooted in small, intimate gatherings,
in informal, face to face encounters; and (unfortunately) the sources
which shed light on such occasions are extremely thin. The closer we
approach the most commonplace experiences of labouring people in the
eighteenth century, the more meagre our information becomes. We can
speculate and offer general impressions, but detailed discussions are not
possible. In contrast, the aspects of plebeian culture which are much more
fully documented are those which involved public performances: those
occasions when the labouring people were likely to be noticed by seekers
after news and by the guardians of law and order. Our evidence, then,
relates largely to special festive assemblies, to large gatherings of people,
and to events which attracted the attention of gentlemen. The importance
of the more intimate kinds of leisure should not be forgotten, but the
sources themselves necessitate an account of recreations which highlights
the holiday calendar and the more organized and visible forms of sports
and pastimes.[3]

One of the most important holidays for the common people was the
occasion of the annual parish feast, sometimes known as the wake or the
revel. Many of the contemporary local histories and descriptive accounts
alluded to the celebration of an annual wake, and country diarists often
mentioned the local feasts which they or their servants attended. Wakes
were major recreational events, and observers of popular customs were
agreed on their prevalence and widespread appeal. 'I am now in the
Country,' wrote a contributor to the *Gentleman's Magazine* in September
1738, 'and at that Season of the Year in which Parish Feasts abound.'[4]
In 1710 Daniel Hilman noticed that the parish wake 'in a great many

[2] White Kennet, *Parochial Antiquities Attempted in the History of Ambrosden, Burcester, and
other Adjacent Parts in the Counties of Oxford and Bucks.* (Oxford, 1695), pp. 18–19
and 22.
[3] A. R. Wright, *British Calendar Customs*, ed. T. E. Lones (3 vols.; London, 1936–40) is
a useful source on the traditional holiday calendar. The first volume covers the move-
able feasts, the second and third volumes the fixed festivals; the bulk of the descriptive
material is drawn from the period after the early nineteenth century. See also the
collections assembled by William Hone: *The Every-Day Book* (2 vols.; London, 1825–7),
The Table Book (2 vols.; London, 1827–8), and *The Year Book* (London, 1832).
[4] *Gentleman's Magazine*, VIII (1738), 465.

places continues still to be observ'd with all sorts of rural Merriments; such as Dancing, Wrestling, Cudgel-playing, etc.'.[5] Writing of Cornwall in 1758, William Borlase claimed that 'every parish has its annual feast', and in 1778 it was said that 'many are yet celebrated' in County Durham; several observers remarked on the many wakes which continued to be held in Derbyshire.[6] The people in south-west Leicestershire, in the vicinity of Claybrook, were reported in 1791 to be 'much attached to the celebration of wakes'.[7]

There is other evidence concerning parish feasts which allows us to be more precise about their incidence. One of the most useful sources, a history of the county of Northampton, was based on material collected in the early eighteenth century, mostly between 1719 and 1724, by John Bridges, a retired barrister, though the work was not actually published until 1791.[8] Bridges, it seems, personally visited all parts of the county, and for the majority of the parishes his notes indicated whether or not a wake was held, and if so the time of its celebration. Of the 290 parishes which he investigated, 198 were explicitly stated to have an annual feast; in 11 cases he reported that no wake survived, and in 81 others no reference was made to the subject. A feast was observed, then, in at least two-thirds of Northamptonshire's parishes; since 6 parishes had two wakes and 1 had three, Bridges's total for the county came to 206. The material which is available from other areas also points to the prevalence of wakes. In the northernmost hundred of Buckinghamshire, which comprised 28 parishes (a number of them with very small populations), there were at least 14 wakes around the middle of the eighteenth century.[9] Of 15 Berkshire parishes which were specially investigated in 1759, some of them very incompletely, 7 were found to have one wake and 1 had three.[10] A later source, dating from the mid-1840s, included a list of the wakes in the vicinity of Stamford, apparently compiled for the benefit of itinerant tradesmen. Although the area under view was not precisely delimited – the list focused on a socio-economic rather than an administrative region – our impression of the prevalence of wakes is again reinforced, and this time for a much later period. A total of 118 feasts were included in the

[5] Daniel Hilman, *Tusser Redivivus: Being Part of Mr. Thomas Tusser's Five Hundred Points of Husbandry* (London, 1710), 'June', p. 16.
[6] William Borlase, *The Natural History of Cornwall* (Oxford, 1758), p. 301; Hutchinson, *Northumberland*, II, 26n; James Pilkington, *A View of the Present State of Derbyshire* (2 vols.; London, 1789), II, 55; John Farey, *General View of the Agriculture of Derbyshire* (3 vols.; London, 1811–17), III, 628; and Stephen Glover, *The History and Gazetteer of the County of Derby* (2 vols.; Derby, 1831), I, 262.
[7] Aulay Macaulay, *The History and Antiquities of Claybrook* (London, 1791), p. 128.
[8] *The History and Antiquities of Northamptonshire. Compiled from the Manuscript Collections of the Late Learned Antiquary John Bridges* (2 vols.; Oxford, 1791); the compiler was Peter Whalley.
[9] Browne Willis, *The History and Antiquities of the Town, Hundred, and Deanery of Buckingham* (London, 1755).
[10] *Collections Towards a Parochial History of Berkshire* (London, 1783), printed by John Nichols and included in his *Bibliotheca Topographica Britannica* (10 vols.; London, 1780–98), IV.

list: 44 in Rutland, 37 in Northamptonshire, 23 in Lincolnshire, 8 in Huntingdonshire, 4 in Leicestershire, and 2 in Cambridgeshire.[11]

Wakes were most often celebrated around the time of the anniversary of the parish church's dedication, commonly on the Sunday after the feast day of the saint to whom the church was dedicated (though there were many exceptions to this general rule: in Northamptonshire around thirty per cent of the wakes mentioned by Bridges were held at a time which was unrelated to the appropriate saint's day). But the most notable feature of the timing of wakes is the manner in which they were distributed throughout the calendar year. Rather than being evenly spread out during the course of the year, they were very much seasonally concentrated, as is shown in the accompanying table. The two most important periods for wakes were the late spring-early summer, and the late summer and first half of the autumn. Wakes were especially prominent in the latter period: there were eighty-two in Northamptonshire, for instance, between late September and early November.[12]

The distribution of wakes during the calendar year		
Period of Time	Wakes from Bridges	Wakes from list of mid–1840s
January–March	0	0
April and early May	1	1
Around Whit and Trinity Sundays	4	15
Late June – early July	38	31
Second half of July	20	6
Early August	1	6
Around 15 August	14	5
Late August and first half of September	22	0
Second half of September	—	16
Around Michaelmas	31	—
October	18	20
Around All Saints' Day	33	7
Rest of November plus December	23	11
	205*	118

* Of the 206 wakes referred to in Bridges, 1 is undated.

Wakes usually began on a Sunday and lasted for part, and sometimes all, of the week. By the eighteenth century they were predominantly secular

[11] George Burton, *Chronology of Stamford* (Stamford, 1846), pp. 175–7; cf. *Sharp's Agricultural Compendium and General Advertiser for 1846* (Stamford, 1845), p. 44.
[12] See also the several references for August and September in Wright, *Calendar Customs*, III. The slight differences in the timing of late summer and early autumn wakes between the early eighteenth century and the mid-1840s are largely a consequence of the calendar change of 1752. In the later period, for instance, many of the traditional Michaelmas feasts were celebrated around the 10th and 11th of October.

festivals; the religious rites, when they did survive, were usually confined to a special church service on the Sunday of the wake. 'The religious tenor is totally forgotten,' complained one observer about the wakes in the North, 'and the Sabbath', he added (probably with a degree of exaggeration), 'is made a day of every dissipation and vice which it is possible to conceive could crowd upon a villager's manners and rural life.'[13] It was clearly the profane and pleasure-seeking atmosphere which dominated the wake. In a great many parishes the feast must have been one of the main occasions each year for good eating and abundant drinking, for music and dancing, for sports and entertainments, and for hospitality. A wake normally included several of the familiar sports and pastimes of the period: wrestling, or boxing, or cudgelling; perhaps donkey racing, a wheelbarrow race (while blindfolded), a smock race for the women; contests might be arranged in hot hasty-pudding eating, grinning through a horse collar (the funniest won), chasing a greased pig, running in sacks, or smoking pipes of tobacco; at some wakes bull-baiting, cock-fighting, or badger-baiting were featured.[14] The wake was a community's own petty carnival. Often there were stalls with gingerbread, nuts, and fruit; sometimes a travelling fiddler attended to play for the dancers; and housewives usually made special preparations for the entertainments which were expected of them. It was said of the three feasts in Stamford that 'they are generally kept up with great spirit and liberality, and all the poor who can entertain their friends on the occasion do so to the utmost of their means. The public-houses in the neighbourhood of the feasts frequently provide prizes to be contended for by athletic exercises or rustic sports.'[15] In most communities the wake would have been attended, not only by all the working people of the parish, but also by the considerable numbers of visitors who came as invited guests; for a wake was the time when scattered friends and relations were accustomed to assemble together in order to reaffirm their social ties. 'This being our Feast at Kettering', wrote the parish's curate on 6 July 1766, 'We had, as usual, large Congregations and many Strangers'.[16] At the wakes in the vicinity of Claybrook 'the cousins assemble from all quarters, fill the church on Sunday, and celebrate the Monday with feasting, with music, and with dancing'.[17]

[13] Hutchinson, Northumberland, II, 26n.
[14] Some of these amusements are described in Strutt, Sports and Pastimes, pp. 275–8. For further details on the diversions at wakes, see John Clare, The Village Minstrel (London, 1821), stanzas 70–84; Withers, Poems, I, 2–3; William Somerville, Hobbinol, or the Rural Games (London, 1740); Hone, Every-Day Book, II, cols. 54–5 and 1,399–403; John Byng, The Torrington Diaries, ed. C. B. Andrews (4 vols.; London, 1934–8), I, 208–9; and Richard Blakeborough, Wit, Character, Folklore and Customs of the North Riding of Yorkshire (2nd edn, Saltburn-by-the-Sea, 1911), pp. 89–90.
[15] Burton, Chronology of Stamford, p. 175.
[16] B. M. 'Diary of the Rev. Abraham Maddock, 1765–1771', Add. MS 40,653, fols. 29–30.
[17] Macaulay, Claybrook, p. 128. See also John Cole, The History and Antiquities of Weston Favell (Scarborough, 1827), pp. 32–3; Gentleman's Magazine, CIII (1833), part i, 116 (on Scopwick, Lincolnshire); W. Harbutt Dawson, History of Skipton (London, 1882), pp. 384–5; William Howitt, The Rural Life of England (2nd edn, London, 1840), pp. 493–5; and below, pp. 52–3.

Important occasions for recreation were also provided by the many fairs which were to be found all through the country. The majority of these fairs were primarily concerned with commercial functions – there were horse fairs, cattle fairs, sheep or hog fairs, cheese fairs, fairs for hardware, or leather, or general merchandise; but a good many of them were also treated as pleasure fairs, and in a few cases pleasure provided their main rationale. At St Faith's Fair near Norwich, for instance, which was one of the most important meetings in the kingdom for the sale of cattle, the first day of the fair was devoted entirely to pleasure and generally attracted a large number of visitors. James Woodforde, who lived in Weston, a few miles north-west of Norwich, often gave his servants leave to take a holiday at St Faith's or one of the other fairs in the neighbour-hood.[18] Similarly, on 27 May 1771 Sylas Neville recorded in his diary, 'My people being gone to Ingham Fair, shall be alone till tomorrow evening.'[19] As the village minstrel in John Gay's *The Shepherd's Week* attested, the provincial fair was not only for merchants and farmers:

> Now he goes on, and sings of Fairs and Shows,
> For still new Fairs before his Eyes arose.
> How Pedlars Stalls with glitt'ring Toys are laid,
> The various Fairings of the Country Maid.
> Long silken Laces hang upon the Twine,
> And Rows of Pins and amber Bracelets shine;
> How the tight Lass, Knives, Combs and Scissars spys,
> And looks on Thimbles with desiring Eyes;
> Of Lott'ries next with tuneful Note he told,
> Where silver Spoons are won and Rings of Gold.
> The Lads and Lasses trudge the Street along,
> And all the Fair is crouded in his Song.
> The Mountebank now treads the Stage, and sells
> His Pills, his Balsoms, and his Ague spells;
> Now o'er and o'er the nimble Tumbler springs,
> And on the Rope the vent'rous Maiden swings;
> *Jack-pudding* in his part-coloured Jacket
> Tosses the Glove and jokes at ev'ry Packet.
> Of *Raree-Shows* he sung, and *Punch's* Feats,
> Of Pockets pick'd in Crowds, and various Cheats.[20]

The mingling of business and pleasure at fairs was a very common phenomenon. At Stourbridge Fair, for instance, which was a noted market place for numerous commodities, there were also 'Coffee-Houses, Taverns, Eating-Houses, Music Shops, Buildings for the Exhibition of Drolls, Puppet Shews, Legerdemain, Mountebanks, Wild Beasts, Monsters, Giants, Rope Dancers, etc. . . . Besides the Booths, there are six or seven brick

[18] *The Diary of a Country Parson: The Reverend James Woodforde*, ed. John Beresford (5 vols.; Oxford, 1924–31), II, 99; III, 22, 221–2, 351, 359, 378; IV, 27, 111–12, 292; and V, 118, 279, 321, 398.
[19] *The Diary of Sylas Neville 1767–1788*, ed. Basil Cozens-Hardy (Oxford, 1950), p. 102.
[20] John Gay, *The Shepherd's Week. In Six Pastorals* (London, 1714), from the sixth pastoral, 'Saturday'; cf. Hone, *Every-Day Book*, II, cols. 1,207–12 and 1,307–10.

Houses . . . and in any of which the Country People are accommodated with hot or cold Goose, roast or boiled Pork, etc.'[21] A similar variety of purpose was evident on a smaller scale at other fairs. An Oxfordshire clergyman wrote of how the August fair at Bampton was noted both as an occasion for the sale of horses and as 'a sort of carnival to all the neighbouring villages'.[22] The July fair at Chesham, Buckinghamshire, in 1761 included, along with its market for cattle, wrestling, backswords, and a women's smock race.[23] In Derbyshire the afternoons and evenings of many fairs were said to be 'more or less devoted to amusement and jollity, among the young folks: if this be the main purpose of the day, it is called a *Gig-fair*'.[24] The fair at Prittlewell in Essex which a doctor referred to in his diary on 15 July 1826 seems to have been one of those occasions at which pleasure was predominant:

> Morning very fine. Arranged the stalls in front of my house. The fair is a very decent one. An exhibition on our right of a Giant, Giantess, an Albiness, a native of Baffins Bay and a Dwarf – very respectable. We had a learned Pig and Punch on our left and in front some Theatrical Exhibition. All in very good order.[25]

Puppet shows, gingerbread stalls, musicians, mountebanks, buffoons (there was a punchinello at Brixworth fair in 1673),[26] wax figures, throwing for prizes, painted panoramas of notable historic events, living curiosities (the pig-faced lady, a pair of dwarfs, the thin man): these were familiar features at pleasure fairs. And at some of the larger fairs in the nineteenth century there might be Adam's Circus, or Wombwell's Menagerie, or one of the other major commercial entertainments.

It is impossible to be precise about the proportion of fairs which were at least partly for pleasure. Reasonably complete lists of fairs are readily obtained, but the difficulty lies in trying to distinguish the fairs which were principally for business from those which combined business with pleasure and those which were mostly for pleasure.[27] All wakes were fundamentally festive occasions but fairs assumed a variety of forms. Consequently, it is often hard to establish the actual texture of a particular fair, especially the smaller ones. Moreover, since many of the sources we rely on were compiled primarily for the use of merchants and traders, they tend to emphasize

[21] Charles Caraccioli, *An Historical Account of Sturbridge, Bury, and the Most Famous Fairs in Europe and America* (Cambridge, 1773), pp. 20–1; cf. Daniel Defoe, *A Tour through the Whole Island of Great Britain* (2 vols.; London, Everyman edn, 1962), I, 85; and Bedfordshire R. O., L.30/9a/2, pp. 13–15 (a letter of 1748 describing the Fair).
[22] J. A. Giles, *History of the Parish and Town of Bampton* (Oxford, 1847), p. lxiv.
[23] *Northampton Mercury*, 20 July 1761.
[24] Farey, *Agriculture of Derbyshire*, III, 630; cf. Howitt, *Rural Life*, pp. 497–501.
[25] L. F. Matthews (ed.), 'The Diary of Jonas Asplin, M.D., of Wakering Hall, Rochford, and Prittlewell', *Essex Review*, no. 258 (January 1957), 42.
[26] *The Journal of Thomas Isham, of Lamport, in the County of Northampton, 1671–1673*, ed. Walter Rye (Norwich, 1875), p. 93.
[27] There are two main sources for fairs: William Owen, *An Authentic Account . . . of all the Fairs in England and Wales* (London, 1756), and John Ogilby and William Morgan, *The Traveller's Pocket-Book* (London, 1759), both of which were published in numerous later editions. I have used chiefly the 1756 edition of Owen and the 1770 edition of Ogilby and Morgan.

the commercial functions of fairs, the commodities in which they special-
ized, and to ignore or depreciate their recreational dimension. Of the
hundreds of fairs extant around 1770 in fourteen selected counties (Bedfordshire, Berkshire, Buckinghamshire, Cambridgeshire, Derbyshire,
Hertfordshire, Huntingdonshire, Leicestershire, Northamptonshire, Nottinghamshire, Oxfordshire, Rutland, Staffordshire, and Warwickshire),
only twenty were explicitly identified as pleasure fairs, or listed as specializing only in 'toys', and another twelve included toys as one of their major
articles of sale.[28] The reference to 'toys' – a term which included jewelery,
buckles, buttons, and other kinds of light ornaments – can usually be
regarded as a clear indication that a particular fair functioned (though not
always exclusively) as a holiday event, for it was when the commodities
of sale tended to be decorative and relatively inexpensive that the commercial and the recreational cultures became most closely intermeshed.
The 'toys' at such fairs often served as Gay had suggested – 'the various
Fairings of the Country Maid'.

Although the majority of fairs probably did centre on the dealings in
livestock, cheese, hardware, and other commercial staples, it is likely that
a substantial minority were distinctly mixed gatherings, occasions when
recreation complemented trade. The Easter Tuesday fair at Daventry was
reported in Owen's *Book of Fairs* to be for horses and horned cattle, the
fair of June 6th and 7th for 'swine and all sorts of goods', and the fair of
October 2nd and 3rd for 'cattle, cheese, onions, etc.'; but a local source
indicates that all three were 'also frequented for pleasure'.[29] Various
articles of sale were featured at the Nottingham Goose Fair, but the fair
was even more renowned as an occasion for recreation.[30] The fair at
Boughton Green, Northamptonshire, which was said to be noted for
'timber, poles, ladders, cooper's ware, tunnery, braziery, china, etc.' and
for 'ready made cloaths, hats, and stockings', also had a high reputation
as a pleasure fair, in both genteel and plebeian society; the recreational
attractions of the fair – the races, raffling, wrestling, and singlestick
matches – were usually emphasized in the published advertisements.[31]
On Whit Thursday 1766 William Cole recorded that 'Tom went with his
Uncle and almost all the young People of the Parish, to Buckingham Fair',
and one assumes that they were not principally attracted to the fair because
of its cattle market, the only feature which is mentioned in the commercial
lists.[32]

It should be noted as well that in one region of the country, East Anglia,

[28] Ogilby and Morgan, *Traveller's Pocket-Book.*
[29] George Baker, *The History and Antiquities of the County of Northampton* (2 vols.; London, 1822–41), I, 326–7.
[30] *Creswell and Burbages' Nottingham Journal*, 9 October 1784 and 8 October 1785.
[31] Ogilby and Morgan, *Traveller's Pocket-Book*; John Britten, *A Topographical and Historical Description of the County of Northampton* (London, 1810), p. 114; Bridges, *Northamptonshire*, I, 411; Baker, *County of Northampton*, I, 36–7; and *Northampton Mercury*, 1 June 1730.
[32] *The Blecheley Diary of the Rev. William Cole 1765–1767*, ed. F. G. Stokes (London, 1931), p. 51.

pleasure fairs appear to have been particularly prominent. Of the 111 fairs in Essex around 1756, 63 were cited as specializing in toys and another 9 included toys as one of their specialties; of the 92 fairs in Suffolk, 42 were identified exclusively with toys and 23 included toys as one of their principal articles of sale. The predominance of pleasure fairs in Norfolk may have been rather less pronounced – of the 101 fairs, 16 were exclusively and 29 partly for toys – though many of the fairs were said to be noted for 'petty chapmen', and pedlars were probably most conspicuous at the smaller pleasure fairs.[33] This emphasis on pleasure fairs may have been largely a consequence of the apparent absence of parish feasts in the three counties; fairs, it seems, functioned to a greater extent in East Anglia as festive events, and they provided some of the recreational attractions which in the Midlands and the North were normally associated with wakes. Woodforde's servants in Weston, Norfolk, always got leave to visit their friends at fairs, never at wakes. This regional peculiarity was implied in a comment by William Marshall, when he was remarking on the social character of so many of the fairs in Norfolk: Yorkshire, he said, 'has its *feasts*; other counties their *wakes*; and Norfolk its *fairs*'.[34] Indeed, sociableness was the common ingredient of all such occasions, and it was provided for in some form or other in all parts of the country.

Hiring fairs (see Plate 1), which were popularly known as 'stattis' or 'mops', were always observed as festive events. The statute sessions for hiring servants were supposed to be held under the supervision of the chief constables, but by the end of the eighteenth century in many areas this official involvement had been largely abandoned. The fairs themselves, however, normally survived, partly because they continued to be serviceable for both masters and servants, and partly because publicans and stall-keepers were active in giving them encouragement. Statute fairs functioned most obviously as labour exchanges, but the evidence suggests that they were of at least equal importance as social occasions. John Clare, for instance, was a witness to the holiday mood at hiring fairs:

> He knew the manners too of merry rout
> Statute and feast his village yearly knew
> And glorious revels too without a doubt
> Such pastimes were to Hob and Nell and Sue
> Milkmaids and clowns that statute joys pursue
> And rattle off like hogs to London mart
> Weary of old they seek for places new
> Where men hail maidens with a frothing quart
> And Hodge with sweetheart fix'd forgets his plough and cart[35]

'In the evening they turn to a kind of holiday romp,' said one writer of the statute fairs he had seen in Leicestershire; on 3 October 1791 James Woodforde saw 'a great many Lads and Lasses' going to the hiring fair at

---

[33] Owen, *Fairs*.

[34] William Marshall, *The Rural Economy of Norfolk* (2 vols.; London, 1787), II, 261.

[35] *Village Minstrel*, stanza 61. The punctuation has been removed from these and other verses by Clare since it was clearly a result of the publisher's intervention.

Reepham.[36] Some of the many newspaper notices of statute fairs drew attention to the intended diversions: 'Ten-Bell Ringing' at the fair in Stonham Aspal, Suffolk, in 1757; bell ringing and a match at singlesticks at Stony Stratford, Buckinghamshire, in 1765; backswords and a variety of races at Berkhamstead, Hertfordshire, in 1751; morris dancing at Great Brington, near Northampton, in 1747; bell ringing, morris dancing, and a match at singlesticks at the statute in Towcester, Northamptonshire, in 1766.[37] Some statute fairs were very substantial events, like the one at Polesworth, Warwickshire, which William Marshall noticed in 1784: 'farm servants, for several miles round', he said, 'consider themselves as liberated from servitude on this day; and, whether they be already hired, or really want masters, hie way, without leave, perhaps, to the statute'.[38] Michaelmas was the most common time for hiring fairs, though they were also held around Martinmas (in Yorkshire), Christmas (in the south-west), and occasionally in May (in Cumberland and parts of Lincoln-shire).

One gets the strong impression from the contemporary sources that hiring fairs were very widely established – William Marshall, for instance, thought that in Leicestershire 'most towns and many villages have their statutes'.[39] In September and early October 1757 the *Ipswich Journal* carried advertisements for twenty statute fairs in the county of Suffolk. Lists of fairs from the late eighteenth century indicate that there were at least ten places with statutes in Oxfordshire – two at each of Woodstock, Chipping Norton, Witney, Bicester, and Thame; and one at Burford, Banbury, Deddington, Watlington, and Wheatley.[40] There is positive evidence that fourteen hiring fairs were held in Northamptonshire in 1805, and it is probable that there were several more.[41] In general it would appear that during the eighteenth and early nineteenth centuries most counties had about one hiring fair for every one to two hundreds.

It is important to emphasize the extent to which wakes and fairs were intimately involved in the seasonal rhythms of agricultural life. To a con-siderable degree they were dependent on and given form by these rhythms. In many instances they were fitted into the cycles of agricultural labour at times of convenience, during those intervals between the completion of one set of tasks and the beginning of another. There was a concentration of festive occasions during the later spring and early summer because this was a period of partial relaxation between the spring sowing and the summer

---

[36] William Pitt, A General View of the Agriculture of the County of Leicester (London, 1809), p. 303, and Diary of a Country Parson, ed. Beresford, III, 303; cf. Gentleman's Magazine, LXXV (1805), part i, 202.

[37] Ipswich Journal, 17 September 1757; Northampton Mercury, 30 September 1765, 26 August 1751, 7 September 1747, and 6 October 1766.

[38] William Marshall, The Rural Economy of the Midland Counties (2 vols.; London, 1790), II, 19. There is a detailed description of the large hiring fair at Studley, Warwickshire, in Hone's Table Book, I, cols. 171–8; cf. Howitt, Rural Life, pp. 495–7.

[39] Marshall, Midland Counties, II, 20n; cf. Pitt, Agriculture of the County of Leicester, p.302.

[40] J. Bridges, A Book of Fairs, or, A Guide to West-Country Travellers (n.p., n.d.), p. 13, and Owen, New Book of Fairs (1792).

[41] Northampton Mercury, September and October 1805.

harvest. But easily the most important release from labour came with the completion of the corn harvest. In late summer the agricultural year in arable areas was brought to an end: the harvest itself was frequently concluded with a festive dinner for the workers who had helped to bring in the crops, and during the next few weeks, as the pressures of work slackened off, many of the labouring people were able to enjoy a period of relative leisure. The necessity to gather in the crops imposed overriding demands on most of the farming population, and the intensification of labour during these weeks ensured that it would be generally regarded as an especially unpropitious time for recreation. In Surrey in 1671 a man was prosecuted for baiting a bull, not because the sport was thought to be cruel, but on the grounds that by practising it during the harvest-time he caused 'divers labourers and other poore persons to leave their work'.[42] There was a marked decline in the number of East Anglian pleasure fairs during August, and in the area around Stamford during the 1840s it appears that not a single wake was celebrated between the end of August and the middle of September. But in the autumn there were fewer pressing demands and as a result it was a convenient and welcome time for feasts and fairs. White Kennet pointed out that many wakes 'are now celebrated near the time of Michaelmass, when a vacation from the labours of harvest and the plough, does afford the best opportunity for visits and sports'.[43] Most people would have had more money than usual – the labourers with their harvest wages, the servants whose terms ended at Michaelmas with their newly settled accounts – and some of the money was spent on pleasure and hospitality, or it was used to buy clothing, finery, and household effects at one of the autumn fairs. The autumn was an interim season, socially and economically, between the peak period of labour and the discomforts, hardships, and dreariness which were often suffered during the winter; and winter was very much the off-season for wakes and pleasure fairs. Autumn, then, brought a welcome respite from labour, and spring brought a sense of renewal after the tribulations of winter: one of the stanzas of a ballad known as 'The Mayer's Song' spoke of how

Life with us is in its spring,
We enjoy a blooming May,
Summer will its labour bring,
Winter has its pinching day.[44]

For those communities which were intimately involved in arable farming, the many fairs and feasts which followed the harvest would have served as the principal holidays of the autumn. The only other autumn holiday of general significance was Guy Fawkes Day, the 5th of November. One observer referred in 1686 to the 'rejoicings and sports on gunpowder treason night' and 'the privilege of haveing some merriment' which the common people enjoyed.[45] Special festivities were commonly observed

[42] Quoted without reference in Govett, *King's Book of Sports*, p. 73.
[43] Kennet, *Parochial Antiquities*, p. 611.   [44] Hone, *Every-Day Book*, II, col. 571.
[45] *The Diary of Abraham de la Pryme*, ed. Charles Jackson (Publications of the Surtees Society, LIV, 1870), p. 10.

in the larger towns. At Northampton in 1742 the 5th of November was marked by the 'Ringing of Bells at all the Churches' and ceremonial processions, and 'the Evening concluded with Bonfires, Fireworks, and other Demonstrations of Joy'.[46] There were similar celebrations at Gloucester in 1740, and the day was also brought to a close with diversions which would have been partly for the benefit of the common people, in particular bonfires and fireworks.[47] The anniversary was also observed in rural areas: 'The rustic feasts were celebrated according to custom', noted Thomas Isham of Lamport on the 5th of November, 1671; and on the same day in 1766 Wlliam Cole wrote in his Bletchley diary of 'Bonfires on the Green'.[48] Most of the customary amusements of Guy Fawkes Day centred on the various uses of fire – bonfires, firearms, squibs, firebrands, and fireworks. At Weston Favell, Northamptonshire, 'the revelry of the day' was 'anticipated for several weeks previous', and fuel was specially collected in order to provide for a large bonfire.[49] At Lincoln, November the 5th was one of the main holidays of the year, and it was distinguished, according to a correspondent in 1818, 'by the usual disgraceful proceedings of the populace – bull baitings, throwing of serpents, squibs, etc.: every parish too had its bonfire and "Old Guy".' [50] Around 1800 at Middleton, according to Samuel Bamford:

> Most people ceased from working in the afternoon, and children went from house to house begging coal to make a bon-fire . . . At night the country would be lighted up by bon-fires . . . tharcake and toffy were distributed to the younger members of families, whilst the elder clubbed their pence and at night had 'a joynin' in some convenient dwelling. The lord of the manor made the young men a present of a good two-horse load of coal, with which a huge fire was lighted on The Bank, near the church, and kept burning all night and most of the day following. The young fellows also joined at ale from the public-house, and with drinking, singing, and exploding of fire-arms, they amused themselves pretty well . . . [51]

Depending on the customs of the locality, the festivities of the Christmas season occurred at various times during the period between Christmas itself and Twelfth Day. 'This was Twelfth-day,' wrote James Boswell in his journal for 6 January 1763, 'on which a great deal of jollity goes on in England'.[52] 'Feasting and rural amusements take place at several seasons of the year', said one observer of Cumberland, 'but the principal are at Christmas, when the greatest hospitality prevails among the villagers; every family is provided with goose pies, minced pies, and ale.'[53] In

---

[46] *Northampton Mercury*, 8 November 1742.   [47] *Gloucester Journal*, 11 November 1740.
[48] *Journal of Thomas Isham*, p. 17, and *Diary of William Cole*, p. 146.
[49] Cole, *Weston Favell*, p. 59.
[50] *Stamford Mercury*, 13 November 1818; cf. the *Mercury* for 10 November 1809, 10 November 1815, 12 November 1819, 10 November 1820, and 9 November 1821.
[51] *The Autobiography of Samuel Bamford*, vol. I: *Early Days*, ed. W. H. Chaloner (London, 1967), pp. 159–60.
[52] *Boswell's London Journal 1762–1763*, ed. Frederick A. Pottle (London, 1950), p. 125.
[53] John Housman, *A Topographical Description of Cumberland, Westmoreland, Lancashire, and a part of the West Riding of Yorkshire* (Carlisle, 1800), pp. 76–7.

Northumberland 'the celebration of New Year's Day is preserved . . . as a rural festival. Gifts are made to children, servants, and dependants, called New Year's Gifts'.[54] Much of the recreation during the Christmas season was taken in small groups – with the family, in intimate gatherings with friends and neighbours – rather than in large public assemblies. Servants were sometimes allowed to attend special parties. Hospitality, sociability, good eating and drinking: these were the dominant features of the season. 'The mirth of the [Twelfth] day here consists of feasting and social intercourse between neighbouring families', said Hutchinson of Northumberland.[55] 'With the generality,' an essay of 1754 suggested, 'Christmas is looked upon as a festival in the most literal sense, and held sacred by good eating and drinking. These, indeed, are the most distinguishing marks of Christmas.'[56] Understandably enough, men whose ordinary diet was poor and monotonous had a particular appreciation for the lavish fare and special delicacies which were made available at such times as the Christmas season and the week of the annual wake.

There were also several public recreations of the Christmas season, most notably mumming and ceremonial dancing. On 2 January 1769 at Castle Cary in Somerset James Woodforde recorded in his diary, 'We had the fine Mummers this evening at the Parsonage'; at Witney, Oxfordshire, mummers were still performing at Christmas time around the middle of the nineteenth century.[57] In 1769 John Wallis wrote of the special Christmas rituals which were observed in parts of Northumberland:

> Young men march from village to village, and from house to house, with music before them, dressed in an antic attire, and before the . . . entrance of every house entertain the family with . . . the antic dance . . . with swords or spears in their hands, erect, and shining. This they call, The *sword*-dance. For their pains they are presented with a small gratuity in money, more or less, according to every house-holder's ability. Their gratitude is expressed by firing a gun.[58]

Mumming plays and sword dancing were said to be common during the season in the North of England.[59] Other Christmas customs were also observed in various areas, including wassailing, carolling, and other forms of ritual processions, and the decorating of houses. Woodforde, for instance, wrote on 24 December 1768 of the carolling which was customary at Castle Cary, and in December 1790 at Weston, Norfolk he gave 1s. 6d. to 'Willm Mason of Sparham who used to go about at Christmas with 10 Bells, and has this Year got a Bell-Harp'.[60]

[54] Hutchinson, *Northumberland*, II, Appendix, p. 4.
[55] *Ibid.* II, Appendix, p. 5; cf. George Young, *A History of Whitby* (2 vols.; Whitby, 1817), II, 879–80.
[56] *London Magazine*, XXIII (1754), 535.
[57] *Diary of a Country Parson*, I, 83, and J. A. Giles, *History of Witney* (London, 1852), p. 62.
[58] John Wallis, *The Natural History and Antiquities of Northumberland* (2 vols.; London, 1769), II, 28; cf. C. J. D. Ingledew, *The History and Antiquities of North Allerton, in the County of York* (London, 1858), pp. 342–3.
[59] Brand, *Popular Antiquities*, pp. 175–6; Christopher Clarkson, *The History and Antiquities of Richmond in the County of York* (2nd edn, Richmond, 1821), pp. 290–1.
[60] *Diary of a Country Parson*, I, 82, and III, 239.

Plough Monday, which fell on the first Monday after Twelfth Day, was by tradition, if no longer always in practice, the time when agricultural work was resumed following the festivities of Christmas, and in many places it served as a holiday for the farm labourers. 'On Plow Monday', wrote Aulay Macaulay, 'I have taken notice of an annual display of Morrice-dancers at Claybrook, who come from the neighbouring villages of Sapcote and Sharnford.'[61] During the late 1760s at Waterbeach, Cambridgeshire, William Cole was visited by the ploughmen on their holiday (on 11 January 1768 he wrote of 'Plow Monday. All the Boys in the Parish with Hurdy Gurdy's, black'd Faces, Bells and Plows'); and at Barnack, Northamptonshire, during the 1720s the rector's accounts included annual gifts on Plough Monday.[62] Plough Monday celebrations were also to be found in other villages in Northamptonshire, and in parts of Derbyshire, Staffordshire, Lincolnshire, and Yorkshire; for the most part they were confined to the east-central regions of England, the area encompassing Yorkshire, the East Midlands, and East Anglia.[63] The customs of the day often included mumming, or ceremonial dancing, and usually a procession by the agricultural labourers, and the small donations which were collected during the day were laid out for an evening's feasting and drinking. It was said that the most common practice was 'to drag a plough from door to door, soliciting *plough money*, wherewith to defray the expences of a feast, and a dance in the evening'.[64] A contributor to the *Gentleman's Magazine* reported that 'the young men yoke themselves, and draw a plough about with musick, and one or two persons, in antic dresses, like jack-puddings, go from house to house, to gather money to drink; if you refuse them, they plough up your dunghill'.[65]

Shrove Tuesday was the only other major winter holiday. It was especially noted as a holiday for apprentices, though many other labouring people observed it as well. Brand mentioned it as the apprentices' 'particular holiday' and noticed how, 'At Newcastle upon Tyne, the great Bell of St Nicholas' Church is tolled at Twelve o'clock on this Day; Shops are immediately shut up, Offices closed, and all Kind of Business ceases; a Sort of little Carnival ensuing for the remaining Part of the Day.'[66] It

[61] Macaulay, *Claybrook*, p. 128.
[62] W. M. Palmer, *William Cole of Milton* (Cambridge, 1935), p. 47; B.M., 'Diary of Rev. William Cole', Add. MS 5835, pp. 369 and 398; and A. Tindal Hart, *Country Counting House: The Story of Two Eighteenth-Century Clerical Account Books* (London, 1962), p. 67.
[63] Anne E. Baker, *Glossary of Northamptonshire Words and Phrases* (2 vols.; London, 1854), II, 123–4; Thomas James, *The History and Antiquities of Northamptonshire* (London, 1864), p. 15; *Derby Mercury*, 1 February 1816 and 9 January 1817; J. E. Brogden, *Provincial Words and Expressions Current in Lincolnshire* (London, 1866), pp. 151–2; *Stamford Mercury*, 14 January 1848 and 15 January 1864; Clarkson, *Richmond*, p. 293; and Thomas Davidson, 'Plough Rituals in England and Scotland', *Agricultural History Review*, VII (1959), 30.
[64] John Brady, *Clavis Calendaria: or, A Compendious Analysis of the Calendar* (2 vols.; London, 1812), I, 153.
[65] *Gentleman's Magazine*, XXXII (1762), 568; cf. Brand, *Popular Antiquities*, p. 409, and Howitt, *Rural Life*, pp. 471–2.
[66] Brand, *Popular Antiquities*, pp. 331 and 333.

was said that during the early nineteenth century at Filey in the East Riding the 'apprentices and servants are on this day privileged with a holiday, for recreation'.[67] On Shrove Tuesday at Messingham, Lincolnshire, in the later eighteenth century 'cock fights were held at the public house in the morning. In the afternoon foot-ball was played, and the day was concluded with dancing and cards.'[68] Eating pancakes, as a number of observers pointed out, was one of the most distinctive of the Shrovetide customs. Samuel Bamford, for example, recalled that at Middleton in the early nineteenth century 'we had always a holiday on [Shrove] Tuesday, when we went to each other's houses to turn our pancakes'; it was reported that on Shrove Tuesday at Claybrook 'a bell rings at noon, which is meant as a signal for the people to begin frying their pancakes'.[69] The sporting attractions of the day were most commonly associated with football and throwing at cocks, both of which are considered in the following chapter.

During the holidays of the Easter season, said Henry Bourne, 'it is customary for Work to cease, and Servants to be at Liberty'.[70] Easter was a time for general festivity and relaxation. 'From time immemorial', remarked the *Manchester Chronicle* in 1841, 'the Easter week has been a season of mirth and festivity amongst the sons and daughters of toil in this neighbourhood'.[71] The holidays were marked by a variety of standard diversions. At Richmond in the North Riding football, fives, and cricket were practised; there were 'revels' and pugilism at Bristol in 1822, handbell-ringing at Oakingham, Berkshire, in 1829, and a steeplechase race at East Kirby, Lincolnshire, in 1841.[72] At Waterbeach on Easter Tuesday 1769 William Cole wrote of 'A Dancing at Rose Denson's where Tom and Molly went at 8 and Jem at 10 when I went to Bed'.[73] On Easter Monday at Hallaton, Leicestershire, it was customary to have a 'scrambling' for ale and meat pies, a sort of licenced free-for-all, and the afternoon was 'spent in festivity, ringing of bells, fighting of cocks, quoits, and such like exercises, by Hallaton and the neighbouring youth'.[74] There was also a considerable concentration of fairs around Easter, some of which were at least partly for pleasure. According to William Owen's guide to fairs, in the middle of the eighteenth century there were 113 English and Welsh fairs during the week before and the week after Easter, 63 of them on Easter Monday and Tuesday.[75]

[67] John Cole, *The History and Antiquities of Filey* (Scarborough, 1828), p. 132; cf. Young, *Whitby*, II, 881, and Dawson, *Skipton*, p. 375.
[68] *John MacKinnon's Account of Messingham in the County of Lincoln*, ed. Edward Peacock (Hertford, 1881), p. 10.
[69] Bamford, *Early Days*, p. 136, and Macaulay, *Claybrook*, p. 128.
[70] Bourne, *Antiquitates Vulgares*, p. 196.
[71] Quoted in the *Derby Mercury*, 21 April 1841; cf. *Leicester Journal*, 27 April 1821 and 31 March 1826.
[72] Clarkson, *Richmond*, p. 294; John Latimer, *The Annals of Bristol in the Nineteenth Century* (Bristol, 1887), p. 97; *Berkshire Chronicle*, 25 April 1829; and *Lincolnshire Chronicle*, 23 April 1841.
[73] B. M., 'Diary of William Cole', Add. MS 5835, p. 404.
[74] John Nichols, *The History and Antiquities of the County of Leicester* (4 vols.; London, 1795–1811), II, part ii, 600.   [75] Owen, *Fairs*, pp. 172–3.

May Day was one of the principal holidays of the spring, especially for the young people. On the first of May, wrote Henry Bourne,

> the juvenile Part of both Sexes, are wont to rise a little after Mid-night, and walk to some neighbouring Wood, accompany'd with Musick and the blowing of Horns; where they break down Branches from the Trees, and adorn them with Nose-gays and Crowns of Flowers. When this is done, they return with their Booty home-wards, about the rising of the Sun, and make their Doors and Win-dows to Triumph in the Flowery Spoil. The after-part of the Day, is chiefly spent in dancing round a Tall-poll, which is called a May-Poll . . .[76]

These were the essential elements of the May Day festivities: gathering flowers and shrubbery, decorating houses, ritual dances, and general merry-making. In Northumberland, said William Hutchinson, the 'young people of both sexes go out early in the morning of the 1st of May, to gather the flowering thorns and the dew of the grass, which they bring home with music and acclamations; and having dressed a poll on the town-green with garlands, dance around it'.[77] In 1672 an apprentice from Woburn, Bedfordshire, who had been charged with a theft was supported by the parishioners in pleading that he '(with divers other youths of our said parish) had upon May day in the morninge last past stucke severall May bushes at the doores of divers people in our said Towne, and at the very instant (as is supposed) when the money was lost, were drinkinge and makinge merry at those houses where the May bushes were formerly stuck'.[78] There was a 'May-pole hill' near Horncastle in Lincolnshire, and according to William Stukeley, 'the boys annually keep up the festival of the *Floralia* on May Day, making a procession to this hill with *May gads* (as they call them) in their hands', and 'at night they have a bonefire and other merriment'.[79] A cottager in Waterbeach, Cambridgeshire, recalled that in the late eighteenth century May Day 'was our grandest holiday': special garlands were made up and hung in the street, bells were rung, and the day was concluded with dancing, ball games, and various other diver-sions.[80]

While the majority of these May celebrations were held on the first day of the month, it seems that in some places they were customarily observed on the 29th ('Oak-Apple Day'), the anniversary of Charles II's birthday and his return to London in 1660. In these cases the May Day festivities had been transferred to the later date after the Restoration, complete with garlands, maypoles, and traditional dancing, but it is difficult (if not im-possible) to determine the extent of this shift.[81] On 29 May 1761 at Nuneham Courtenay, Oxfordshire, James Newton wrote in his diary of 'Oaken Boughs set at many Peoples' Doors', a practice which may have

[76] Bourne, *Antiquitates Vulgares*, pp. 200–1; cf. Borlase, *Cornwall*, p. 294.
[77] Hutchinson, *Northumberland*, II, Appendix, p. 14.
[78] Bedfordshire R.O., H.S.A. 1672 S50 (24 July 1672).
[79] William Stukeley, *Itinerarium Curiosum* (London, 1724), p. 29.
[80] John Denson, *A Peasant's Voice to Landowners* (Cambridge, 1830), pp. 17–18.
[81] For some evidence on this change, see Wright, *Calendar Customs*, II, 254–70.

been derived from the May Day custom of the same character.[82] A similar custom was still being observed at Lyme Regis, Dorset, in the early nineteenth century.[83] At Normanton, Derbyshire, John Byng came across a maypole in 1789 which was, 'as others of this county, richly adorn'd by garlands, composed of silk, gauze, and mock flowers; and around which (a woman told me) they danced in the Morris-way; but not in honor of the goddess Maia on the 1st of her month, but, rather in memory of the Restoration, upon the 29th of May'.[84]

The Whitsun holidays, along with those at Christmas and Easter, were probably the most widely observed of the yearly celebrations. Whit Monday, said one observer, 'is a universal festival in the humble ranks of life throughout the kingdom'.[85] In previous generations the Whitsun period had been one of the usual times for parish 'ales', and though the religious significance of such ales had largely disappeared by the eighteenth century, their secular spirit lived on, often under the traditional name. In a deposition from Oxfordshire in 1763 one informant 'saith that on Wednesday in Whitsun week last, there being a Whisun ale at Haly . . . he went to sell cakes to the company then assembled there'; another deponent referred to the gathering as 'a Whisun Sport'.[86] In May 1743 at Shalstone, Buckinghamshire, the squire of the parish gave 2s. 6d. to 'the Whitsun-ale folks'.[87] 'A Revel called a Whitsun-Ale' was customary at Eynsham, Oxfordshire, in the 1730s; a similar occasion at Cumner, Berkshire, had to be abandoned in 1753 because of an outbreak of smallpox.[88] A Whitsun ale was held at Towcester in 1766, and a festivity in the Cotswolds which was known by the same name was said in 1779 to be attended 'by great numbers of young people of both sexes'.[89]

The literature of the eighteenth and early nineteenth centuries is full of references to Whitsun festivities. Parson Woodforde's diary, for instance, includes frequent references to the Whitsun recreations in Weston: 'This being Whit Monday', he wrote on 5 June 1786, 'there was running for a Shift, plowing etc. etc. this Afternoon at the Heart'; and on 12 May 1788, 'Merry doings at the Heart to day being Whit Monday, plowing for a Pair of Breeches, running for a Shift, Raffling for a Gown etc.'.[90] During the Whitsun week of 1758 at Shepperton, Surrey, there was a punting match, cudgelling, wrestling, and a smock race for women; at Hornsea in the East Riding during the early nineteenth century the week was noted for

[82] Bodleian Lib., 'Diary of Rev. James Newton of Nuneham Courtenay, Oxon, 1761–62', MS. Eng. misc. e. 251, fol. 10.

[83] George Roberts, The History and Antiquities of the Borough of Lyme Regis and Charmouth (London, 1834), p. 257.

[84] Torrington Diaries, II, 29.

[85] Hone, Every-Day Book, II, col. 666.

[86] Oxfordshire R.O., Quarter Sessions Rolls, Trinity 1763 (Depositions).

[87] Quoted in Purefoy Letters 1735–1753, ed. G. Eland (London, 1931), p. xxv.

[88] H. A. Lloyd Jukes (ed.), Articles of Enquiry Addressed to the Clergy of the Diocese of Oxford at the Primary Visitation of Dr. Thomas Secker, 1738 (Oxfordshire Record Society, XXXVIII, 1957), p. 61; Jackson's Oxford Journal, 26 May 1753.

[89] Northampton Mercury, 12 May 1766; Samuel Rudder, A New History of Gloucestershire (Cirencester, 1779), pp. 23–4.

[90] Diary of a Country Parson, II, 248, III, 24; cf. II, 137, 188; III, 276; V, 316.

feasting and dancing.[91] On Whit Monday 1766 at Bletchley William Cole recorded that the 'Woburn Abbey Morrice Dancers' visited the parish and that 'Tom went to the Alehouse with the young People of the Parish'; the next year Tom and another man 'went to a Wrestling Match at Thornborough' on the Monday and on the Tuesday the Woburn dancers again performed.[92] Whitsuntide, in fact, was one of the principal times of the year for ceremonial dancing. Morris dancers were noticed by Nicholas Blundell at Hatherop, Gloucestershire, in 1703 and by John Byng at Wallingford, Berkshire, in 1781, on both occasions during Whitsun week.[93] Henry Purefoy of Shalstone made donations to the Whitsun morris dancers in 1735 and 1742, and an anonymous account book from Warwickshire records payments to the holiday dancers in 1775 and 1776.[94] Morris dancing was also a part of the special festivities which were annually observed at Kidlington in Oxfordshire:

> on Monday after Whitson week, there is a fat live Lamb provided, and the Maids of the Town, having their thumbs ty'd behind them run after it, and she that with her mouth takes and holds the Lamb, is declared *Lady of the Lamb*, which being dress'd with the skin hanging on, is carried on a long Pole before the Lady and her Companions to the Green, attended with Musick and a *Morisco Dance* of Men, and another of Women, where the rest of the day is spent in dancing, mirth and merry glee. The next day the Lamb is part bak'd, boyld and rost, for the Ladies feast, where she sits majestically at the upper end of the Table and her Companions with her, with musick and other attendants . . . [95]

Around Whitsuntide, as at Easter, there was a large number of fairs. William Owen listed a total of 314 English and Welsh fairs which fell during the fortnight before and the fortnight after Whit Sunday, 79 of them on Ascension Day and 113 on Whit Monday and Tuesday.[96] In Essex alone there were 10 Whitsun pleasure fairs and another 2 just after Trinity Sunday. An unofficial fair was held on Trinity Monday at Naseby, Northamptonshire – it was known as 'Rothwell-fair Monday' – 'the inhabitants inviting their friends, and making merry; the young people assemble, and spend the afternoon and evening, with ringing of bells, dancing, etc.'.[97] At Leicester during the 1830s Whitsun week was still regarded as 'a general holiday' by the common people, and here as in many other towns and

[91] John Brand, *Observations on Popular Antiquities*, revised by Henry Ellis (2 vols.; London, 1813), from a copy annotated with notes and clippings by Joseph Haslewood which is held in the British Museum (shelf mark: 142.e.1, 2), vol. II, facing p. 226 (hereafter cited as B. M. Brand); E. W. Bedell, *An Account of Hornsea, in Holderness, in the East-Riding of Yorkshire* (Hull, 1848), p. 89.

[92] *Diary of William Cole*, pp. 51, 222, and 223

[93] *The Great Diurnal of Nicholas Blundell of Little Crosby, Lancashire*, ed. J. J. Bagley, transcribed and annotated by Frank Tyrer (2 vols.; Record Society of Lancashire and Cheshire, 1968–70), I, 35, and II, xiv; *Torrington Diaries*, I, 5.

[94] *Purefoy Letters*, p. xxv; Warwickshire R.O., CR 125B/4 (for 5 June 1775 and 2 June 1776).

[95] Thomas Blount, *Fragmenta Antiquitatis* (London, 1679), p. 149.

[96] Owen, *Fairs* (1756), pp. 173–6.

[97] John Mastin, *The History and Antiquities of Naseby* (Cambridge, 1792), pp. 77–8.

villages it had become the main time of festivity for the large number of clubs and friendly societies which had grown up since the later eighteenth century.[98] This, for example, was clearly the case in the counties of Northampton, Derby, and Norfolk (in Woodforde's parish the 'Weston Purse-Club' had its annual perambulation on Whit Tuesday), as well as in many parts of the West Country.[99]

[98] *Leicester Journal*, 27 May 1831; Howitt, *Rural Life*, pp. 444–50.
[99] Baker, *Northamptonshire Words*, ii, 435; *Derby Mercury*, 10 June 1840, 5 June 1844, 10 June 1846; Hone, *Every-Day Book*, ii, cols. 669–70; *Diary of a Country Parson*, v, 119, 316, 393; and Margaret D. Fuller, *West Country Friendly Societies* (Reading, 1964), p. 89.

3

Sports and pastimes

We have already had occasion to refer to many of the sports and pastimes of the eighteenth century. The variety of recreational activities was reasonably impressive: there were athletic sports and animal sports, team sports and individual sports, games of skill and games of chance, casual kinds of play and more formal and structured diversions, events at which most people were spectators and others which allowed a wider participation. In 1720 John Strype indicated that in London 'the more common sort divert themselves at Foot ball, Wrestling, Cudgels, Ninepins, Shovelboard, Cricket, Stow-ball, Ringing of Bells, Quoits, pitching the Bar, Bull and Bear baiting, throwing at Cocks, and lying at Alehouses'.[1] Many of the recreations of the period have continued to the present day, though usually in a very modified form, and others are now defunct. Some sports and pastimes were frequently documented; others were seldom mentioned, partly because they were closely associated with the low-keyed, informal relaxations of everyday life; others still were confined to particular localities. The more notable of these diversions, those which appear to have been practised in many parts of the country, are the subjects of this chapter.

Football play in the twentieth century has taken three basic forms: soccer, rugby football, and American football. The rules and organization of each game are now, of course, elaborately systematized, and the sport has become a prominent fixture in modern society, both nationally and internationally. In earlier times, however, when social outlooks were considerably more parochial, this sort of standardization did not exist: the peculiarities of local customs and circumstances exercised a very great influence on the recreational activities of the common people. Those games which we can recognize as some form of football play were practised in a variety of ways, for they were all distinctively shaped by the particular traditions of their own localities. In some games kicking was the main exercise of the sport, in others carrying and throwing were allowed, and in a few cases there was very little kicking at all. Some games were played with an inflated bladder which was usually encased with leather; others, especially those which emphasized throwing and carrying, made use of a smaller hard ball. There were different sets of rules which determined the character of fair play: in some places the rules were comparatively sophisticated in the restrictions they placed on aggressive behaviour, while in others the

---

[1] A *Survey of the Cities of London and Westminster: by John Stow*, ed. John Strype (London, 1720), Book I, p. 257; cf. Edward Chamberlayne, *Angliae Notitia, or the Present State of England* (London, 1669), p. 46.

players were allowed a good deal of discretion. 'When the exercise becomes exceeding violent,' said Joseph Strutt, 'the players kick each other's shins without the least ceremony, and some of them are overthrown at the hazard of their limbs.'[2] A contest might be over an extensive stretch of countryside, with one goal perhaps the village well and the other a church a mile or two distant in an adjacent parish (the annual match between the students of the Bromfield free school, for example, was played between the eastern and western parts of the parish, a distance of two or three miles, 'every inch of which ground was keenly disputed');[3] or it could be in a convenient enclosed field, the goals a pair of stakes, or any other handy markers, a few yards apart. There were also considerable differences in the degree to which the sport was formalized and incorporated into an established local tradition. At one extreme was the impromptu, fairly casual play through the streets of a town or village or in an untilled field; at the other were the big matches on festive occasions, matches which were frequently soaked in ritual and organized to the point of being an institutionalized element in the community's pattern of life. Somewhere in between were many of the games in the countryside of village against village or hundred against hundred, or perhaps between the two ends of a parish at its annual wake. Some matches called for teams of ten to fifteen a side, while others, the less regulated affairs, permitted numbers unlimited.

The East Anglian version of football was known as 'camping'. 'Camping is Foot-ball playing, at which they are very dextrous in Norfolk', wrote Daniel Hilman in 1710; later in the century it was said that 'in some parts [of Suffolk] this active game of our ancestors is still much in fashion'.[4] A camping ground had two goals (around ten yards in width) 150 to 200 yards apart, and when play was to begin,

> An indifferent spectator . . . throws up a ball, of the size of a common cricket ball, mid-way between the confronted players [of ten to fifteen a side], and makes his escape. It is the object of the players to seize and convey the ball between their own goals . . . he who can catch or seize it speeds therefore home pursued by his opponents (thro' whom he has to make his way) aided by the jostlings and various assistances of his own *sidesmen*. If caught and held, or in imminent danger of being caught, he *throws* the ball – but must in no case *give* it – to a less beleagured friend, who, if it be not arrested in its course or he jostled away by the eager and watchful adversaries, catches it; and he hastens homeward, in like manner pursued, annoyed, and aided – winning the notch (or snotch) if he contrives to *carry* – not *throw* – it between his goals. But this in a well matched game, is no easy achievement, and often requires much time, many doublings, detours, and exertions . . . if the holder of

---

[2] Strutt, *Sports and Pastimes*, p. 79.

[3] William Hutchinson, *The History of the County of Cumberland* (2 vols.; Carlisle, 1794), II, 323n.

[4] Hilman, *Tusser Redivivus*, 'November and December', p. 15; Sir John Cullum, *The History and Antiquities of Hawsted, in the County of Suffolk* (London, 1784), p. 113.

the ball be caught with the ball in his possession, he loses a *snotch*, if, therefore, he be hard pressed, he *throws* it to a convenient friend, more free and in breath than himself. At the loss (or gain) of a *snotch*, a recommence takes place, arranging which gives the parties time to take breath. Seven or nine notches are the game – and these it will sometimes take two or three hours to win.[5]

A football was used for the modified game of 'kicking camp' and shoes were worn for what was quaintly known as 'savage camp'. There seems to have been a further distinction between two basic styles of camping, rough-play and civil-play: the former included boxing as one of its tactics while the latter allowed only wrestling and kicking.[6] Cornish hurling was somewhat similar to camping, though in the western parts of the county the play was normally over open countryside and permitted an indefinite number of participants.[7]

In many places the principal football match of the year was on Shrove Tuesday. During the earlier nineteenth century there were still scores of Shrovetide games, many of which were played through the streets of town. Among the recorded holiday matches were the ones at Alnwick, Chester-le-Street, Sedgefield, Derby, Ashbourne, Nuneaton, and Corfe Castle; Twickenham, Teddington, and Bushey Park in Middlesex; and Dorking, Richmond, Kingston-upon-Thames, Hampton Wick, East Mousley, Hampton, and Thames Ditton, all in Surrey.[8] 'From time immemorial', observed *The Times* of 6 March 1840, 'it has been the custom in most of the parishes and places in the western portions of the counties of Middlesex and Surrey, for the inhabitants on Shrove Tuesday in every year to devote the greater part of the day to the *manly sport* of foot-ball, which has not been confined to the open spaces of the respective towns and villages, but the ball has been pursued by hundreds through the most public thoroughfares, the shops and houses of which were customarily closed, and the windows barricaded with hurdles, to prevent their being broken.' In some places the contests were associated with other holidays. Devonshire games were often on Good Friday; at Workington and Eakring, Nottinghamshire, the main match of the year was on Easter Tuesday; and at Kirkham, Lancashire, it was customarily played on Christmas Day.[9]

Since each holiday match had its own special customs and playing arrangements, no one case can be regarded as completely typical; however,

[5] Edward Moor, *Suffolk Words and Phrases* (London, 1823), pp. 63–6.

[6] R. W. Ketton-Cremer, 'Camping – a forgotten Norfolk Game', *Norfolk Archaeology*, xxiv (1932), 88–92.

[7] Borlase, *Cornwall*, pp. 300–1.

[8] See Francis P. Magoun, Jr, *History of Football from the Beginnings to 1871* (Bochum-Langendreer, 1938), pp. 101–2 for a list of the references to Shrovetide games which he had collected; and Wright, *Calendar Customs*, i, 26; Hone, *Every-Day Book*, i, 245; and Charlotte S. Burne (ed.), *Shropshire Folk-lore: A Sheaf of Gleanings* (London, 1883), p. 319.

[9] *Devon and Cornwall Notes and Queries*, x (1918–19), 113; *Notes and Queries*, 10th series, 1 (1904), 194 and 230, and W. Litt, *Wrestliana; or, An Historical Account of Ancient and Modern Wrestling* (Whitehaven, 1823), pp. 52–4; V. C. H. *Nottinghamshire*, ii, 412; Henry Fishwick, *The History of the Parish of Kirkham, in the County of Lancashire* (Publications of the Chetham Society, Old series, xcii, 1874), p. 206.

we can at least examine one of them, the well documented Derby game, both as an interesting case in its own right and as an illustration of the general character of a Shrovetide match. In theory the Derby competition was between the parishes of St Peter's and All Saints, but in practice the rest of the borough was allowed to take part, and the townsmen were usually joined by a large influx of holidayers from the countryside. Business was suspended for the afternoon and play began at two o'clock from the market place. The objective of each team (there were 500 to 1,000 a side in the early nineteenth century) was to carry the ball to a goal about a mile outside the town, St Peter's the gate of a nursery ground towards London and All Saints the wheel of a watermill to the west. In most matches the St Peter's side tried to get the ball into the River Derwent and swim with it, a circuitous approach to their own goal but a tactical removal of the ball in the opposite direction from the All Saints' watermill. If the Peter's men could overpower their rivals in the water, the ball was landed at a point near their goal and carried home; if the defence was too strong it would be hidden until dark, sometimes to be relieved of its cork shavings and the covering smuggled in under someone's smock or petticoat. Occasionally, when one side had uncommon muscle, the offence was straight overland, but this strategy obliged the Peter's team to cross the brook which led to their opponents' goal, an approach which could easily backfire. New ploys for attack or defence were warmly received: on one occasion, for instance, an enterprising fellow was reputed to have escaped with the ball into a sewer and passed under the town, only to be surprised as he surfaced by a party of opponents. Towards the finish of the match, when the drift of the contest was clear, the climax centred on the stratagems around one goal, such as starting up the All Saints' water-wheel. The player who ended the game was chaired through the winners' home territory and was given the honour of throwing up the ball at the start of the next year's play. A similar match for the youth of the town was staged on Ash Wednesday under the supervision of their elders.[10]

Although the Derby game probably attracted an unusually large following, many of the other holiday matches would also have been recreational highlights in their own, usually smaller communities. The entry for Shrove Tuesday 1767 in William Cole's Bletchley diary mentioned 'Football playing on the Green',[11] and in a case like this a significant proportion of the able-bodied men in the parish would have had to turn out just in order to make up the teams. There were numerous places in which organized games were planned or traditionally anticipated for some special occasion. 'Seven bouchers should have play'd at foot-ball with seven glovers, being Tuesday, this year above', wrote Jacob Bee of Durham on 18 September 1683, 'and my man Christopher went without leave to play.'[12] In October

[10] This account is based particularly on Glover, *County of Derby*, I, 262–3; Llewellyn Jewitt, 'On Ancient Customs and Sports of the County of Derby', *Journal of the British Archaeological Association*, VII (1852), 204; an article in the *Penny Magazine*, 6 April 1839; and a report in the *Derby Mercury*, 20 February 1827.
[11] *Diary of William Cole*, p. 191.
[12] 'Diary of Jacob Bee of Durham', in *Six North Country Diaries* (Publications of the Surtees Society, CXVIII, 1910), p. 47.

1735 a match was being planned in London 'for 12 Norfolk Men to play against 12 of any other County or Country whatsoever'; and on 2 February 1742 Richard Kay of Baldingstone, Lancashire, wrote in his diary: 'in the Afternoon took a Walk to Bury with great Numbers beside to see a Foot-Ball Match betwixt Town and Country'.[13] Camping and football matches were sometimes advertised in East Anglia, and during the 1770s there were reports of organized games in parts of Devon, at Rochdale, Lancashire, between some of the hamlets in the parish, and at Hitchin in Hertford-shire.[14] There was a report in 1722, which we may hope was not apocryphal, that on a Sunday in the fall at a village near Eastlow, 'during the usual time of Divine Service, there happened such a violent Hurricane, that a great part of the Steeple of the Church was blown down; which would have done very considerable Damage to the Parishioners had they been at Church: But they happened to be luckily at a Foot-Ball Match, by which means their Lives were probably saved'.[15]

Along with these more formalized, more structured matches, there must have been a good many relatively informal and spontaneous games, on the lines of the football play in Covent Garden described in John Gay's *Trivia* (see Plate 2). On 12 January 1723, for instance, an impromptu game was reported from Smithfield, and on 23 April 1711 Nicholas Blundell spent some time teaching a few of the villagers 'to play at Penny prick with the Foot balle'.[16] In Chichester 'Footballing in the streets day after day in frosty weather' was said to be a familiar sight in the earlier eighteenth century; on 3 January 1665 Samuel Pepys noticed that a street in London he rode through was 'full of footballs, it being a great frost'.[17] In 1792 the Moravians in Bedford were complaining of the games which were played just outside their single brethren's house.[18] In these cases the people's recreation would have been taken during a brief respite from work, in the evening perhaps, or at some time during the weekend. A cottager in Waterbeach, Cambridgeshire, spoke of how, 'as the days lengthened, in the evening, after our work was done, we assembled on our village-green to spend our time in some rustic amusements, such as wrestling, football, etc.'; and in 1759 a resident of Shifford, Berkshire, referred to the main sports of the village as 'football, wrestling, and

[13] *Suffolk Mercury*, 27 October 1735; *The Diary of Richard Kay, 1716–1751, of Baldingstone, near Bury: A Lancashire Doctor*, ed. W. Brockbank and F. Kenworthy (Publications of the Chetham Society, 3rd series, XVI, 1968), p. 47; cf. B. T. Barton, *History of the Borough of Bury and Neighbourhood* (Bury, 1874), p. 41.

[14] *Norwich Gazette*, 2 May 1741, quoted in John Glyde, *The Norfolk Garland* (London, 1872), p. 165; *Ipswich Journal*, 19 October 1754, quoted in the *East Anglian Daily Times*, 21 September 1901, p. 12; *Chelmsford Chronicle*, 19 June 1789; William Chapple, *A Review of Part of Risdon's Survey of Devon* (Exeter, 1785), pp. 37–8; Henry Fishwick, *The History of the Parish of Rochdale* (London and Rochdale, 1889), p. 536; and Reginald L. Hine, *The History of Hitchin* (2 vols.; London, 1927–9), II, 244.

[15] *St James's Journal*, 1 December 1722.

[16] *St James's Journal*, 19 January 1723; *Diurnal of Nicholas Blundell*, I, 287.

[17] *The Memoirs of James Spershott*, ed. Francis W. Steer (Chichester Papers, no. 30, 1962), p. 14; *The Diary of Samuel Pepys*, ed. Henry B. Wheatley (8 vols.; London, 1904–5), IV, 303; cf. M. Misson's *Memoirs and Obesrvations in His Travels over England*, ed. John Ozell (London, 1719), pp. 306–7.

[18] Bedfordshire R.O., M.O. 35 (meeting of 21 February 1792).

cudgelling'.[19] John Clare recalled some of his own recreational experiences: 'I never had much relish for the pastimes of youth', he confessed; 'instead of going out on the green at the town end on Winter sundays to play football I stuck to my corner stool poreing over a book'.[20]

Whatever form it might have taken, however organized or casual it might have been, it is clear that football was a very common and widespread recreation. On 4 July 1696 Sir William Trumbull wrote from Whitehall to a correspondent with regard to 'the numerous meetings of People at Football Matches etc.'.[21] On some occasions the sport was even employed as a camouflage for an instance of popular protest. In the fenland, for example, some of the attempts to resist the various schemes for enclosure and drainage were initiated and organized under the guise of a football game. The Isle of Ely was the scene of such protests in June 1638 when a camping match provided the excuse for several hundred men to assemble together and then proceed to destroy the drainage ditches.[22] A letter of 9 March 1699 from the Privy Council to the Lord Lieutenants of Cambridgeshire, Norfolk, Huntingdonshire, and Northamptonshire revealed a similar use of the sport:

> After our very hearty Commendation to your Grace, The Governor, Bayliffs and Commonalty of the Company of Conservatiors of the Great Levell of the Fenn called Bedford Levell having by their Petition this day Read at the Board humbly set forth that being very Sensible of the Ruyne and Destruction lately committed by divers desperate and malitious Persons that have destroyed in a great Measure the works of Draining in Deeping Levell, adjacent to the Petitioners Levell, under Colour and pretence of Foot Ball Playing; They the Petitioners have lately received notice of the like Design against the works of Bedford Levell, Humbly praying that Such orders and directions may be given as may secure the Petitioners and the Countrys Estates in the said Levell from any Violence or Destruction. And it appearing . . . that Publick notice has been given by a Paper affixed on march Bridge of a Foot Ball Play and other Sports on or about the Fourteenth of this instant March on Coats Green by Wittlesea, and that Severall Persons had been heard to say that the Captain or Chief of the Mobb in the late Ryat in Deeping Fenns was to be at the said Foot Ball Play, and that they would pull down the mills and Cutt the Banks as had been already done in Deeping Fenns. Wee have thought fit to acquaint your Grace therewith, and that wee have sent directions to the High Sheriff and Justices of the Peace to hinder and obstruct all Riotous or

---

[19] Denson, *Peasant's Voice to Landowners*, p. 17; *Collections Towards a Parochial History of Berkshire*, p. 55.

[20] *Clare: Selected Poems and Prose*, ed. Eric Robinson and Geoffrey Summerfield (London, 1966), p. 65; cf. Clare's *The Shepherd's Calendar*, ed. Robinson and Summerfield (London, 1964), p. 5.

[21] P.R.O., S.P. 44/99, p. 285.

[22] *Calendar of State Papers, Domestic Series, Charles I, 1637–1638* (London, 1869), pp. 503–4.

Tumultuous meetings in or near Bedford Levell upon account of Foot Ball Play or otherwise and to suppress and disperse the Same, Recommending to your Graces particular Care to use all proper means for the preventing and Suppressing any Such Riotous or Tumultuous assembly whereby the Publick Peace may be disturbed or Endangered.[23]

Later still, in 1768, the prolonged resistance to the enclosure of Holland Fen included the staging of football games on parts of the disputed land, though in this case the exercise may have been largely a symbolic gesture of communal defiance.[24]

Football play was also involved in other instances of protest. During the 1740 food riots, for example, an informant from Northamptonshire reported to the Secretary of State that 'a Mach of Futtball was Cried at Ketring of five Hundred Men of a side but the [real] Desighn was to Pull Down Lady Betey Jesmains Mills'.[25] Similarly, in late July 1765 the *Northampton Mercury* carried an announcement of a football game to be played at West Haddon –

This is to give N O T I C E to all Gentlemen Gamesters and Well-Wishers of the Cause now in Hand, That there will be a Foot-Ball Play in the Fields of Haddon aforesaid, on Thursday the 1st Day of August, for a Prize of considerable Value; and another good Prize to be play'd for on Friday the 2d. All Gentlemen Players are desired to appear at any of the Publick-Houses in Haddon aforesaid each Day between the Hours of Ten and Twelve in the Forenoon, where they will be joyfully received, and kindly entertained, etc.

but the next issue of the newspaper was obliged to report, with some embarrassment, that

We hear from West-Haddon, in this County, that on Thursday and Friday last a great Number of People being assembled there, in order to play a Foot-Ball Match, soon after meeting formed themselves into a tumultuous Mob, and pulled up and burnt the Fences designed for the Inclosure of that Field, and did other considerable Damage.[26]

Football play, it would seem, was a convenient and sometimes effective pretence for gathering together a large assemblage of local dissidents; and it could only have functioned in this way, as a convincing shield for rebellious intentions, if it were a familiar, accepted, and relatively ordinary reason for drawing together a considerable crowd.

The social position of cricket in England was quite different from that of football. Football was predominantly a popular pastime: the sport was certainly encouraged at some of the public schools (where gentlemanly conduct was often loosely construed), and occasionally at Cambridge

[23] P.R.O., P.C. 2/77, p. 309.
[24] W. Marrat, *The History of Lincolnshire* (3 vols.; Boston, 1814), i, 138–46.
[25] P.R.O., S.P. 36/50, fol. 418. I am indebted to Mr E. P. Thompson for this reference.
[26] *Northampton Mercury*, 29 July and 5 August 1765; see also J. W. Anscomb, 'An Eighteenth Century Inclosure and Foot Ball Play at West Haddon', *Northamptonshire Past and Present*, iv, no. 3 (1968/9), 175–8.

University,[27] and gentlemen were sometimes involved in popular contests as match-makers and gamesters, but for the most part football was regarded as too rough and uncivil for adults of good breeding. Cricket, on the other hand, had acquired an enthusiastic genteel following since the beginning of the eighteenth century. Having easily made the transition from a more humble social idiom, it had become one of the most favoured sports in fashionable society. One finds, in fact, that most of the numerous references to cricket in eighteenth-century sources are concerned with this genteel taste for the sport. Publicity for cricket grew to rival that for cocking and horse-racing.[28] Betting, of course, was a major attraction, though gentleman-players were much more prominent in cricket than in most of the other athletic sports. Cricket was able to be absorbed more readily into a culture of refinement and restraint, for its structure of rules allowed for a nice blend of energetic activity and dignity of behaviour, and in this way it satisfied the disposition to compete without infringing on the normal standards of genteel propriety.

It is clear, however, that genteel society had no monopoly on the game (see Plate 3). An essay of 1743, for instance, complained of the mingling of ranks at cricket matches: 'can there be any thing more absurd,' it asked, 'than making such Matches for the sake of Profit, which is to be shared amongst People so remote in their Quality and Circumstances?'[29] César de Saussure claimed of cricket that 'everyone plays it, the common people and also men of rank', a view which was shared by other observers.[30] It was said in 1829 that at Beverley 'the lower classes of the people have their quoits, their foot-ball, and their cricket'.[31] In 1755 an Oxfordshire manservant 'was absent by his Masters Consent one day in April to go and see a Cricket Match at Whitam in the County of Berkshire'; and on 30 October 1766 William Cole's servant 'engaged himself to go with Mrs Willis's Servants and others to Dinner at a Cricket Match at Fenny-Stratford'.[32] Many of the contests which gentlemen organized or publicans promoted must have attracted a considerable body of plebeian spectators. The matches were often much publicized, and some of them were held during a holiday period or at the time of a fair; moreover, they were

[27] E. G. Dunning, 'The Evolution of Football', *New Society*, 30 April 1964; *Fifth Report of the Historical Manuscripts Commission* (London, 1876), p. 483, col. 2; Hart, *Country Counting House*, p. 18.

[28] See especially two works by George B. Buckley: *Fresh Light on 18th Century Cricket: A Collection of 1,000 New Cricket Notices from 1697 to 1800* (Birmingham, 1935), and *Fresh Light on Pre-Victorian Cricket: A Collection of New Cricket Notices from 1709 to 1837* (Birmingham, 1937).

[29] *Gentleman's Magazine*, XIII (1743), 486.

[30] *A Foreign View of England in the Reigns of George I and George II: The Letters of Monsieur César de Saussure to his Family*, ed. Madame Van Muyden (London, 1902), p. 295; Chamberlayne, *Angliae Notitia* (1708 edn), p. 252; Mary Russell Mitford, *Our Village: Sketches of Rural Character and Scenery* (5 vols.; London, 1824–32), I, 146–8.

[31] George Oliver, *The History and Antiquities of the Town and Minister of Beverley* (Beverley, 1829), p. 432; cf. Joseph Lawson, *Letters to the Young on Progress in Pudsey during the Last Sixty Years* (Stanninglen, 1887), pp. 62–3.

[32] Oxfordshire R.O., Quarter Sessions Rolls, Epiphany 1764 (examination of John Collyer, 25 October 1763); *Diary of William Cole*, p. 143.

normally played in a place which was open to public view, on the downs, on a moor, or on the village green.

One of the ancestors of cricket was 'stool-ball', a game which was played mostly by the common people.[33] Oliver Heywood found cause to complain on Easter Sunday 1681 that 'as my hearers went from us through Halifax there was hundreds of people at Clark brig, in the church yard, on the green, and all along the town of young people and others playing at Stool-ball, and other recreations, without any controll'.[34] The sport was still to be found in some localities during the eighteenth century. In 1702, for example, a member of the Bunyan Congregation in Bedford was under admonition for various 'light unbecoming actions', one of which was playing stool-ball; and on 14 May 1715 Nicholas Blundell noted that 'the Young Folks of this Town had a Merry-Night at James Davis, Tatlock played to them; the Young Weomen treated the Men with a Tandsey as they had lost to them at a Game at Stoole Balle'.[35]

Pugilism (see Plate 5) was one of the sports which cut very much across class lines. Its patronage extended from labourer to lord, and in many instances both social extremes were to be found at the same match. Fighting, of course, was a long-standing social reality, but it only gradually became established as an acknowledged and organized recreation. When two working men 'have a disagreement which they cannot end up amicably', wrote de Saussure in 1727, they sometimes

> retire into some quiet place and strip from their waists upwards. Everyone who sees them preparing for a fight surrounds them, not in order to separate them, but on the contrary to enjoy the fight, for it is a great sport to the lookers-on, and they judge the blows and also help to enforce certain rules in use for this mode of warfare. The spectators sometimes get so interested that they lay bets on the combatants and form a big circle around them. The two champions shake hands before commencing, and then attack each other courageously with their fists, and sometimes also with their heads, which they use like rams. Should one of the men fall, his opponent may, according to the rules, give him a blow with his fist, but those who have laid their bets on the fallen man generally encourage him to continue till one of the combatants is quite knocked up and says he has had enough.[36]

Fights of this sort were well on the way to becoming organized sporting events. By the mid-eighteenth century the practise of pugilism was being increasingly systematized: formal rules of play were developed, the 'scientific' principles professed by the best fighters were set forth, and

[33] Robert MacGregor, *Pastimes and Players* (London, 1881), pp. 5–7; Rowland Bowen, *Cricket: A History of its Growth and Development throughout the World* (London, 1970), pp. 33 and 46.

[34] *The Rev. Oliver Heywood, B.A., 1630–1702: His Autobiography, Diaries, Anecdote and Event Books*, ed. J. H. Turner (4 vols.; Brighouse and Bingley, 1881–5), II, 279.

[35] G. B. Harrison (ed.), *The Church Book of Bunyan Meeting 1650–1821* (London and Toronto, 1928), p. 103; *Diurnal of Nicholas Blundell*, II, 134.

[36] *Letters of de Saussure*, p. 180.

championship matches were arranged, often with the support of interested members of the gentry. By the end of the century the newspapers were carrying frequent and sometimes detailed reports of the more notable fights. Some were arranged by professional promoters or publicans, others by gentleman-patrons. Prominent boxers, who were almost always of humble social origins, were local and perhaps even national celebrities, and several thousand enthusiasts were often on hand for a major battle. Sylas Neville, a spectator at a match in Norwich in 1772, remarked on 'what a concourse of people of all ranks there was to see this fight and what gambling'.[37] Small-scale matches were sometimes arranged at wakes or fairs, and at the larger fairs professionals might exhibit their skills in a sideshow.

There were numerous other athletic diversions of reasonable prominence. Wrestling was very popular in many regions, particularly in Cornwall, Devon, Bedfordshire, Northamptonshire, Norfolk, Cumberland, and Westmoreland. It could arise informally, outside an alehouse or after work on a summer evening; sometimes formal tournaments were promoted – the Boughton Green Fair in Northamptonshire, for instance, featured wrestling as one of its customary attractions. It was said that at a match at Botley, Berkshire, in 1737 'there was the greatest Concourse of People that has been known on such an Occasion, for tho' in the middle of Harvest, it's modestly computed there were 10,000 People, some of whom came 40 Miles to see the Diversion'.[38] Quoits, skittles and nine-pins (both varieties of bowling) were probably common, though they received only limited notice, largely because they would have been associated with casual social gatherings (see Plate 4). Foot races and pedestrian contests where often arranged, the latter from the later eighteenth century and the former all through the period, and both served as further outlets for gambling. Instances of such contests recur in contemporary sources. To take only one illustration: in 1770, after an Italian had succeeded in walking fifty miles in twelve hours, 'he was conducted to Nottingham by a large Concourse of People with Cockades, preceded by a Hand-Organ, and a Band of Music. And the same Evening he walked seven Miles to a Country Wake, and back again to Nottingham'.[39]

Eighteenth-century provincial newspapers included a good many references to matches of cudgelling, backsword, and singlestick, all of which were forms of duelling which made use of simple sticks (see Plate 7). The object of the contest was 'to break a head', which was interpreted to mean the drawing of blood: 'No Head to be deemed broke unless the Blood runs an Inch', stipulated an advertisement for a match in 1753.[40] A contributor to Hone's *Year Book* provided details on the sports:

[37] *Diary of Sylas Neville*, p. 173.
[38] B. M. Brand, *Popular Antiquities* (1813), II, facing p. 310.
[39] *Northampton Mercury*, 18 June 1770. During the early nineteenth century the newspapers were full of reports on pedestrian matches. Examples of running matches may be found in *Oliver Heywood*, II, 294; *Six North Country Diaries*, p. 49; and Christopher Morris (ed.), *The Journeys of Celia Fiennes* (London, 1947), pp. 359–60.
[40] *Jackson's Oxford Journal*, 29 September 1753.

Single-stick playing is so called to distinguish it from cudgelling, in which two sticks are used: the single-stick player having the left hand tied down, and using only one stick both to defend himself and strike his antagonist. The object of each gamester in this play, as in cudgelling, is to guard himself, and to fetch blood from the other's head; whether by taking a little skin from his pericranium, or drawing a stream from his nose, or knocking out a few of . . . the teeth . . .

In cudgelling, as the name implies, the weapon is a stout cudgel; and the player defends himself with another having a large hemisphere of wicker-work upon it. This is called the *pot* . . . [41]

Some players exhibited considerable expertise, and could attack an opponent with great speed and pinpoint accuracy. A typical announcement for this sort of sport appeared in *Sarah Farley's Bristol Journal* for 7 May 1774:

To be played for at Back Sword at Wotton under Edge, on the Tuesday and Wednesday in the Whitsun Week, Twenty guineas, viz. 8 guineas the first day by nine men on each side, and 12 guineas the second day by eleven men on each side. Each couple to play 'till one of their heads is broken. The side which gets the odd head to have the prize. No padding allowed. [42]

Mention should also be made of the widespread custom of bell-ringing. 'Ringing of Bells is one of their great Delights,' thought Henri Misson, 'especially in the Country'. [43] The ringing was either of church or hand bells, and many places had their own groups of ringers who performed on special occasions: 'the people are so fond of this amusement', said de Saussure, 'that they form societies among themselves for carrying it out'. [44] In June 1770 it was reported that 'the Sherwood Company of Change-Ringers in Nottingham (who generally go to spend two or three Holidays in the Country at Whitsuntide) went this Year to amuse themselves upon the melodious Peal of eight Bells at Burton-upon-Trent, in Staffordshire, but were greatly disappointed in finding the Bells in very bad Order . . . On their Return they performed upon the Sett of ten Bells at All-Saints Church in Derby'. [45] Competitive ringing between parishes was also popular. On New Year's Day 1735 six hats were 'to be rung for at Hepworth, and to meet at the White Swan; to be Rung for by four Companies of Ringers, putting in one Shilling a Man, and every Company to Ring three Book-Peals of their own chooseing'; a similar event was held at the Red Lyon in Aylsham, Norfolk, in July 1752. [46] In Cornwall,

---

[41] Hone, *Year Book*, col. 1525; cf. Misson, *Memoirs and Observations*, p. 308, and John Eyles, 'Backsword or Singlestick?', *Country Life*, 8 July 1965, p. 108. Backsword seems to have been the same as singlestick.

[42] Quoted in *Gloucestershire Notes and Queries*, IV (1890), 85. I am indebted to Mr Malcolm Thomas for this reference.

[43] Misson, *Memoirs and Observations*, p. 306.

[44] *Letters of de Saussure*, p. 295.

[45] *Northampton Mercury*, 18 June 1770.

[46] *Suffolk Mercury*, 16 December 1734; *Norwich Mercury*, 11 July 1752; cf. R. M. Wiles, *Freshest Advices: Early Provincial Newspapers in England* (Columbus, Ohio, 1965), pp. 346–7.

according to one historian, ringing 'became as common and keen as hurling matches or wrestling bouts'.[47]

Human beings, it seems, have always had a strong disposition to manipulate animal life for 'sporting' purposes. Of the animal sports in eighteenth-century England, several of which no longer exist, bull-baiting was undoubtedly one of the most prominent (see Plate 8). It was a common diversion at many wakes, especially at those in the West Midlands, and in some localities it was closely associated with one of the other major holidays: with a Whitsun fair perhaps, or the 5th of November, or the festivities at a local election. For some communities it may even have been a fairly regular recreation. The common people of early eighteenth-century Chichester, for example, were said by one resident to have been 'much given to mean diversions such as bull-baiting, which was very frequent, and for which many bulldogs were kept in the town to the great torture and misery of those poor animals'.[48] Butchers were sometimes required to have a bull baited before killing it, and fines could be levied on those who neglected to do so.[49] The most detailed and probably most accurate description of a bull-bait was provided by the French observer, Henri Misson, at the end of the seventeenth century:

> They tie a Rope to the Root of the Horns of the Ox or Bull, and fasten the other End of the Cord to an Iron Ring fix'd to a stake driven into the Ground; so that this Cord, being about 15 Foot long, the Bull is confin'd to a Sphere of about 30 Foot Diameter. Several Butchers, or other Gentlemen, that are desirous to exercise their Dogs, stand round about, each holding his own by the Ears; and when the Sport begins, they let loose one of the Dogs: The Dog runs at the Bull; the Bull, immoveable, looks down upon the Dog with an Eye of Scorn, and only turns a Horn to him to hinder him from coming near: The Dog is not daunted at this, he runs round him, and tries to get beneath his Belly, in order to seize him by the Muzzle, or the Dewlap, or the pendant Glands . . . The Bull then puts himself into a Posture of Defence; he beats the Ground with his Feet, which he joins together as close as possible, and his chief Aim is not to gore the Dog with the Point of his Horn, but to slide one of them under the Dog's Belly, (who creeps close to the Ground to hinder it) and to throw him so high in the Air that he may break his neck in the Fall. This often happens: When the Dog thinks he is sure of fixing his Teeth, a turn of the Horn, which seems to be done with all the Negligence in the World, gives him a Sprawl thirty Foot high, and puts him in Danger of a damnable Squelch when he

[47] H. L. Douch, *Old Cornish Inns, and their Place in the Social History of the County* (Truro, 1966), p. 136.

[48] *Memoirs of James Spershott*, p. 14.

[49] W. H. D. Longstaffe, *The History and Antiquities of the Parish of Darlington* (Darlington and London, 1854), p. 295; Dawson, *History of Skipton*, p. 386; George Tate, *The History of the Borough, Castle, and Barony of Alnwick* (2 vols.; Alnwick, 1866–9), I, 432. Baiting a bull was thought to make its flesh more tender.

comes down. This Danger would be unavoidable, if the Dog's Friends were not ready beneath him, some with their backs to give him a soft Reception, and others with long Poles, which they offer him slant-ways, to the Intent that, sliding down them, it may break the Force of his Fall. Notwithstanding all this Care, a Toss generally makes him sing to a very scurvy Tune, and draw his Phiz into a piti-ful Grimace: But unless he is totally stunn'd with the Fall, he is sure to crawl again towards the Bull, with his old Antipathy, come on't what will. Sometimes a second Frisk into the Air disables him for ever from playing his old Tricks: But sometimes too he fastens upon his Enemy, and when once he has seiz'd him with his Eye-teeth, he sticks to him like a Leech, and would sooner die than leave his Hold. Then the Bull bellows, and bounds, and kicks about to shake off the Dog; by his Leaping the Dog seems to be no Manner of Weight to him, tho' in all Appearance he puts him to great Pain. In the End, either the Dog tears out the Piece he has laid Hold on, and falls, or else remains fix'd to him, with an Obstinacy that would never end, if they did not pull him off.[50]

Bull-baits usually took place in a publican's yard, an accessible open field, or a market place – in 1794 the chamberlain's account at Leominster, Herefordshire, included a payment of 1s. 6d. on the day after November 5th 'to a labourer for cleansing the Corn Market after Bull-baiting'; some towns – Harewood, Darlington, and Hornsea are cases in point – even had an iron ring permanently fixed in the ground to which the bull's rope could be fastened.[51] The place-name 'bull-ring' is, in most instances, an indication of a former bull-baiting site.

The other two animals which were used for baiting, though less often than bulls, were bears (see Plate 9) and badgers. Different techniques, of course, were used by the bear for self-defence. 'As soon as the dogs had at him,' noted a German tourist, the bear 'stood up on his hind legs and gave some terrific buffets; but if one of them got at his skin, he rolled about in such a fashion that the dogs thought themselves lucky if they came out safe from beneath him.'[52] The relative infrequency of bear-baiting was largely due to the scarcity of bears. Badgers, however, like bulls, were in much more ample supply, and consequently were more often baited. The objective of badger-baiting, according to one sporting writer, was to see (and bet on) how many times 'the dog will draw the badger from his box, within a given space of time . . . It is almost incredible, considering the strength and powers of offence, with the sharp teeth of the Badger, how often he will be drawn within the usual time, by a well-bred

---

[50] Misson, *Memoirs and Observations*, pp. 24–7; Misson's work was first published in French in 1698.

[51] Quoted in George F. Townsend, *The Town and Borough of Leominster* (Leominster, n.d.), p. 196; John Jones, *The History and Antiquities of Harewood, in the County of York* (London, 1859), p. 168; Longstaffe, *Darlington*, p. 295; Bedell, *Hornsea*, p. 88.

[52] *London in 1710, From the Travels of Zacharias Conrad von Uffenbach*, ed. and trans. W. H. Quarrell and Margaret Mare (London, 1934), p. 59.

and thoroughly trained dog.'[53] In all baiting sports the testing of a dog's skill and courage was one of the principal points of the exercise.

Bull-running was a prominent diversion in Tutbury, Staffordshire, Stamford, Lincolnshire, and perhaps one or two other towns. The bull-running in Stamford, held on the 13th of November, was a major festive occasion for the town and its surrounding countryside which attracted each year hundreds of spectators and participants. The sport was essentially a free-for-all bull-fight without weapons, or at best with only sticks and heavy staffs; it seems to have been much like some of the bull-runnings recently (or still) found in parts of France and Spain, and it was characterized by a similar sort of carnival atmosphere. On the morning of the 13th the entrances to the main streets were barricaded, shops were shut up, and at eleven o'clock, with the bells of St Mary's tolling his arrival, a bull was released from a stable to the swarms of onlookers and participants (called 'bullards') who packed the street. The excitement was provided by the ensuing confusion and disorder, and by displays of daring in tormenting the bull – by throwing irritants at him, perhaps, or by baiting him with a red effigy and then manoeuvring out of his way. A talented bullard might pack himself in an open-ended barrel and roll it at the bull: the objective here was to provoke him to toss the barrel, and yet at the same time to avoid getting dislodged or mauled. 'If he be tame,' wrote a hostile observer in 1819, 'he is soon surrounded by the *canaille*, and *loaded*, as the bullards express it; that is, some have hold of his horns, and others his ears, some are beating his sides with bludgeons, and others are hanging at his tail.'[54] A man in trouble would be aided by diversionary antics from his friends. Sometimes the bull was stormed by groups, and often he was simply chased through the streets. After an intermission for lunch the bull was again let loose, but this time he was driven towards the main bridge spanning the Welland River. The bullards surrounded him on the bridge and together lifted him over the parapet and into the water: this was known as 'brigging' the bull. He would shortly make his way to the adjacent meadow where a few dogs might be set upon him (though he was not tied down), and where bullards would give chase for a while around the muddy lowland. In late afternoon he was escorted back to town, frustrated and fatigued no doubt, but not usually mutilated. He was then slaughtered and sometimes the meat was sold cheaply to the poor or served up in the public houses. The odd bull which had refused to be 'brigged' was spared his life.[55]

[53] Henry Alken, *The National Sports of Great Britain* (London, 1821), caption for the plate 'A Match at the Badger'; cf. William Youatt, *The Obligation and Extent of Humanity to Brutes* (London, 1839), p. 173.

[54] *Fireside Magazine; or Monthly Entertainer* (Stamford), February 1819, pp. 46–7.

[55] This account is based largely on material from the local press, especially the *Stamford Mercury*, during the period 1785–1840. The evidence available on the Tutbury bull-running is comparatively slight, partly because it was suppressed at a relatively early date (in 1778). It was held annually in August, and by the eighteenth century it seems to have occasioned a general carnival for the nearby parishes in Staffordshire and Derbyshire. Details are provided in Robert Plot, *The Natural History of Staffordshire* (Oxford, 1686), pp. 436–40; Stebbing Shaw, *The History and Antiquities of Stafford-*

Throwing at cocks was principally a Shrovetide recreation, though occasionally it might have been practised at a wake or fair. On Shrove Tuesday 1708 Nicholas Blundell recorded in his diary that 'My Wife and I saw them throw at the Cock in the Townfield', and the next year at the same time he complained that 'My Tenant Thomas Warton should have comne [here for dinner] . . . but he was so busy shooting at the Cock he could not come, but after dinner he came and eat some Pancakes etc: with us.'[56] At Lamport, Northamptonshire, Thomas Isham noted that 'this is the usual day for cock killing' and 'a great slaughter of cocks at our place' on the Shrove Tuesdays of 1672 and 1673; at York on Shrove Tuesday 1673 'the prentices of the city being at liberty for recreation, plaid in the minister-yeard, throwing at a cock'.[57] At Shrovetide in 1722 a newspaper spoke of how 'several People got together in St George's Field to throw at Cocks according to the ancient and barbarous Custom at this Season of the Year'.[58] The method of the amusement, which was a precursor of many modern fairground entertainments, was stark and uncomplicated: a cock was tied to a stake by a cord, and the competitors, standing some twenty yards away, tried to knock it down by throwing some kind of missile, normally a cudgel or a broom-stick. In most instances the sport was run as a private enterprise, with the owner of the cock charging about twopence for three throws. If a thrower could knock the cock down and run and secure the bird before it regained its feet, the cock was his; sometimes he would then set himself up as the promoter. A well trained cock was a difficult target and could earn good money for its owner. Writing in the early 1780s, James Spershott of Chichester described how, during the second quarter of the century,

> on Shrove Tuesday the most unmanly and cruel exercise of 'cock scailing' was in vogue everywhere, even in the High Church 'lighten' and many other places in the city and in the country. Scarcely a churchyard was to be found but a number of those poor innocent birds were thus barbarously treated. Tying them by the leg with a string about 4 or 5 feet long fastened to the ground, and, when he is made to stand fair, a great ignorant merciless fellow, at a distance agreed upon and at two pence three throws, flings a 'scail' at him till he is quite dead. And thus their legs are broken and their bodies bruised in a shocking manner . . . And wonderful it was that men of character and circumstance should come to this fine sight and readily give their children a cock for this purpose.[59]

César de Saussure complained in 1728 that 'it is even dangerous . . . to go near any of those places where this diversion is being held; so many

shire (2 vols.; London, 1798–1801), i, part ii, 52–5; and Sir Oswald Mosley, History of the Castle, Priory, and Town of Tutbury (London, 1832), pp. 88–90. Wisbech appears to have had a more limited form of bull-running: see Frederic J. Gardiner, History of Wisbech and Neighbourhood, During the last Fifty Years 1848–1898 (Wisbech and London, 1898), pp. 25 and 52.
[56] Diurnal of Nicholas Blundell, i, 163 and 204.
[57] Journal of Thomas Isham, pp. 27 and 85; Oliver Heywood, i, 345.
[58] B. M. Brand, Popular Antiquities (1813), i, following p. 62.
[59] Memoirs of James Spershott, p. 14.

clubs are thrown about that you run a risk of receiving one on your head'.[60]

Cock-fighting is probably the best known of the traditional blood sports. It was certainly mentioned very frequently in eighteenth-century sources: the newspapers, for instance, were full of advertisements for cock-fights. Although most of the well publicized matches of the period were organized for gentlemen (and usually by gentlemen), it is clear that the common people were by no means uninvolved in the sport. Shropshire, for example, was noted for its plebeian cock-fights, and miners in many areas were known to be enthusiastic cockers. Cocking, in fact, was one of the diversions which cut sharply across class lines. Hogarth's famous engraving emphasized the mingling of ranks in a cock-fighting crowd (see Plate 6), and Oliver Heywood attested to the same phenomenon in a hostile depiction of the sport which he confided to his diary:

> Upon Monday May 31, 1680, there was to begin a great cocking at Halifax, the place was on the back side of the Crosse, at Halifax, the inne is kept by widow Mitchel where a cocking house is built that cost 32 li, many gentlemen came to it upon the munday, that day was spent in appointing judges to sit and match the cocks which they did with great authority, on the tuesday the poorer sort of Halifax brought their cocks which were to fight first, but Mr. Tho. Thornhil said what had beggars to doe to fight their cocks among gentlemen upon which Tho. Cockrofts son tript up his heels, so they fell to blows, and they took sides and all fought desperately a long while, Ab. Mitchel taking the poor mens part: at last Jo. Mitchel drew his rapier and swore he would run him through that struck another stroke, so they were quieted – then they fell to cocking, and the Halifax cocks generally beat the gentlemens, then on the wednesday, thursday, friday the gentlemens cocks fought, abundance of money was lost and won, – they drunk all night and were so high in swearing, ranting at the Crosse that they were heard far in the town.[61]

Most of the more substantial cock-fights were held in an inn which was specially fitted up for the sport, or at an actual cockpit. A cockpit resembled a small amphitheatre: it had a round platform in the centre and was surrounded by tiered benches for the gamesters. Before a battle the cocks were matched by weight, their beaks were filed down, and their wings and tails were clipped. The German tourist, von Uffenbach, described the way in which a fight was conducted:

> When it is time to start, the persons appointed to do so bring in the cocks hidden in two sacks, and then everyone begins to shout and wager before the birds are on view. The people, gentle and simple (they sit with no distinction of place) act like madmen, and go on raising the odds to twenty guineas and more. As soon as one of the bidders calls 'done' . . . the other is pledged to keep his bargain. Then the cocks are taken out of the sacks and fitted with silver spurs

[60] *Letters of de Saussure*, p. 294.
[61] *Oliver Heywood*, II, 271–2; cf. *Pierce Egan's Book of Sports and Mirror of Life* (London, 1832), p. 146, col. 2.

... As soon as the cocks appear, the shouting grows even louder and the betting is continued. When they are released, some attack, while others run away ... [and some] are impelled by terror to jump down from the table among the people; they are then, however, driven back on to the table with great yells (in particular by those who have put their money on the lively cocks which chase the others) and are thrust at each other until they get angry. Then it is amazing to see how they peck at each other, and especially how they hack with their spurs. Their combs bleed terribly and they often slit each other's crop and abdomen with the spurs. There is nothing more diverting than when one seems quite exhausted and there are great shouts of triumph and monstrous wagers; and then the cock that appeared to be quite done for suddenly recovers and masters the other. When one of the two is dead, the conqueror invariably begins to crow and jump on the other ... Sometimes, when both are exhausted and neither will attack the other again, they are removed and others take their place; in this case the wagers are cancelled. But if one of them wins, those who put their money on the losing cock have to pay up immediately, so that an hostler in his apron often wins several guineas from a Lord. If a man has made a bet and is unable to pay, for a punishment he is made to sit in a basket fastened to the ceiling, and is drawn up in it amidst peals of laughter.[62]

Although individual pairings tended to be the norm, the most spectacular (and notorious) kind of fight was the Welsh main, a match-play competition involving a large number of cocks, commonly 32, out of which only one was able to survive.

There were a number of other prominent animal sports. Dog-fighting existed in some areas; and field sports, though more difficult to assess, were certainly not entirely unknown to the common people. They were, of course, predominantly a part of a gentleman's culture, and by law they were reserved for his enjoyment; but menservants sometimes went coursing with their masters or hunted with their approval – the diaries of Cole, Blundell, and Woodforde testify to this – and on the other side of the law, a good many casual poachers must have hunted for pleasure as well as for gain.[63] It was said that in Cheshire and Lancashire hunting the foumart 'is a common diversion amongst the lower sort of people, who have a peculiar breed of dogs for this purpose ... This diversion is always followed in the night-time; and those who are once initiated are said to be extremely fond of the sport.'[64] Some gentlemen's hunts attracted a considerable number of plebeian foot followers.

Horse racing, another of the gentry's favourite diversions, also had an appeal for the common people. Although its organization was largely

[62] *Travels of von Uffenbach*, pp. 48–9; cf. Count Frederick Kielmansegge, *Diary of a Journey to England in the Years 1761–1762*, transl. Countess Kielmansegg (London, 1902), pp. 241–2.

[63] See for example C. J. Hunt, *The Lead Miners of the Northern Pennines in the Eighteenth and Nineteenth Centuries* (Manchester, 1970), pp. 223–4.

[64] *Gentleman's Magazine*, LIV (1784), 836.

under the control of the governing class, the followers of the sport were drawn from all social levels. Indeed, the crowds which appeared at some of the major meetings could hardly have been so substantial without the attendance of plebeian spectators. Parson Woodforde's servants were in the habit of going to the Lenewade Races, and in 1795 one of the diarist's entries referred to the Bruton Races which 'a vast Concourse of People attended, both gentle and simple'.[65] Oliver Heywood mentioned on several occasions the large crowds which were present at local races, and in one instance he complained of how 'One race begets another, that at Rastrick . . . begot one at Halifax, September 25, 1678; it was given out that many races would be run, to gather the countrey to drink their ale, for it was hoped it would be as profitable to the town as a fair, . . . [and] the countrey came in freely'.[66] The common spectators at some of the races around London were disapprovingly acknowledged: they were, complained the *Craftsman* in 1738, 'frequented chiefly by Apprentices, Servants, and the lowest Sort of Tradesmen'.[67] In August 1749, when 'there was no Horse-Races in Tothill-Fields, Westminster . . . as was expected', the common people became 'so enraged . . . that they pulled down the Starting-post, Booths, Benches, etc. and made a large Bonfire with them in the Middle of the said Fields'.[68] Even if there had have been a concern to keep the populace away from race meetings, it would have been quite impracticable to attempt to exclude them from the open spaces which served as the courses – the commons, heaths, pastures, meadows, and waste lands.[69]

[65] *Diary of a Country Parson*, v, 208, 267, 327; iv, 230.
[66] *Oliver Heywood*, ii, 246. The tensions which such promotions could generate were revealed in a notice in the *Gloucester Journal* for 1 June 1736. 'Whereas it has been reported, that the Alehouse Keepers of Melksham, have an Intention to have a petty Horse-Race in Melksham-Common, contrary to the Approbation of the principal People that have Right of Feeding in the Common of Melksham: And whereas the said Common is a stinted Common, and that the Proprietors are apprehensive that these Diversions will be prejudicial to the Feed and Cattle: This therefore is to give Notice, that whoever brings Horses to run, or erects Booths in the Common of Melksham aforesaid, will be prosecuted as the Law directs.'
[67] *Craftsman*, 26 August 1738, reprinted in the *London Magazine*, vii (1738), 447.
[68] Reprinted from a London paper in the *Ipswich Journal*, 26 August 1749.
[69] It was pointed out by John Lawrence, *A Philosophical and Practical Treatise on Horses, and on the Moral Duties of Man towards the Brute Creation* (2 vols.; London, 1796–8), ii, 23, that 'the course has from very early times, been the proper theatre of amusement to the most exalted ranks of society, and there need [be] no laws to restrain the middling and lower classes from engagements thereon, since their expensiveness will, in general, confine such to their proper place as spectators'. It had been found necessary, however, in order to discourage popular involvement in horse racing, to make illegal all races for stakes of less than fifty pounds (13 George II c. 19).

4

Social contexts

Many recreations arose directly out of the fabric of common interests and common sentiments among the working people themselves. The fundamental social basis for several of the calendar festivities was the relatively small, tightly-knit rural community, and it was in this kind of community that a large number of labouring men spent most of their time and developed their basic sense of social identity. It was a world of face-to-face contacts, deriving its unifying forces from the common experiences of daily (and yearly) routine and a shared oral culture. The people's social relationships stemmed mostly from the ties of family, the ties of neighbourhood (a village, a hamlet, one end of town), and the ties which were formed in the course of their work. The range of their social encounters was normally fairly limited; in most rural areas, aside from the market towns, they would have had relatively infrequent contact with complete strangers. Some of their recreations reflected the personal character of their day-to-day experiences. During the Christmas season friends from the parish, and perhaps relatives from nearby, were in the habit of gathering together at a public house or in each others' cottages. It was said that on Christmas Day 'at Danby Wisk in ye North-Riding of Yorkshire, it is the custom for ye Parishioners after receiving ye Sacrament, to goe from Church directly to the Ale House and there drink together as a testimony of Charity and friendship'.[1] A morris dance in the market place or through the village streets would have attracted an audience from the bulk of the inhabitants, many of whom would have known one another personally. There was a communal basis for the ritual. The community's sense of solidarity might also have been expressed in some athletic competition – the village hero contending in a wrestling match, a football game against a neighbouring parish. Some festive occasions arose out of a consciousness of mutual interests among people of the same trade. St Crispin's feast, the 25th of October, was regularly celebrated by the shoemakers in Knaresborough; Plough Monday was an occupational holiday for the ploughmen, St Andrew's Day (November 30th) for the lacemakers; February 3rd was widely observed by the woolcombers with parades and merry-makings, in honour of their patron saint, Bishop Blaze.[2]

The ties of kinship, friendship, and neighbourliness among the common people were especially important as supports for the annual wake, prob-

[1] John Aubrey, *Remaines of Gentilisme and Judaisme*, ed. James Britten (London, 1881; repr. 1967), p. 5.
[2] Ely Hargrove, *The History of the Castle, Town, and Forest, of Knaresborough* (Knaresborough, 6th edn, 1809), p. 84; Wright, *Calendar Customs*, III, 186–7, and II, 130–5; Hone, *Every-Day Book*, I, cols. 209–12, and *Year Book*, cols. 1,202–3; and Enid Porter, *Cambridgeshire Customs and Folklore* (London, 1969), p. 396.

1 *The Statute* (1787) by John Nixon

2 *Football, Played at the Market Place, Barnet*

3 *A Country Cricket Match* (from P. F. Warner (ed.), *Imperial Cricket* (London and Counties Press Association Ltd, 1912)

ably the principal occasion for individuals to come together in order to reaffirm their social relationships. Henry Bourne remarked that at the time of a wake the people 'deck themselves in their gaudiest Clothes, and have open Doors and splendid Entertainments, for the Reception and Treating of their Relations and Friends, who visit them on that Occasion, from each neighbouring Town'; and in September 1738 a contributor to the *Gentleman's Magazine* declared that 'I hear of one [parish feast] every Sunday kept in some Village or other of the Neighbourhood, and see great Numbers of both Sexes in their Holiday Cloaths, constantly flocking thither, to partake of the Entertainment of their Friends and Relations, or to divert themselves with the rural Games and athletick Exercises'.[3] John Clare also wrote of the social connections which underlay the wake:

> The woodman and the thresher now are found
> Mixing and making merry with their friends
> Children and kin from neighbouring towns around
> Each at the humble banquet pleas'd attends
> For though no costliness the feast pretends
> Yet something more than common they provide
> And the good dame her small plum pudding sends
> To sons and daughters fast in service tied
> With many a cordial gift of good advice beside[4]

The feast was pre-eminently a time of hospitality and generous provision. It was said in 1759 that in Fallow, a hamlet of the parish of Sparsholt in Berkshire, 'the feast day at the old chapel at Fallow, now demolished, had been on the Sunday following the feast of St James, which day the neighbourhood of Fallow keep in the way of having better cheer and open hospitality'.[5] At the wakes in Stamford, 'An abundance of good cheer, which every individual in the parish provides, whose circumstances will permit him to obtain it, supplies his table nearly the whole of the week, to which a host of ready cousins, friends, and neighbours, are welcome: and on the Saturday night, the round of festivity is commonly concluded with ass races and dancings.'[6] Similarly, Samuel Bamford recalled that on the Sunday of the wake 'the very best dinner which could be provided was set out . . . and the guests were helped with a profusion of whatever the host could command. It was a duty at the wakes to be hospitable, and he who at that time was not liberal according to his means, was set down as a very mean person.'[7]

On many festive occasions the most active participants, as one might expect, were men and women in their teens and early twenties. John Aubrey reported that the Michaelmas fair at Kington St Michael, Wiltshire was 'much resorted unto by the young people',[8] a feature which was

[3] Bourne, *Antiquitates Vulgares*, p. 225; *Gentleman's Magazine*, VIII (1738), 465; cf. Borlase, *Cornwall*, p. 301.

[4] Clare, *Village Minstrel*, stanza 74 (punctuation omitted).

[5] *Parochial History of Berkshire*, p. 37.

[6] John Drakard, *The History of Stamford* (Stamford, 1822), p. 428.

[7] Bamford, *Early Days*, pp. 154–5.

[8] *Aubrey's Collections for Wiltshire*, ed. Sir T. Phillipps (2 parts; London, 1821–38), part I, p. 96.

noticed of many other fairs. 'Here met the village youths on pleasure bent,' wrote James Withers of the annual petty fair in his Cambridgeshire village.[9] Since almost all servants were single, young people were especially prominent at hiring fairs. Guy Fawkes Day seems to have been particularly associated with the revelries of younger men; Shrove Tuesday was traditionally the special holiday of apprentices, and May Day was primarily for the benefit of young men and women.

The most important reason for the prominent involvement of young people in recreational events was the fact that they served as occasions for courtship and sexual encounters. This was most noticeably the case at fairs and feasts. On 29 October 1781 Sylas Neville referred in his diary to the 'country Beauties and their sweethearts enjoying themselves at the fruit stalls and mountebank's stage' at a fair in Burton-upon-Trent; and at Norwich on 8 April 1784 he wrote of a 'fair on Tombland for toys etc., full of Beaux and Belles before dinner'.[10] An observer of the hiring fair at Studley, Warwickshire, noticed that 'towards evening each lad seeks his lass, and they hurry off to spend the night at the public houses'.[11] It was said that at the fairs and statutes in Cumberland 'it is customary for all the young people in the neighbourhood to assemble and dance at the inns and alehouses'; after a hiring, with 'fiddlers tuning their fiddles in public houses, the girls begin to file off, and gently pace the streets, with a view of gaining admirers; while the young men . . . follow after, and having eyed the lasses, pick up each a sweetheart, whom they conduct to a dancing room, and treat with punch and cake'.[12] The feast at Pudsey was reported to be a major occasion for match-making.[13] Dancing was always a standard attraction at wakes and pleasure fairs and it provided a focal point for courting and flirtation. John Clare, for instance, wrote of the dancing at a village feast:

> Where the fond swain delighteth in the chance
> To meet the sun tann'd lass he dearly loves
> And as he leads her down the giddy dance
> With many a token his fond passion proves
> Squeezing her hands or catching at her gloves
> And stealing kisses as chance prompts the while[14]

It would have been strange if many holiday gatherings had not catered to the special interests of unmarried men and women. Festive assemblies offered them some of the best opportunities for establishing new contacts and for pursuing acquaintances already made; they widened the range of choice, and because of their free and easy and relatively uninhibited textures, they encouraged the kinds of gallantries and personal displays which were not usually possible in everyday life. Eustace Budgell must have had this sort of setting in mind when, in his portrayal of a football game

[9] Withers, Poems, I, 2.
[10] Diary of Sylas Neville, pp. 279 and 316; cf. 'Woodcombe Wake' in The Poems of William Barnes (2 vols.; London, 1962), ed. Bernard Jones, II, 650–1.
[11] Hone, Table Book, I, col. 176.
[12] Housman, Description of Cumberland, pp. 70–1.
[13] Lawson, Progress in Pudsey, pp. 11–15.
[14] Clare, Village Minstrel, stanza 72 (punctuation omitted).

at a country wake, he noted that one 'Tom Short behaved himself so well, that most People seemed to agree it was impossible that he should remain a Batchelour till the next Wake'.[15] Sir Thomas Parkyns was assuming a similar set of circumstances when he was publicizing the satisfactions which were to be gained from his favourite sport:

> For the most Part our Country Rings for Wrestlings, at Wakes and other Festivals, consist of a small Party of young Women, who come not thither to choose a Coward, but the Daring, Healthy, and Robust Persons, fit to raise an Offspring from: I dare say, they sufficiently recommend themselves to their Sweet-hearts, when they demon-strate that they are of hail Constitutions, and enjoy a perfect state of Health, and like the Fatigue of that Day . . . [16]

In the same vein, John Gay's *The Shepherd's Week* had the maid Marian speak warmly of how

> Young *Colin Clout*, a Lad of peerless Meed,
> Full well could dance, and deftly tune the Reed;
> In ev'ry Wood his Carrols sweet were known,
> In ev'ry Wake his nimble Feats were shown.
> When in the Ring the Rustic Routs he threw,
> The Damsels Pleasures with his Conquests grew;
> Or when aslant the Cudgel threats his Head,
> His Danger smites the Breast of ev'ry Maid . . . [17]

However, although the young may have been particularly active on many holidays and even dominant on a few, they seldom monopolized the pleasures of a festive gathering. On most occasions there would have been ample room for the participation, in some form or other, of the middle-aged and the elderly. On 9 July 1715 Nicholas Blundell reported that at Little Crosby 'the Little Boyes and Girles of this Town diverted themselves with Rearing a May-pole in the West-Lane, they had Morrys dansing and a great many came to it both old and young'.[18] Similarly, John Denson of Waterbeach claimed that 'both old and young partici-pated' in the afternoon diversions of May Day – the rites of the morning were exclusively for the young people – 'and those whom age and infirmity prevented, appeared to enjoy our sports as they sat at their cottage doors'.[19] On those occasions when youth enjoyed the limelight there was nothing to prevent the older people from looking on. At the annual harvest feast in Warton, Lancashire, during the early eighteenth century 'the Old People after Supper smoak their Pipes, and with great Pleasure and Delight behold the younger spending the Evening in Singing, Dancing, etc.'.[20] On Midsummer Eve, according to Henry Bourne,

---

[15] *Spectator*, No. 161, 4 September 1711.
[16] Sir Thomas Parkyns, *The Inn-Play: or, Cornish-Hugg Wrestler* (London, 3rd edn, 1727), p. 20.
[17] Gay, *Shepherd's Week*, from the second pastoral, 'Tuesday'.
[18] *Diurnal of Nicholas Blundell*, II, 140.
[19] Denson, *Peasant's Voice to Landowners*, pp. 17–18.
[20] *John Lucas's History of Warton Parish*, ed. J. Rawlinson Ford and J. A. Fuller-Maitland (London, 1931), p. 126.

> it is usual in the most of Country Places, and also here and there in Towns and Cities, for both Old and Young to meet together, and be Merry over a large Fire, which is made in the open Street. Over this they frequently leap and play at various Games, such as Running, Wrestling, Dancing, etc. But this is generally the Exercise of the younger Sort; for the old Ones, for the most Part, sit by as Spectators, and enjoy themselves and their Bottle.[21]

Matrons would watch the games and dancing at a wake and older men would be keen observers at a match of football, wrestling, or cudgelling. 'Aged men also, hardly able to walk, were to be seen moving towards this scene of riot,' complained a clergyman of the bull-running at Stamford, 'anxious to witness a repetition of such exploits as they, when young, had often performed.'[22]

Even when the young were the most vigorous participants, then, it is clear that a good many older people attended a festive event as spectators – often to gossip, to pronounce judgements, and to display the wisdom of experience. James Withers wrote of how at a village fair, 'The old folks talked of times when they were young, / And the same songs, year after year, were sung'.[23] Indeed, the crowds at many fairs and most feasts were drawn from all age groups of the population. Moreover, there were a number of holidays and diversions which placed no special premium on youth. The celebrations of the Christmas season, for instance, were appropriate for people of all ages. Several of the principal pastimes favoured no particular age group: bull-baiting and cock-fighting retained an appeal for many older men, and bell-ringing could be enjoyed and practised by people of almost any age. Sex, in fact, was probably a social determinant of greater weight than age, for while many of the major holidays involved women almost as much as men, most of the sporting events assumed that women would attend only as spectators, or not at all.

While some of the traditional popular recreations were conducted fairly autonomously and had their fundamental roots in the common people's own culture of social interdependence, many others were at least partly dependent on the patronage, or interest, or acquiescence of persons with greater authority, usually the gentry. In certain recreations the involvement of gentlemen was of the first importance. Most horse races would not have existed without them; and hiring fairs obviously assumed employers. Gentlemen also participated actively in cricket, cock-fighting, and pugilism: they served as patrons for the boxers of their choice and commonly were responsible for the purses; they bred most of the best fighting cocks and often arranged the mains; and they not only watched cricket but also played it with enthusiasm. Patronage, of course, was traditionally one of the major social functions of the governing class, and

---

[21] Bourne, *Antiquitates Vulgares*, pp. 210–11.

[22] J. F. Winks, *The Bull Running at Stamford . . . ; Being the Substance of a Sermon Delivered in the General Baptist Meeting-House, on Lord's Day Evening, Nov. 15, 1829* (London, n.d.), p. 14.

[23] Withers, *Poems*, I, 3; cf. 'Woodcom' Feast' in the *Poems of William Barnes*, I, 79–80.

it extended into many areas of social activity. Behind a large number of recreational events was the supporting prestige or largess, often conspicuously displayed, of some prominent figure. Gentlemen frequently provided the prizes for sporting contests and rural diversions: in June 1721, for example, it was announced that

> the Earl of Stafford has been pleas'd to give a Hat, Value one Guinea, to be play'd for on the Monday at Cudgels; and another of the same Price, as also 6 Pair of Buckskin Gloves, at 5s. a Pair, to be wrestled for on Tuesday; and a Silver Cup of 5 Guineas Price, to be run for on the Wednesday, by Maiden Galloways, not exceeding fourteen Hands, during the time of Boughton Green Fair.[24]

Some of the traditional popular sports were patronized by the gentry for their own diversion. The gentlemen subscribers to the bowling green at Kingsthorp, Northamptonshire, gave notice in September 1751 of the wrestling and singlestick matches which they were organizing; and in July 1753 at Bristol, where a grand cudgelling match (of some 70 competitors) was promoted, it was said that the 'whole Expence' was 'borne by a voluntary Subscription of the Gentlemen frequenting the Hot-Well'.[25] These were familiar kinds of occurrences, and it is clear that one of their principal attractions was the gambling involved. Gentlemen were seldom inclined to support a popular diversion very eagerly unless they could bet on its outcome. At a widely attended wrestling match at Botley, Berkshire, in 1737 it was said that 'there were many Hundred Pounds won and lost upon the Match'.[26] An announcement for a wrestling match at Highworth, Wiltshire, in the autumn of 1740 pointed out that 'if any Person is inclin'd to lay any Sums of Money against the Berkshire Boys, they may have Bets'.[27] The prominence of boxing and cock-fighting was very much related to their suitability for gambling. Pedestrian contests relied almost entirely on the willingness of gentlemen to lay bets, and wagers often depended on the outcome of foot races. On all such occasions, then, the gentlemen gamesters and the plebeian sportsmen found interests in common.

Sometimes gentlemen were relied on to make donations towards the support of a particular holiday or pastime. When aid was solicited on certain traditional occasions, they were expected to contribute a modest sum to the people's ceremonial fund; such solicitations were an integral part of the mumming and dancing rituals of Christmas, Plough Monday, and Whitsuntide. An account book which was kept in the early eighteenth century for the Throckmorton family of Weston Underwood, Buckinghamshire, includes records of payments to morris dancers, mummers, wassailers, and musicians during the Christmas season.[28] On 20 October 1714 Claver Morris, a physician in Wells, gave a shilling to some morris

---

[24] *Northampton Mercury*, 5 June 1721.
[25] *Northampton Mercury*, 23 September 1751; B. M. Brand, *Popular Antiquities* (1813), i, facing p. 783.
[26] *Ibid.* ii, facing p. 310.
[27] *Gloucester Journal*, 21 October 1740.
[28] Berkshire R.O., D/EWeA1.

dancers.[29] During the 1760s the Earl of Gower was giving a guinea twice each year, around Whitsuntide and New Year's Day, to the Lichfield morris dancers.[30] Most of these kinds of payments would have been regarded by both the donors and recipients as customary aids. Around 1720 the rector at Landbeach in Cambridgeshire was paying 'by custom' 2s. 6d. 'on Shrove Tuesday for the Football men'.[31] Often the donations were collected in the course of a procession: the procession of ceremonial dancers, or the bearers of May garlands, or perhaps of football players before a traditional match. On Christmas Day at King's Cliffe, Northamptonshire, during the earlier eighteenth century 'the parishioners with the clerk assemble at the church, at three o'clock in the morning, and sing a Psalm; then they proceed to the cross, and to every gentleman's house in the town, for which they receive a largess in the holidays'.[32]

In some places the traditional parish perambulations of Rogation week survived into the eighteenth century, and they, too, often relied on the participation of propertied householders in support of the customary feasting. The parish register of Ashampstead, Berkshire, for the eighteenth century included a 'Memorandum of such Tenures, by whose Tenants or Under-Tenants, and of those Places, where by Antient Custom, Refreshments are to be provided on the Day of perambulation in the Rogation Week within the parish of Ashampstead, either of Bread, Cakes, Cheese, Butter or Cheesecake, Some one thing, some another, according to the abilities of the several Persons concerned in this provision.'[33] In Shalstone, Buckinghamshire, the squire of the parish made a note on 24 May 1731 of the activities on 'Rogation Monday – Shalstone folks went on Processioning – eight pounds of Cheese and a twelve penny loaf and one dozen and a half of penny loaves serves Them for Eating' – he paid the baker 2s. 6d. 'for bread for the processioners' – 'And two Bushell of Malt and half a pound of hops serves Them for Drinking.' He added significantly, 'N.B. This is no Custom but my free gift only', but the practice was continued: in 1746 the donation included two twelve penny loaves of bread, six white penny loaves, nine or ten pounds of cheese, and two bushels of malt and half a pound of hops; and on the Rogation Tuesday of 1795 the processioners (26 men and 11 boys) started at 8 a.m. from Shalstone House, were refreshed 'with Bread and Cheese and Ale' at 11, and finished 'at 3 O'Clock in the Afternoon when they were regaled with a plenty of Bread and Cheese and five Horns of Ale to each Man's Share'.[34] A memorandum book kept by Sir Thomas Sclater includes an account

[29] *The Diary of a West Country Physician 1684–1726*, ed. Edmund Hobhouse (London, 1934), pp. 19–20.

[30] Staffordshire R.O., D. 593/F/3/12/2/1.

[31] Quoted in William K. Clay, 'A History of the Parish of Landbeach in the County of Cambridge', *Publications of the Cambridge Antiquarian Society*, VI (1861), 60n.

[32] Bridges, *Northamptonshire*, II, 432.

[33] Berkshire R.O., D/P8 1/1, p. 1.

[34] 'Purefoy Memorandum Book', in the possession of Mr Geoffrey Purefoy of Shalstone Manor, Buckinghamshire. I am grateful to Mr Purefoy for allowing me to examine some of his family papers.

of the perambulation at Linton, Cambridgeshire, on 18 May 1680, an occasion which included a feast given at Sclater's house for around a hundred men of the parish. According to his notes,

> the anciestest were first in ye Hall to drink and eate Cake, about 16 or 20, and after about 5 or 6 of ye clock in ye parlor had with me a Supper, viz 4 or 5 joints of Meats and a cold Gammon of English Bacon stuft. And some 20 persons more were in ye kitchin and had Beer and Cake . . . and stayed about 2 Hours . . . And the 3rd Company being about 40 or 60 were in ye Court next the kitchin and brick stables and after every one was served with the —— [one word illegible] Beer and a piece of Cake of half a peck cut into 14 or 16 pieces being given, severally set out into ye outermost Court next ye Barn and meadow and stayed about 1 Hour and a Half or 2 Hours.[35]

The recreations of servants were particularly dependent on the favour and interest of their employers. At the very least servants had to get leave from their masters and mistresses in order to take time off. Servants' lives, of course, were governed by a great many constraints; however, if the diaries of Nicholas Blundell, William Cole, and James Woodforde are any indication, it would appear that servants were given permission to attend a fair, or a feast, or some sporting event on quite a number of occasions. In 1708, for instance, Blundell's servants went to at least three plays, one of which was held in the hall of his house.[36] On both the 11th and 12th of July 1768 William Cole's servantman was allowed to go dancing in the evenings, and on 11 January 1769 he 'Gave Tom, Molly and Jem Leave to meet Mr Mason's Sons and Daughters and Mr Hall's Sons and Kitty Huckle at John Denson's: they stay'd late'.[37] On 7 May 1792 Woodforde wrote about a 'frolic given to the Servants etc. at Weston House this After-noon, Tea and Supper etc. Our Servants were invited, Betty and Briton went about 5 in the Afternoon and stayed till 11 at Night . . . Our People said they never were at a better frolic'.[38] In mid October 1776 he had allowed some free time to several of his servants: on the 12th Betty went with her boy friend to another town to stay overnight; on the 17th Will Coleman went to St Faith's Fair; and on the 18th Molly was given leave to stay away overnight.[39] Even a guidebook for the good behaviour of servants, which was at pains to emphasize the need for industriousness and a careful use of time, accepted that a certain amount of free time for recreation was only right and proper. 'But those you live with must be very unreasonable indeed', it advised, 'that would not permit you some-times to see your Friends on other Days than those which ought to be devoted to Heaven alone: Few Servants but are allowed one Holiday at each of the great Festivals of the Year, and in the Time of Fairs, and it is

---

[35] Cambridgeshire R.O., R. 59/5/3/1, p. 120.
[36] *Diurnal of Nicholas Blundell*, I, 167, 181, and 183.
[37] B.M., 'Diary of William Cole', Add. MS 5835, pp. 386 and 398.
[38] *Diary of a Country Parson*, III, 350.
[39] Bodleian Lib., 'Diary of Rev. James Woodforde', MS. Eng. misc. f. 149, leaf 16.

then expected that you should go to your Relations, or take what other Recreation you think proper.'[40]

Sometimes the gentry's support for their servants' recreations was rather more active. At Little Crosby the servants were occasionally allowed to have dancing: on 4 September 1706, for example, Blundell reported, 'I played at Tables with my Lord Gerard. John my Lords Brewer played on his Pips in the Kitchen and some of the Servants dansed'; and on 10 September 1709, 'The Miller played here after Supper and some of the Servants etc: dansed.'[41] Servants would at times be provided with pocket money if they were going to a recreational event. Around 1770 the memorandum book of the agent for the Aston estates in Shropshire included allowances given to the farm servants to spend at wakes, 'merry nights', bull-baits, and cock-fights.[42] On 25 July 1707, when the family went to a fair in Liverpool, Blundell gave 1s. 2d. as 'Fairings for the Servants'.[43] William Cole noted on 26 January 1767 that 'I gave Tom and Jem leave to go to see the Montabank at Fenny-Stratford, and gave each of them with Sarah something to try their Luck at the Lottery. Jem and Sarah who went Shares got a large Pair of Silver Buckles.'[44]

Certain festive events were actively arranged by the gentry or farmers as a result of their role as employers of agricultural labour. At the end of a major agricultural task – the corn harvest was easily the most important – it was standard practice for the employer to provide a feast for his workers. 'When the Fruits of the Earth are gather'd in,' wrote Henry Bourne, 'and laid in their proper Receptacles, it is common, in the most of Country Places, to provide a plentiful Supper for the *Harvest-Men*, and the Servants of the Family; which is called a *Harvest-Supper*, and in some Places a *Mell-Supper*, a *Churn-Supper*, etc.'[45] In Northumberland the harvest dinner was called 'the Mell-Supper, at which there are dancing, masquing, and disguising, and all other kinds of rural mirth'; and in parts of Yorkshire, as John Brand was told by a local clergyman, 'when all the Corn is got home into the Stack-yard, an entertainment is given called the Inning Goose'.[46] The harvest dinner, wrote Daniel Hilman in 1710,

> the poor Labourer thinks crowns all, a good Supper must be provided, and every one that did anything towards the Inning, must now have some Reward, as Ribbons, Lace, Rows of Pins to Boys and Girls, if never so small for their Encouragement, and to be sure plumb Pudding. The men must now have some better than best Drink, which with a little Tobacco, and their screaming for their Largess, their Business will soon be done . . . [47]

[40] A Present for a Servant-Maid: or, The Sure Means of Gaining Love and Esteem (London, 1743), p. 39.
[41] Diurnal of Nicholas Blundell, I, 118 and 229.
[42] Burne (ed.), Shropshire Folk-Lore, p. 463n.
[43] Diurnal of Nicholas Blundell, I, 145n.
[44] Diary of William Cole, p. 179.
[45] Bourne, Antiquitates Vulgares, p. 229.
[46] Hutchinson, Northumberland, II, Appendix, p. 17; Brand, Popular Antiquities (1813), I, 444n.
[47] Hilman, Tusser Redivivus, 'August', pp. 9–10.

(The tone of voice is clearly that of the reluctant landlord.) Stephen
Duck had the labourer's experience in mind when he wrote of the feasting
which followed the harvest:

>Our Master joyful at the welcome sight,
>Invites us all to feast with him at Night,
>A Table plentifully spread we find,
>And Jugs of humming Beer to cheer the Mind;
>Which he, too generous, pushes on so fast,
>We think no Toils to come, nor mind the past.
>But the next Morning soon reveals the Cheat,
>When the same Toils we must again repeat:
>To the same Barns again must back return,
>To labour there for room for next Year's Corn.[48]

Certainly the harvest dinner must have been one of the most widely
observed of all the calendar festivities. At Warton, Lancashire, the celebrations were organized on a communal basis: 'When Harvest is over they
have a Merry Night as they call it, against which each Family of the better
sort contributes, some Time before, it's [sic] Quota of Malt, which is
brewed into Ale, of which, and of a plentiful Entertainment provided at
the joynt Expences of the Masters of Families, the whole Village are
Partakers.'[49] On 6 September 1737 at Baldingstone, Lancashire, Richard
Kay noted in his diary that 'this Evening we ended our Shearing, and
according to Custom we gave our Reapers this Evening a Treat'.[50] James
Woodforde wrote on 14 September 1776 of being 'Very busy all day with
my Barley, did not dine till near 5 in the afternoon, my Harvest Men dined
here to-day, gave them some Beef and some plumb Pudding and as much
liquor as they would drink'.[51] When the harvest was completed in 1706,
Nicholas Blundell 'killed a Bull for the Workfolks' on September 12th,
and the next day he noted that 'Many of the Workfolks and most of the
Servants went at night to be Mery at Great Crosby'.[52] When he finished the
harvest in 1768, Francis Prior of Ufton, Berkshire, 'Gave all the people
that work'd at Cart that day their supper and plenty of Ale and I intend
if please God I live till the next harvest and remain in the same mind I now
am to provide on this Ocation a Large Round of Beef.'[53] At Bletchley,
Waterbeach, and Weston the rectors' servants were frequently invited to
other men's harvest dinners. On 27 August 1801, for example, Woodforde
mentioned that 'Our Servant Maid, Sally Gunton, had leave to go to Mr
Salisbury's Harvest Frolic this Evening and to stay out all Night. Our

[48] Stephen Duck, 'The Thresher's Labour', in his *Poems on Several Subjects* (London,
1730), pp. 24–5.
[49] *Lucas's History of Warton*, p. 126.
[50] *Diary of Richard Kay*, p. 13.
[51] *Diary of a Country Parson*, I, 187.
[52] *Diurnal of Nicholas Blundell*, I, 119.
[53] Frederic Turner (ed.), *A Berkshire Bachelor's Diary: Being the diary and letters of Francis
Prior, recusant and gentleman farmer of Ufton, Berks., in the latter half of the 18th century*
(Newbury, 1936), p. 17. In 1769 he gave the intended dinner, for which he killed a
bull (*ibid.* p. 24).

Servant Man, Bretingham Scurl, had also leave to be at Mr Bridewell's Harvest Frolic this Evening'; and on 6 September 1766 Cole noted that 'Tom and Jem went to Master Holdom's Harvest Home last Night after they put me to Bed at 10.'[54] In the arable parishes of England harvest feasts would have involved a large proportion of the active, adult members of the community.

Although the finishing of the corn harvest occasioned the most important of the agricultural festivities, there were other farming tasks which might also be concluded with recreations, usually at the employer's expense. On the final day of the hay harvest in 1766 William Cole noted that the labourers 'made a sort of Procession, with a Fiddle and German Flute, Jem dressed out with Ribbands and Tom Hearne dancing before the last Cart, I giving a good Supper to all my Hay makers and Helpers, being above 30 Persons in the Kitchin, who staid 'till one'.[55] Meadow-mowings in Leicestershire were sometimes concluded with sports and diversions which, at the very least, would have assumed the employers' acquiescence.[56] On 14 September 1714 Nicholas Blundell had 'a great Breaking of Flax as grew in the Little More-hey . . . there was 12 Breakers, 12 Scutchers, 11 Slansers, 4 to tend two Gigs and one to take up the Flax, in all 40 Persons; . . . I gave a good Supper to my own Breakers and Swinglers. Tatlock played to them at Night, we had 4 Disgisers and a Garland from Great Crosby, and a deal of Dansing.'[57] In many of the pastoral areas of England festivities were associated with the sheep-shearing of early summer. John Aubrey observed that 'Sheep-sheerings, on the Downes in Wiltshire, and Hampshire etc: are kept with good Cheer, and strong beer'; Thomas Hardy's knowledge of these festivities was put to good use in *Far from the Madding Crowd*.[58] 'The Feast of Sheep-sheering, is generally a Time of Mirth and Joy, and more than ordinary Hospitality', wrote Henry Bourne, 'for on the Day they begin to sheer their Sheep, they provide a plentiful Dinner for the Sheerers, and for their Friends who come to visit them on that Occasion; a Table also, if the Weather permit, is spread in the open Village, for the young People and Children.'[59]

Perhaps the most interesting instance of an employer making provision for his labourers' recreation is the marling celebration which was arranged in 1712 by Nicholas Blundell. During the spring he had been marling some of his fields and as the work was nearing completion in July he wrote of the festivities with which he was actively concerned. The details are worth quoting at length:

> July 4. Some of the Young Foulks of this Town met those of the
> Morehouses and of Great Crosby to consider about the Flowering

[54] *Diary of a Country Parson*, v, 334; *Diary of William Cole*, p. 114; cf. B.M., 'Diary of William Cole', Add. MS 5835, pp. 390 and 416, where four harvest feasts in Waterbeach are mentioned.
[55] *Diary of William Cole*, p. 75.
[56] John Throsby, *Select Views in Leicestershire* (2 vols.; London, 1790), II, 83–4.
[57] *Diurnal of Nicholas Blundell*, II, 110.
[58] Aubrey, *Remaines*, p. 34; *Far from the Madding Crowd*, chaps. 22 and 23.
[59] Bourne, *Antiquitates Vulgares*, p. 126; cf. Hone, *Table Book*, II, cols. 559–61, and *Year Book*, cols. 812–14.

of my Marl-pit, some of them met at Weedows and others at my Mill . . .

July 7. I was very busy most of the after-noone shaping Tinsall etc: for the Garland for my New Marl-pit and after Supper the Women helped to Paste some things for it. I began to teach the 8 Sword Dancers their Dance which they are to Dance at the Flowering of my Marl-pit, Dr. Cawood played to them . . .

July 8. I was very busy in the after Noone making Kaps etc: for my Marlers and Dansers, severall of Great Crosby Lasses helped me. The Young Women of this Town, Morehouses and Great Crosby dressed the Garlands in my Barne for Flowering of my Marl pit. I tought my 8 Sword Dancers their Dance, they had Musick and Danced it in my Barn.

July 9. I was extreamly busy all Morning making some things to adorn my Marlers Heads. My Marl-pit which was made in the Great Morehey out of which I Marled the Picke and Little Morehey was flowered very much to the Satisfaction of the Spectators, there was present Ailes Tickley, Mrs Molineux of the Grange, Mr Burton, Mr Shepperd of Ince, etc:, they Suped here, all the 14 Marlers had a Particular Dress upon their Heads and Carried each of them a Musket or Gun, The six Garlands etc: were carried by Young Women in Prosestion, the 8 Sword Dancers etc: went along with them to the Marl-pit where they Dansed, the Musick was Gerard Holsold and his Son and Richard Tatlock, at Night they Danced in the Barne, Thomas Lathord of Leverpoole brought me to the Marl-pit a Dogg Coller against my Bull Bate as is to be in the Pit . . .

July 15. I Baited a Large Bull in the Bottom of my New Marl-pit in the Great Morehey, he was never baited before as I know off, yet played to admiration, there was I think 8 or 9 Doggs played the first Bait and onely two the 3rd Bait, I think there was not above two Doggs but what were very ill hurt, some Sticked into the Side or Lamed or very ill Brused, I gave a Coller to be played for but no Dogg could get it fairly, so I gave it to Richard Spencer of Leverpoole being his Dogg best deserved it, There was present at the Bait old Robert Bootle, John Fooler, John Tarlton, John Knowles of Leverpoole, etc: . . .

July 18. Mr Aldred began to make some kaps for some of my Sword Dansers against the Finishing day . . .

July 28. William Kennion, Christopher Parker, and their Wives, Sera Atherton, John Mather etc: dined here, they came some of them to give to my Marlers and others to present my Wife against the Finishing of my Marling, I went with them to the Marl pit . . .

July 23. I had my Finishing day for my Marling and abundance of my Neighbours and Tenants eat and drunk with me in the after noone, severall of them had made presents to my Wife of Sugar, Chickens, Butter, etc:. All my Marlers, Spreaders, Water-Baylis and Carters din'd here except one or two Carters as I think were absent, I payed off my Marlers, and Spreaders and some of my Carters. We fetched home the May powl from the pit and had Sword Dansing and a Merry Night in the Hall and in the Barne, Richard Tatlock played to them . . . [60]

There were other times too when the gentry might commemorate some special event by providing food and drink and entertainment for the common people. These kinds of festivities were normally occasioned either by an event of state – a coronation, a royal birthday or wedding, a military victory, the ending of a war – or by a development of importance for a particular family – the birth of a son, the heir to an estate coming of age. Celebrations of this type are reasonably well known: certainly they were often recorded, sometimes in considerable detail, by the newspapers of the period. At Northampton, to commemorate the coronation of George III,

an Ox was roasted whole on the Market-Hill, and at Noon given to the Populace, with several Hogsheads of Strong Beer, by the Worshipful the Mayor and Corporation – a very handsome Coronation-Pole, upwards of 100 Feet high, was erected in the Centre of the Hill, on the Top of which is fixed an Imperial Crown and Sword, finely gilt and painted . . . At Night the Town was illuminated in a grander Manner than ever was before known . . . [61]

After the recovery of George III from his illness in 1789, the country was full of celebrations which were organized by the gentry. At Exton in Rutland, for example, 'the right hon. the Earl of Gainsborough, entertained the whole parish in a most bountiful manner; the town was illuminated, a large bon-fire made, and a pipe of ale given to the people in the streets'; at Morton, Lincolnshire, 'a liberal subscription having been made by the inhabitants of Morton and Hanthorp; the two inferior public houses were opened for the reception of every householder who chose to partake of the same, the number of whom amounted to one hundred and sixty, who were regaled with an excellent supper of beef and ale'.[62] Many of the great national events were acknowledged in the conventional manner: music, illuminations, perhaps bonfires and fireworks, an assembly for the gentility, beef and beer distributed among the common people. Peace festivals were widely observed to commemorate the ending of the Napoleonic Wars; the festivities at Bury St Edmunds, which included a variety of traditional sports, ended with 'a Bon-Fire, and the Burning of Bonaparte's Effigy'.[63]

[60] *Diurnal of Nicholas Blundell*, II, 25–7. Marling feasts are also mentioned in Edwin Butterworth, *An Historical Account of the Towns of Ashton-under-Lyne, Stalybridge, and Duckinfield* (Ashton, 1842), pp. 37–8.
[61] *Northampton Mercury*, 28 September 1761.
[62] *Stamford Mercury*, 13 March and 1 May 1789.
[63] West Suffolk R.O., 864.

Family celebrations were sometimes accompanied by similar gala displays. 'Made an entertainment at Esholt to all the neighbouring gentlemen and their ladyes,' wrote Sir Walter Calverley on 11 September 1707, 'and on Saturday after, being 13th same Sept., had my tenants and neighbours and wives at another entertainment provided on purpose. Both the said entertainments were upon the account of my wife's coming to Esholt.'[64] (He had just been married in the previous January.) In a letter of 14 October 1761, the Earl of Breadalbane described to his daughter the reception which had been given his family on their arrival in Staffordshire:

> The street of Eccleshall thro which we pass'd was adorned with Boughs and Flowers which cover'd every house to the top. An arch was erected of the same materials, with our arms and those of Lord Niddesdale . . . hanging in the middle, under which our Coach pass'd. Several girls dress'd in white strew'd flowers as we went, and morrice dancers preceeded us. The windows and streets were crowded, and a great deal of ale given, by subscription, to the mob. Our neighbour Mr. Bosvile sent a machine drawn by one of his coach horses with a Hogshead of ale on it, and his coachman riding on the Cask like a Bacchus; the horse, machine, Hogshead, and man were all dress'd with flowers. This stood in the street and was soon emptied. Several sheep were roasted whole and many Bonfires and the Bells of different parishes rang all the next day. Besides the subscription made by the principal Inhabitants and the neighbouring Farmers, it cost me £20 but luckily 'tis a Case which happens seldom . . . [65]

The birth of a son and heir to Sir Michael Newton in 1732 prompted him to give 'a splendid Entertainment' at Leominster: '30 Dozen of Wine, 10 Hogsheads of Cyder, an Ox roasted whole in the Street, and 20s. to every Publick-house in Town'.[66] Birthdays, the heir's coming of age, weddings, even funerals: all these family occasions often involved food and drink for all, sports (at times of rejoicing), and much ceremonial display. The coming of age of George Eliot's Arthur Donnithorne is an enriched reconstruction of the type of celebration which was, as many sources attest, a common event in actual experience.[67]

Other sorts of important local developments could also be the occasion for a special treat. It was reported in November 1736, for instance, that

> The Lower Road leading from Marlborough to Beckhampton, Sandy-Lane, and Bristol, (which is much the warmest, safest, and nearest Way) being finish'd, Thomas Smith, of Kennet, Esq; made a handsome Entertainment for his Neighbours, on a very high, large, and beautiful Hill, called Celbury Hill, which lies in the

---

[64] 'Memorandum Book of Sir Walter Calverley, Bart.', in *Yorkshire Diaries and Autobiographies in the Seventeenth and Eighteenth Centuries* (Publications of the Surtees Society, LXXVII, 1886), p. 117.

[65] Bedfordshire R.O., L 30/9/17/15.

[66] *Weekly Worcester Journal*, 17 November 1732.

[67] *Adam Bede*, Book III.

Lower Road; and in a very loyal and affectionate Manner all the Company drank a Health to his Majesty King George, the Queen, the Prince . . .

After Dinner a Bull was baited at the Top and Bottom of the said Hill, and between 4 and 5000 People sate at the Bottom of that and another steep Hill opposite to it, which made a very agreeable Appearance, and seemed to be as pleasing to the Company as the other Diversion. There was also Backsword, Wrestling, Bowling, and Dancing. The same Diversions were repeated on the 2d Day, and also running round the Hill for a Petticoat. The 3d Day the Bull was divided by Mr Smith amongst his poor Neighbours on the Top of the Hill, where they diverted themselves with Bonfires, Ale and Roast Beef, for several Hours, and concluded with drinking the Royal Family's and several other loyal Healths.[68]

Election contests were frequently accompanied by sports and festivities as the candidates vied with each other for electoral support. During the months preceding the notoriously expensive Oxfordshire election of 1754, for example, the county was lavishly treated to a variety of entertainments by the opposing parties.[69] Elections, in fact, whenever they were held in the more open constituencies, were as much festive spectacles, distractions from normal routine, as they were occasions for the considered exercise of political choice.

Sometimes men of substance were involved in promoting or patronizing certain recreations by virtue of the local offices of authority which they held; in these cases the persons who occupied particular positions in local government, usually in the parish or the borough corporation, were obliged by custom to make disbursements for recreational purposes. Bull-baiting seems to have been the most common of these public provisions. At Alnwick, for example, the corporation records indicate that money was being spent to support the sport during the later seventeenth century; as late as 1750 a workman was paid ten pence 'for going to Alemouth for a rope to bait a Bull'.[70] At times during the late seventeenth and early eighteenth centuries bull-baiting was also being supported by the corporations of Cambridge, Bristol, Northampton, Nottingham, and Truro.[71] At Skipton in the mid-eighteenth century the constables' accounts included a charge every few years for buying a new bull rope.[72] In all these cases it seems to have been the custom for the local government to contribute towards the exercise of the sport. A similar situation may have existed at Stamford with regard to the bull-running: in 1710 the chamberlain paid the constables to stop up the streets on 'ye Bull running day';

[68] Gloucester Journal, 9 November 1736.
[69] See Jackson's Oxford Journal for 1753 and early 1754.
[70] Tate, History of Alnwick, i, 432.
[71] Porter, Cambridgeshire Customs, p. 229; John Latimer, The Annals of Bristol in the Eighteenth Century (n.p., 1893), pp. 26–7; Christopher A. Markham and J. Charles Cox (eds.), The Records of the Borough of Northampton (2 vols.; Northampton, 1898), ii, 222; Records of the Borough of Nottingham (9 vols.; 1882–1956), vi, 83; Douch, Old Cornish Inns, p. 51.
[72] Dawson, History of Skipton, p. 386.

and around 1740 at least two of the town's parishes made allowances to their churchwardens for expenses at the bull-running.[73] As late as 1821 it was reported that the two bulls which were baited on the 5th of November at Lincoln had been provided by the city's chamberlains.[74] Sometimes, too, a local election was the occasion for a sponsored animal sport. Around 1760 at Liverpool it was usual to provide a bear for baiting on the day of the mayor's election; and at Beverley during the eighteenth century it was

> the custom, from time immemorial, for every Mayor of this town on his election, to give a bull to the populace, for the purpose of being baited, on the day of his being sworn into office; and which was always done either in the Market-place, or at the door of the donor – several of the Aldermen of those days having rings fixed in the pavement, opposite their houses, for that purpose.[75]

Most of the kinds of dependence which we have mentioned lay stress on the active participation of gentlemen in the recreational life of the common people. But there were more subtle ways too in which many of these recreations assumed support from above. It was not always active assistance which they especially needed, financial or otherwise, but rather the support which was derived from the passive acquiescence of the gentry in the people's traditions and customs. Customary practices, in order to flourish, not only had to be preserved by the common people themselves: they also had to be approved of, or at the very least tolerated, by people with authority. Unless there was a widespread consensus within the governing class which was more or less in favour of these popular traditions, they could not be easily retained. The customs involved sometimes imposed certain limitations on a gentleman's freedom of action, for they were customary *privileges*, rights which the people claimed for themselves; and unless these privileges were acceded to by the gentry, even though particular sacrifices might be involved, the recreations which they sustained would have been placed in jeopardy. If both the people and the gentry were inclined to accept these customs, whatever reservations there may have been, the recreational practices were relatively secure; if, on the other hand, the gentry were to become hostile, this hostility was sure to pose a serious threat to their survival.

During much of the eighteenth century the dominant attitude of the gentry towards the recreations of the people seems to have been one of acquiescence and tolerance. To a certain extent gentlemen shared some of the same recreational interests as the common people, and there was only limited room for conflict when their tastes were often so similar. The common denominator was particularly noticeable in the practice of animal sports. Although there were murmurings of disapproval before the middle

[73] George H. Burton (ed.), *Old Lincolnshire, A Pictorial Quarterly Magazine* (Stamford, 1883–5), p. 166; Burton, *Chronology of Stamford*, p. 51; Stamford Town Hall, Phillips Collection, No. 183.

[74] *Stamford Mercury*, 9 November 1821.

[75] Thomas Troughton, *The History of Liverpool* (Liverpool, 1810), pp. 92 f; *Hull Advertiser*, 1 November 1817; cf. the *Advertiser* for 11 October 1817 and 13 October 1820, and Oliver, *History of Beverley*, p. 422.

of the century, there is no indication that any substantial number of gentlemen had as yet become seriously opposed to them; in fact, they were more likely to be keen spectators, and sometimes even participants. 'My Black-Bull was Baited at Mrs Ann Rothwells,' wrote Nicholas Blundell on 8 September 1712, 'there played but three right Doggs and two of them were ill hurt:'[76] On 20 October 1714 the physician Claver Morris gave 1s. 6d. for the bull-baiting at a public house; and on 5 September 1759 James Woodforde wrote that 'I went to the Bear-baiting in Ansford' (his father was rector of the parish).[77] During the festivities on the day of the mayor's election in Liverpool it was said that 'every house and window in the vicinity of the spot where the bear was baited, was adorned by the appearance of the most elegant ladies and gentlemen in the town'; and an observer of the Stamford bull-running probably had men of substance in mind when he claimed in 1785 that 'I have heard some of the natives, who have lived in the metropolis, aver that they never saw any diversion there comparable to it, and if they were to pay a visit to their friends, have construed to come down a little before this day in order to become actors in it'.[78] Cock-fighting drew its followers from genteel as much as from plebeian sportsmen; and the informal field sports, especially fishing and coursing, sometimes brought together a diversity of social ranks.

The point to bear in mind is that, during the first half of the eighteenth century in particular, many gentlemen were not entirely disengaged from the culture of the common people. They frequently occupied something of a half-way house between the robust, unpolished culture of provincial England and the cosmopolitan, sophisticated culture which was based in London. Most of the country houses were not yet principally seasonal extensions of a polite and increasingly self-conscious urban culture, and many of their occupants remained relatively uncitified. They still retained some of the characteristics of rusticity, traits which they shared with the common people. The fact that the drama of the late seventeenth and earlier eighteenth centuries was full of booby-squires (boobies from London's point of view) is an indication, not that the characterization was necessarily accurate, but that there actually were a large number of gentlemen whose modes of thought and behaviour were deeply imbedded in the experiences of rural life.[79] There were points at which genteel and plebeian experiences overlapped, and many a gentleman must have been prepared to accept the traditional customs of that community on which he himself depended for some of his satisfactions – not only economic, but psychic and social as well. He too was often a traditionalist, a cultural as well as a political conservative. Moreover, as one student of the period has justly

[76] Diurnal of Nicholas Blundell, II, 33.
[77] Diary of a West County Physician, pp. 19–20; Diary of a Country Parson, I, 12; cf. Wiles, Freshest Advices, p. 346.
[78] Troughton, History of Liverpool, p. 93; W. Harrod, The Antiquities of Stamford and St. Martin's (Stamford, 1785), pp. 193–4.
[79] John Loftis, Comedy and Society from Congreve to Fielding (Stanford, 1959), especially pp. 68–76.

observed, 'to an English landowner popularity was of real importance',[80] and the less social insulation was possible, the more was popularity valued. Nicholas Blundell cannot be regarded as a typical squire of the early eighteenth century – he was a Catholic and he lived in a relatively remote part of the country – but his diary is certainly an instructive testimony of the extent to which one gentleman was involved in those traditional activities which were also shared by the common people of the community. An intimate involvement in rural culture imposed certain common experiences on lord and labourer alike.

The paternalism and tolerance which did exist were not, of course, entirely disinterested. Sometimes it was very much in a gentleman's own interest to accommodate himself to the customary expectations of the common people. Despite the reservations which he may have held, it would often have been inexpedient to fly in the face of popular tradition. It was just this kind of self-interest which one observer had in mind when he wrote in 1759 of the custom of providing harvest feasts:

> These rural entertainments and usages . . . are commonly insisted upon by the reapers as customary things, and a part of their due for the toils of harvest, and complied with by their masters perhaps more through regards of interest, than inclination. For should they refuse them the pleasures of this much expected time, this festal night, the youth especially, of both sexes, would decline serving them for the future, and employ their labours for others, who would promise them the rustic joys of the harvest supper, mirth, and music, dance, and song.[81]

There was, in other words, the need to accept a certain amount of give and take. It is often difficult, however, to determine how much of the gentry's behaviour was motivated by an awareness of their own self-interest and how much resulted from their uncritical acceptance of traditional practice. At times certainly there must have been a tension between the conflicting pulls of two inclinations, the one traditional and the other 'progressive'. Sir Joseph Banks seems to have felt this sort of tension when he wrote from Revesby, Lincolnshire, on 20 October 1783 that 'This is the day of our fair when according to immemorial custom I am to feed and make drunk everyone who chooses to come, which will cost me in beef and ale near 20 pounds'.[82] His conformity to the customary obligations was probably prompted largely by the desire to maintain his reputation. Certainly some popular traditions must have been ambivalently regarded by the gentry: although many customs served to keep the people contented and sympathetically attached to their social superiors, they also assumed the expenditure of time and money. The crucial distinction, it seems, was between those who accepted the traditional practices, more

---

[80] G. E. Mingay, *English Landed Society in the Eighteenth Century* (London and Toronto, 1963), p. 284.

[81] *The Genuine Account of the Life and Trial of Eugene Aram, for the Murder of Daniel Clark* (London, 1759), p. 71; from a short account by Aram of 'The Melsupper, and Shouting the Churn'.

[82] Royal Society of Arts, Banks to Sir Charles Blagden, Misc. MSS, B.22. I have Mr David Mackay to thank for this reference.

or less willingly and without much consideration (probably the more common disposition), and those who regarded them as impediments to their freedom of action, as unacceptable and anachronistic popular impositions. The latter view, as we shall see, was to become increasingly powerful as the century advanced.

The dominant attitude during at least the first half of the eighteenth century reflected a subtle blend of tolerance, self-interest, and the paternalistic habit. The judiciousness of this delicate mixture is especially evident in an article of 1736 entitled 'Reflections on Wakes and other Times of Publick Diversion':

'Tis well known that such Diversions are chiefly enjoy'd by the common People; who being fatigued by labouring continually for a sorry Living, find a Relaxation highly necessary for them. For several Months before these Festivals come, they please themselves with the Expectation of approaching Joys. Then, think they, we shall not only rest from our mean Employments, but shall act the Part of Richer and more Creditable People; we shall appear with our best Clothes, and with the Help of our Savings not only live well, but divert ourselves with the merry Humours of Harlequin and Punchanello. These Imaginations brighten their Thoughts, dispel the Clouds of Melancholy, and make them dispatch their Business with Pleasure and Alacrity. When the Festival is over, the Idea of it dwells long in their Imaginations, and is every Day revived by their Memories. But what would be the Consequence, if all such Diversions were entirely banished? The common People seeing themselves cut off from all Hope of this Enjoyment, would become dull and spiritless, and lose not only the Support of their Labour, but even the Comfort of Life: And not only so, but thro' the absolute Necessity of diverting themselves at Times, they would addict themselves to less warrantable Pleasures. Let it not be objected, that they ought rather to addict themselves to such Relaxations as are edifying and apt to promote Virtue. 'Tis true, they ought so to do; but every Thing cannot be so as it ought to be, nor indeed much otherwise than it is. From all this it follows, that the Government is not at all to be blamed for suffering publick Diversions, tho' in some Respects not strictly warranted by Religion, with Design to guard against more pernicious Consequences.[83]

The same attitude of moderation was adopted by the author of a guide-book for the good behaviour of servant girls: 'Innocent Merriment', it was advised, 'will make you afterward work with more Alacrity, ought to be sometimes indulg'd, and is never blameable, but when the Heart is set too much upon it'.[84] Similarly, in the course of advocating increased genteel patronage of certain traditional recreations, the author of a letter to the London Magazine in 1738 declared that

[83] This essay first appeared in the Dutch Spectator, but it was regarded as sufficiently relevant to English circumstances to justify republication in at least two English journals, the Daily Gazetteer of 2 October 1736, and the London Magazine, v (1736), 560–1.
[84] Present for a Servant-Maid, p. 39.

I would not confine rural Diversions to Trials of Strength and Courage; I would admit other Amusements, from which the inferior Part of the other Sex might not be excluded. Dancing on the Green at Wakes, and merry Tides, should not only be indulg'd but incourag'd; and little Prizes being allotted for the Maids who excel in a Jig or Hornpipe, would make them return to their daily Labour with a light Heart, and grateful Obedience to their Superiors.[85]

Here, then, was the essence of the paternalism of the period: tolerance and a disposition towards traditionalism were strongly reinforced by an awareness of the methods for maintaining social control. 'For a Sort of civil and political Reasons,' confessed a contributor to the *Gentleman's Magazine* in 1738, 'as well as out of my natural Candor and Humanity, I am no Enemy to the Recreations of the Populace.'[86] Adam Smith was to touch on the relationship between social control and recreations in his discussion of the potentially subversive character of popular religious sects. One of the ways to guard against their dangerous tendencies, he suggested, was to provide 'public diversions':

The state, by encouraging, that is by giving entire liberty to all those who for their own interest would attempt, without scandal or indecency, to amuse and divert the people by painting, poetry, music, dancing; by all sorts of dramatic representations and exhibitions, would easily dissipate, in the greater part of them, that melancholy and gloomy humour which is almost always the nurse of popular superstition and enthusiasm. Public diversions have always been the objects of dread and hatred, to all the fanatical promoters of those popular frenzies. The gaiety and good humour which those diversions inspire were altogether inconsistent with that temper of mind, which was fittest for their purpose, or which they could best work upon.[87]

Similarly, in the preface to his pioneering study of popular customs, John Brand pointed out that 'Shows and Sports have been countenanced by the best and wisest of States . . . The Common People, confined by daily Labour, seem to require their proper Intervals of Relaxation; perhaps it is of the highest political Utility to encourage innocent Sports and Games among them.'[88] The functions of bread and circuses, if kept within reasonable bounds, were not misconstrued by paternalistic gentlemen.

The other principal social support for popular recreations was the publican and the public house. Indeed, for the exercise of many recreations the participation of publicans was often very useful and sometimes even essential. Aside from the family household, the public house was the

---

[85] *London Magazine*, vii (1738), 139–40.
[86] *Gentleman's Magazine*, viii (1738), 523.
[87] Adam Smith, *An Inquiry into the Nature and Causes of the Wealth of Natons*, ed. Edwin Cannan (2 vols.; London, 1950), ii, 280–1.
[88] Brand, *Popular Antiquities*, pp. v–vi.

foremost everyday meeting place for off-work social gatherings; it was one of the fundamental social centres of the community (the only others of importance were the market place, the village green, and perhaps the churchyard), and because of this it came to serve as a major focal point around which recreations developed and were cultivated (see Plate 10). It was a natural recreational centre, for men were in the habit of visiting the public house during their free time for refreshment, and conversation, and conviviality. 'The beer-house is an attractive thing to him', said a Hampshire magistrate in 1833 of the working man; 'it is not altogether the beer, but the fellowship they meet with, and the conversation they get into, and the petty publications which are continually carried round to those houses, and which they get to read'.[89] (Even before the advent of popular periodicals and newspapers the alehouse would have been an important centre for the exchange and dissemination of news.) When the Swedish visitor, Peter Kalm, was in Little Gaddesden, Hertfordshire, in April 1748 he noticed that 'the men of this village very often came [to the inn], to pass some hours over some Pint beers . . . There were seen, sometimes both before and after dinner, a number of labouring men and others killing time in this way. Still, the evenings after six o'clock were especially devoted to this, after the carls had finished their regular labour and day's work.'[90] This must have been a familiar kind of scene: certainly it was often mentioned by the social reformers of the period as being all too common.

Quite naturally, the general mood of leisure which was inherent in public house gatherings was frequently given specific content through the provision of particular amusement facilities. A public house could often offer to its patrons decks of cards and other devices for petty gaming, such as a skittle ground, a shuffle board, or a nine pin alley. 'Tom and Jem at the Raffle or Lottery at the Alehouse', wrote William Cole on 7 March 1768.[91] It was observed that in Derbyshire 'Quoits seemed a very prevalent amusement of the lower and more idle part of the manufacturing People, at the Ale-house Doors, in the north of the County, about Sheffield in particular'.[92] If a public house was sufficiently spacious, dancing might be allowed on holiday evenings. In Cumberland, for instance, it was said that many of the village alehouses had several dances a year, in addition to the ones during fairs and statutes.[93] Most hiring fairs were held at some inn or public house, including those which were still run by the high constables, and as a result they inevitably served as the centre for the day's entertainment.

But many publicans did more than just passively preside over the amusements of their clientele: they also actively organized and promoted

---

[89] 'Report from the Select Committee on the Sale of Beer', *Parliamentary Papers*, 1833, xv, p. 9 (evidence of Rev. Robert Wright of Itchin-Abbas).
[90] *Kalm's Account of His Visit to England on His Way to America in 1748*, transl. Joseph Lucas (London, 1892), pp. 333–4.
[91] B. M., 'Diary of William Cole', Add. MS 5835, p. 373.
[92] Farey, *Agriculture of Derbyshire*, III, 630.
[93] Housman, *Description of Cumberland*, pp. 72–3.

popular recreations.[94] They knew that a festive or sporting crowd would assure them of a lively trade. (The sponsors of a horse race in Gloucestershire in 1736, 'G. Chambers at the Three Crowns, and John Halling at the Bear, in Cold-Harbour, and William Nebes of Horsley', were quite explicit about their motives: 'The abovesaid Subscribers have taken the Field, so that all Persons not concern'd are desir'd to bring no Liquors there for Sale.')[95] Publicans were to be found making arrangements for matches of football, cricket, wrestling, cudgelling, and bell-ringing; they sometimes organized baitings of animals and promoted cock-fights. On 12 August 1749 a cricket match was announced to 'be played between Eleven Men from Manningtree, Mistely, and Brightingsea, and Eleven Men of Colchester; to meet at George Johnson's, the Sign of the Fencers in Tenant's Lane, Colchester. Wickets to be pitched at One o'Clock, and play for Eleven Guineas, at Colchester aforesaid; where all Gentlemen Cricketters and others, will meet with a hearty Welcome, from their humble Servant, George Johnson.'[96] Similar notices drew attention to other diversions at public houses: an ass race at the Lion and Castle in Theberton, Suffolk, on 1 October 1743; a wrestling match between Berkshire and Gloucestershire at the Swan Inn in Highworth, Wiltshire on 16 October 1740 ('for the Encouragement of the Gamesters,' it was added, 'the Landlord . . . will give Two Guineas to that Side which shall throw Three Falls out of the Five, and Half-a-Crown to every Man that throws a Fall'); a singlestick match at the Goat Inn in Northampton on 16 August 1765; bull-baiting at the White Hart in Maldon, Essex, on 5 January 1785 and at the Bell in Purleigh on 27 June 1786.[97] The provincial newspapers were full of such advertisements. The efforts of publicans in small villages were probably less ambitious, but most of them would have attempted to provide one or two special attractions on a major holiday. At Weston in Norfolk, for example, the Whitsuntide entertainments normally centred on the local public house, where a variety of rural diversions were arranged. In 1765 one observer spoke of how, 'on occasions of rendezvous and public meetings of merriment in a village, the landlord of the alehouse will give a tup (so they call a ram) or a pig, well soaped, with the tail, and the horns, and the ears, respectively cut off. He that catches the tup is to have him; but if he be not taken, he returns to the landlord'.[98] Some publicans organized their own petty fairs. The publican, in fact, was the only commercial promoter of major significance. There were a few other recreational entrepreneurs, especially the itinerant entertainers – mountebanks, gypsies, travelling players, musicians, exhibitors of curiosities – and by the early nineteenth century some of the fairground amusements

[94] For a summary of the relevant evidence on two counties, see A. F. J. Brown, *Essex at Work 1700–1815* (Chelmsford, 1969), pp. 72–3, and Douch, *Old Cornish Inns*, chap. 3.
[95] *Gloucester Journal*, 20 July 1736.
[96] *Ipswich Journal*, 12 August 1749.
[97] *Ipswich Journal*, 17 September 1743; *Gloucester Journal*, 7 October 1740; *Northampton Mercury*, 12 August 1765; *Chelmsford Chronicle*, 31 December 1784 and 23 June 1786.
[98] Samuel Pegge, 'The Bull-running, at Tutbury, in Staffordshire, considered', *Archaeologia*, II (1773), 90–1 (from a paper read in 1765).

were substantial commercial propositions; but the most regular and most familiar source of promoted recreations had to be a fixed institution, and this could only be the public house.

One of the notable features about the recreational life in eighteenth-century England is the fact that for the most part the Church was only peripherally involved in the traditional festivities of the labouring people. In much of Catholic Europe the Church's participation in these festivities remained vigorous and of fundamental importance; holidays were still in some measure holy days, and the Church continued to be active in sustaining and sanctifying a holiday calendar which was very much of its own making. But in England, where the established Church was largely a senior servant in the machinery of government, much of the religious significance of the periodic festivities had been swept away during the sixteenth and seventeenth centuries.[99] The parish church still retained some association with recreational customs – the wake Sunday, for instance, was commonly marked by a special service, and in some places it was the traditional occasion for strewing the church with rushes (on the feast Sunday at King's Sutton, Northamptonshire, 'it is a custom to cover the floor of the church with rushes', and at Little Oakley and Paston special meadows were set aside for this purpose);[100] however, by the eighteenth century most of these festivities had become, and were widely regarded as, predominantly secular affairs, and when their existence was defended by some gentleman, the defence was usually on grounds of social and political utility. The religious culture of the past was popish and thus to be deplored; the new religious orthodoxy was rational and unencumbered by an overbearing priestcraft. When religious considerations did enter a discussion of popular recreations, it was either because the superstitions of Catholicism were again being condemned, or because a critic of these recreations was drawing attention to the discrepancy between the alleged original religious character of some festive occasion and its contemporary profanity. At those times when the Church actually was associated with a major holiday – around Christmas, at Easter, on the wake Sunday (in 1733 the vicar of Dartford, Kent, referred to 'the great festival days of our church, X'mas, Easter and Whitsunday')[101] – it was really just one of several participants and social supports, and often not the most important. The parson had become much like any other gentleman and his church had given up some of its distinctive functions. For the most part the common people made their own pleasure, and when necessary they looked to secular sources for assistance.

[99] For a discussion of this change see Christopher Hill, *Society and Puritanism*, pp. 146–51 and 209.
[100] Bridges, *Northamptonshire*, I, 180, and II, 330 and 537; cf. Alfred Burton, *Rush-Bearing* (Manchester, 1891), pp. 21–2, and Wright, *Calendar Customs*, I, 181.
[101] Elizabeth Melling (ed.), *Kentish Sources*, vol. IV: *The Poor* (Maidstone, 1964), p. 103.

5

Some social functions

A sociologist has suggested that a 'fundamental characteristic of play, as differentiated from any other sort of behaviour', is 'that play is activity which is by and large *non-instrumental* in character'. 'On a social level', he argues, 'play is relatively "self-contained" activity, which is not linked to consequences lying outside the performance of the activity itself.'[1] This chapter offers a contrary view. It seeks to relate popular recreations to the wider social contexts from which they arose and, in particular, to discern some of the social functions of these recreations for the common people themselves. It attempts to explain some of the less obvious, sometimes latent, appeal of popular recreations and to establish their implications for the social structures and networks of social relations with which they were involved. As a guide to this functional approach we may follow Robert Merton: 'The central orientation of functionalism', he says, is 'expressed in the practice of interpreting data by establishing their consequences for larger structures in which they are implicated'.[2] It should be noted that the 'larger structures' to which our attention is presently directed are primarily those of only one group in society, the labouring people, not the social system as a whole.

It has often been recognized that the experience of play and festivity gives rise to a distinctive world of culture and consciousness. Play has the power to create a coherent sense of experience which is radically different from that of everyday life. It can oppose a new and temporary order to the order of conventional routine; it is able to dissolve normal restraints, sanction what would on other occasions be impermissible, and sometimes allow for fantasies which seem but madness to be actually realized. Play can temporarily overpower the sense of the reality of the everyday world of labour, suffering, and responsibility. It permits the sense of excitement to flourish, offsetting those feelings of boredom and weariness. The experience of gaiety and play is not an ordinary experience: it is extra-ordinary; it involves relief from care, a momentary liberation from those burdens and tribulations which are all too real. 'Carnival', it has been said, 'is not a spectacle seen by the people; they live in it, and everyone participates because its very idea embraces all the people. While carnival lasts, there is no other life outside it. During carnival time life is subject only to its laws, that is, the laws of its own freedom.'[3]

[1] A. Giddens, 'Notes on the Concepts of Play and Leisure', *Sociological Review*, N.S. XII (1964), 74.
[2] Robert Merton, *On Theoretical Sociology: Five Essays, Old and New* (New York, 1967), pp. 100–1.
[3] Mikhail Bakhtin, *Rabelais and His World* (Cambridge, Mass., 1968), p. 7.

Many such social experiences, however, are (and have been) closely related to the different norms which regulate behaviour in ordinary life. The relation has often been one of opposition, of mutual antagonism, though sometimes of mutual sustenance as well. Social scientists have frequently drawn attention to those social activities which, as one writer has put it, 'provide institutionalized outlets for hostilities and drives ordinarily suppressed by the group',[4] occasions when normal constraints are at least partly relaxed; and we can readily see that recreational events have been among the most important of these kinds of occasions. Certain recreations have functioned as outlets for those inclinations which, because of the enforcement of mores governing personal behaviour, were normally repressed. On these occasions some of the ordinary taboos about personal behaviour were set aside and 'licentious' behaviour was temporarily sanctioned. Orgiastic feasts are the classic expressions of the characteristic features of licentiousness – heavy drinking, wild dancing, spontaneous singing and shouting, the loosening of sexual inhibitions – practices which have been observed on such occasions as the Roman saturnalia, the continental and Latin American carnivals, and the Scottish or American New Year's Eve. 'Here the individual,' writes Edmund Leach, 'instead of emphasizing his social personality and his official status, seeks to disguise it. The world goes in a mask, the formal rules of orthodox life are forgotten.'[5]

These kind of events were not at all uncommon in English society. Oliver Heywood, for instance, wrote of how, on a summer Sunday in 1680, 'there was a rushbearing at Howarth and their Tyde (as they call it) on which multitudes of people meet, feast, drink, and commit many outrages in revellings, in rantings, riding, without any fear or restraint'.[6] In Northamptonshire, where the festival of St Andrew continued to be observed by the lacemakers well into the nineteenth century, it was said that 'the day is one of unbridled licence – a kind of miniature carnival . . . the lace-schools are deserted, and drinking and feasting prevail to a riotous extent.'[7] Drink was a basic component of this temporary culture of licentiousness; and drunkenness was a regular and more or less tolerated feature of a large number of festive occasions.[8] Heavy drinking was often reserved for holidays, and it was indulged in by many men who were ordinarily temperate. The liberating powers of drink at fairs and festivities were commonly celebrated in popular stories and songs: moderation, at these times, could be abandoned, restraint thrown aside, and immoderation flaunted to the full.

---

[4] Lewis Coser, *The Functions of Social Conflict* (London, 1956), p. 41. I am indebted to this work for a number of ideas, especially the discussion in Chapter 3 of 'Hostility and Tensions in Conflict Relationships'.

[5] E. R. Leach, *Rethinking Anthropology* (London, 1961), p. 135.

[6] *Oliver Heywood*, II, 272.

[7] Thomas Sternberg, *The Dialect and Folk-Lore of Northamptonshire* (London, 1851), p. 183.

[8] For a discussion of some of the recreational implications of drink, see Brian Harrison, *Drink and the Victorians: The Temperance Question in England 1815–1872* (London, 1971), pp. 40–4.

On such occasions the sobriety which was normally demanded, in order that the everyday business of life could be carried on, was temporarily set aside when the need for discipline was less compelling, and when opportunities became available for relatively harmless insobriety. The observance of sexual proprieties might be similarly weakened: Flaubert once spoke of those 'broad jokes which shocked nobody, since they were all experiencing that sense of relief which follows a fairly long period of restraint'.[9] Since most recreations inherently involved a loosening of ordinary social restraints, and were set in a context which was by nature more permissive, more free and easy[10] – a bathing spot, the fairground, the gatherings around a football pitch – they were particularly suitable settings for the exercise of more radical kinds of licence, for behaviour which was not merely more relaxed but which actually countered the dominant mores of people's working lives. Sexual indulgence was, as it still is, more permissible at a party than in 'normal' circumstances because at a party there were fewer overriding demands which sex could disrupt.

Some holidays were thought to be especially associated with sexual licence. The early morning excursion of May Day into a woods or common in order to 'gather the May' was sometimes held in this light: 'much Wickedness and Debauchery are commited that Night,' claimed Henry Bourne, 'to the Scandle of whole Families, and the Dishonour of Religion'.[11] 'If any kind Sweet-heart left her Maidenhead in a Bush,' remarked a Restoration writer, 'she has good luck if she finde it again next May-day'.[12] Wakes too might be similarly regarded: 'Wherever this sort of feast is yet kept up', said an early nineteenth-century observer of north-east Lincolnshire, 'there is no little drunkenness among the men; and often dancing parties are attended with a rude familiarity towards the other sex near approaching to licentiousness.'[13] John Brand suspected that in the North wakes 'sometimes prove fatal to the Morals of our Swains, and to the Innocence of our rustic Maids'.[14] The smock races which were common at wakes and other rural gatherings could carry a sexual connotation, for the female competitors were often encouraged to come lightly clad.

Fairs were probably the recreational events which were most commonly employed for sexual licence. An apt illustration of this feature is the October fair at Charlton in Kent which was vigorously condemned, but also perceptively observed, by Daniel Defoe. The village, he said,

is . . . infamous for the yearly collected rabble of mad-people, at Horn-Fair . . . The mob indeed at that time take all kinds of liberties, and the women are especially impudent for that day; as if it was a day that justify'd the giving themselves a loose to all manner of in-

[9] Gustave Flaubert, *Sentimental Education* (Penguin edn, 1964), p. 166.
[10] The relative 'looseness' of recreational gatherings is remarked upon in Erving Goffman, *Behavior in Public Places: Notes on the Social Organization of Gatherings* (New York, 1963), chap. 13.
[11] Bourne, *Antiquitates Vulgares*, pp. 200–2.
[12] Matthew Stevenson, *The Twelve Moneths* (London, 1661), p. 22.
[13] Society of Antiquaries, 'Edward James Willson Collection' (Lincoln), vol. xiii, MS p. 62.
[14] Brand, *Popular Antiquities*, p. 302.

decency and immodesty, without any reproach, or without suffering
the censure which such behaviour would deserve at another time.[15]
The fair at Charlton had a particular reputation for licentiousness, but
some degree of permissiveness was a common characteristic of many
fairs. At the March 25th hiring fair in Axbridge, Somerset, it was said
that 'many of the fair filles-de-chambres, dairy-maids, and even fat cooks
and greasy scullion wenches, are so civilly greeted by their amorous
swains, that this fair is productive of much business for the country justices
and their clerks, parish-officers, and midwives, for many miles round'.[16]
'Its effects are seen . . . before the end of the year;' claimed one writer of
the statute fair, 'for, when bastardy cases are being adjudicated, many a
poor girl declares that her ruin was effected at the last Martinmas Hirings.'[17]
At Bromley, Kent, there was a bulge of bastard births each year in December–January, about nine months after the spring fair.[18]

Many fairs provided for the common people what masquerades afforded
to the gentry and nobility. Indeed, the fair as a sexual playground was
something of a literary stereotype. After her first affair, Betty the chamber-
maid in *Joseph Andrews* was said to have been 'long deaf to all the sufferings
of her lovers till one day, at a neighbouring fair, the rhetoric of John the
hostler, with a new straw hat and a pint of wine, made a second conquest
over her'.[19] In Charles Johnson's *The Country Lasses* the same social
assumption emerged from Modely's warning to Heartwell against marry-
ing a peasant girl: 'Ay, ten to one but some Sinewy Thresher, who has
warm'd her brisk Blood at a Mop or a Wake, steps into your Place, and
delivers down a Posterity of young Flail-drivers, known by the name of
Heartwell.'[20] Popular ballads sometimes referred to the permissiveness
which was observed at fairs. A song on the 'Wrekington Hiring', for
instance, told of how

> . . . they danc't agyen till it was day,
> An' then went hyem, but by the way,
> There was some had rare fun they say,
> An' found it nine months after-O . . . [21]

The sexual reputation of fairs was partly a consequence of the social
circumstances of those persons who were most directly involved – servants,
apprentices, and other young bachelors and spinsters. Since almost all of

---

[15] Defoe, *Tour through Great Britain*, I, 97; cf. Hone, *Every-Day Book*, I, cols. 1,386–8,
and William Chappell and J. W. Ebsworth (eds.), *The Roxburghe Ballads* (9 vols.;
London, 1871–99), VII, 194–6, and VIII, 661–8.
[16] *Gentleman's Magazine*, LXXV (1805), part I, 202.
[17] Greville J. Chester, *Statute Fairs: Their Evils and Their Remedy* (York and London,
1856), p. 9; cf. William Sheldrake, *A Picturesque Description of Turton Fair, and its
Pernicious Consequences. A Poem* (London, 1789), pp. 16–17.
[18] *Local Population Studies Magazine and Newsletter*, no. 1 (Autumn 1968), 46.
[19] Henry Fielding, *Joseph Andrews*, Book I, chap. 18.
[20] Charles Johnson, *The Country Lasses* (London, 1715), act IV, scene i.
[21] Two versions of this ballad are included in 'A Collection of Broadsides and Ballads
Printed in Newcastle on Tyne' (c. 1799–1830), B.M., shelf mark 1875.d.13; another
version is in A. L. Lloyd, *Come all ye Bold Miners: Ballads and Songs of the Coalfields*
(London, 1952), pp. 28–30. See also 'Haymaking Courtship' in James Reeves, *The
Idiom of the People: English Traditional Verse* (London, 1958), pp. 122–3.

these people were subordinate to a master or mistress, or perhaps still to their parents, they were ordinarily obliged to submit to a discipline which imposed considerable restrictions on their opportunities for sexual indulgence. Their subordination involved many everyday constraints, and the stronger the constraints, the more a relief from authority was valued. Large social gatherings, such as fairs, allowed them to escape temporarily from some of these restrictions – as the lines from one ballad recommended, 'Come, lasses and lads, take leave of your dads / And away to the fair let's hie'[22] – and gave them a chance to follow more freely their own inclinations in the propitious setting of an abundant sexual market. Hiring fairs were especially appropriate occasions for sexual adventures because they were very much servants' events, holidays which were shaped largely by the servants' own tastes and personal needs. Their employers, of course, were often less enthusiastic. Complaining of what he took to be an increasing licentiousness between the sexes, the rector of Claybrook claimed that 'the practice of hiring servants at public statutes, which prevails universally in Leicestershire, is by many people strongly condemned in a moral point of view, and I believe with reason'.[23] These and other popular assemblies very much encouraged the infringement of important mores which employers were concerned to uphold. Indeed, the uses to which fairs were put illustrate a general feature of many large public gatherings: they tended to undermine the normal means of social control and allow those people who were usually dependent to free themselves from some of the imposed restraints which ordinarily inhibited their personal behaviour.

Festive gatherings could also serve as a medium for the direct expression of hostility against the prevailing structures of authority. In these instances an active defiance was displayed against norms and constraints which were imposed from above; recreations became opportunities for irreverence, occasions for challenging conventional proprieties. This was one of the objections which was advanced against popular festivities by a writer in the mid-seventeenth century.[24] Recreational events sometimes included incidents of aggression specifically intended to embarrass and irritate men of higher rank. The Swiss visitor César de Saussure complained in the 1720s of the populace 'throwing dead dogs and cats and mud at passers-by on certain festival days'.[25] This sort of aggressiveness was commonly observed at the time of Derby's Shrovetide football match, for it was customary for unpopular or just well-dressed persons among the spectators to be 'dusted' with bags of soot or powder.[26] The ritual celebrations of November the 5th were sometimes employed to castigate some prominent individual in the community, usually by substituting the person's effigy for that of Guy Fawkes. On 5 November 1831, for example, the effigies

[22] 'The Humours of Hayfield Fair', in Llewellyn Jewitt (ed.), *The Ballads and Songs of Derbyshire* (London, 1867), pp. 62–4.
[23] Macaulay, *Claybrook*, p. 132.
[24] Hall, *Funebria Florae*, pp. 14–15.
[25] *Letters of de Saussure*, pp. 294–5.
[26] A. W. Davison, *Derby: Its Rise and Progress* (n.p., 1906), p. 212n, and a letter in the *Derby Mercury* of 28 February 1844.

of several bishops were paraded and burnt in a number of towns, a popular protest against their opposition to the Reform Bill.[27]

Popular assemblies were potential threats .to the gentry's tranquility, and occasionally a disturbance materialized. 'I went to drink Tea at Mr Knapp's at Shenley,' reported William Cole on Sunday, 30 August 1767, 'where was the Feast and great Rioting, fighting and quarreling: some of the People affronted Mr Knapp [the rector] as he returned from Church.'[28] On many holidays the common people were animated by a confidence which stemmed in part from numbers (plebeian crowds, they knew, had to be treated more respectfully than plebeian individuals), and as a result they were able to neglect for the moment the habit of deference; they could more easily insult established authorities and mollify, or even reverse, the perquisites of social rank. The kinds of liberties which might be taken were observed in 1761 by a gentleman who witnessed the return of a crowd from the customary Easter Monday festivities in Greenwich Park:

> They set out and continued their journey, preceded by musick of different sorts . . . To this they kept time in country dances . . . Nothing extraordinary happened till they had capered a little beyond the Half Way house; where meeting a single Gentleman on horseback, (who seemed to me to be a Clergyman) holding hands with each other, they formed a line, the extremities of which reached the opposite ditches. When they had thus effectually retarded his progress, they insisted upon his getting down and saluting one of their Nymphs, that they averred, by repeated asseverations, had the most beauty and softest lips of any Girl in the Park. The young Gentleman, sensible of his embarrassment, and probably fearing the consequences of non compliance, shewed his sense in dismounting without hesitation, which, as soon as they perceived his alacrity in doing, he was dismissed with a general plaudit.

> But it fared far otherwise with a fat surly curmudgeon, just behind him in a one horse chair, of whom the same tribute was, in like manner, exacted . . . instead of complying he began to expostulate with them. After a prelude of smart altercation, and abusing him for a woman-hater, they handled him so roughly, that he would have been glad to have kissed a more ignoble part of the Lady than her Face, to have avoided such familiarities.

'I have mentioned these instances,' he added, 'that travellers, whose lot flings them in the way of such mobs, may be warn'd by these example to treat them with civility, as they are too powerful to be awed by threats, and generally too much intoxicated to be prevailed on by the remonstrances of reason.'[29] The usual proprieties of social distance, along with presumptions of personal dignity, were fragile commodites amidst the confusion and excitement of popular festivities, and gentlemen sometimes

---

[27] The Times, 10–12 November 1831; cf. Diary of a Country Parson, i, 81. The Stamford Mercury of 10 November 1820 regretted that the Guy Fawkes holiday 'has served not unfrequently as a vehicle for lampooning some object of private or public obloquy'.
[28] Diary of William Cole, p. 257.
[29] Lloyd's Evening Post, 24 March 1761.

found it expedient to avoid those assemblies where the privileges of 'natural' authority might be publicly undervalued.

Not only, then, might the common people be released from some of the constraints attached to their ordinary subordinate roles; they were able as well, by adopting new and more powerful roles, to establish for the moment a rough and ready social equality. During the early nineteenth century in the area around Bottesford, Lincolnshire, landowners tolerated the privilege which was claimed by the people to shoot game at will, on anyone's land, on the 5th of November.[30] It was said that in the Whitby area December 26th 'is a great hunting day, the game laws are considered as of no force for that day'; a similar custom was observed on Christmas Day around Oldham.[31] Some localities had a traditional holiday during which a special licence was both claimed and practised: the privilege of throwing water on persons who neglected to wear 'a piece of "may" '; the right to capture persons, regardless of their rank, and ride them on a stang until they secured their release with a sixpence.[32] The harvest dinner was widely acknowledged as an occasion for social levelling. John Clare, for instance, wrote of how Lubin

> Join'd with the sun-tann'd group the feast to share
> As years roll'd round him with the change agen
> And brought the masters level with their men
> Who push'd the beer about and smok'd and drank
> With freedom's plenty never shewn till then
> Nor labourers dar'd but now so free and frank
> To laugh and joke and play so many a harmless prank[33]

At the harvest feast, observed Henry Bourne, 'the Servant and his Master are alike, and every Thing is done with an equal Freedom. They sit at the same Table, converse freely together, and spend the remaining Part of the Night in dancing, singing, etc. without any Difference or Distinction.'[34]

Sometimes festive occasions were employed for insulting authority by means of a traditional 'mock mayor' ceremony. At Middleton, for instance, a custom of this sort was observed during the Easter holidays: a drunken man was dressed in ludicrous clothes and chaired through the streets at night as the 'Lord Mayor of Middleton'.[35] The mock mayor in Randwick, Gloucestershire, was elected each year at a revel after Easter 'from amongst the meanest of the people'.[36] Such ceremonies functioned

---

[30] *Notes and Queries*, 7th series, VI (1888), 404–5.

[31] Young, *Whitby*, II, 880; Edwin Butterworth, *Historical Sketches of Oldham* (Oldham, 1856), pp. 108–9. For earlier examples of some other sorts of licence with regard to normal property rights, see Charles Pythian-Adams, 'Ceremony and the citizen: The communal year at Coventry 1450–1550', in Peter Clark and Paul Slack (eds.), *Crisis and order in English towns 1500–1700: Essays in urban history* (London, 1972), p. 68.

[32] Thomas Q. Couch (ed.), *The History of Polperro, by the late Jonathon Couch* (Truro, 1871), p. 153; *Gentleman's Magazine*, LXI (1791), part II, 1,169–70, and LX (1790), part I, 520.

[33] Clare, *Village Minstrel*, stanza 49 (punctuation omitted).

[34] Bourne, *Antiquitates Vulgares*, p. 229.

[35] Bamford, *Early Days*, pp. 138–41.

[36] Rudder, *Gloucestershire*, p. 619.

as a burlesque on the character of the social hierarchy as seen from below; their rituals emphasized the total reversal of roles – as the Bible had put it, 'the last shall be first and the first last'. By slighting authority roles, by indicating that these roles should not be taken too seriously, the people were displaying a regulated disdain for the dominant powers and dominant values.[37] The pretentiousness of the upper ranks could be parodied, their claims to superiority deprecated. At Bideford in Devon the annual election was for the mayoralty of 'Shamwickshire'.[38] It was reported that the person chosen as mayor at Polperro in Cornwall 'is generally some half-witted, or drunken fellow'; at every inn 'he makes a speech full of large promises to his listeners of full work, better wages, and a liberal allowance of beer during his year of mayoralty'.[39] Similar rites were observed at Wooton, Oxfordshire, during the wake and the man selected as mayor was usually one of the biggest drinkers.[40]

Festive events also served as outlets for those personal antagonisms which had been nurtured within the plebeian community: they provided convenient opportunities for individuals to settle their grievances against other individuals. At Middleton, for example, the night of May the 1st was known as 'Mischief-neet': 'any one having a grudge against a neighbour was at liberty to indulge it, provided he kept his own counsel. On these occasions it was lawful to throw a neighbour's gate off the angles, to pull up his fence, to trample his garden, to upset a cart that might be found at hand, to set cattle astray.'[41] In the Huntingdonshire fens during the later nineteenth century Plough Monday was the principal occasion for satisfying such grudges.[42] Sometimes sporting events functioned in a similar manner. Following the game of throwing the hood at Haxey, held annually on Twelfth Day, there was reported to have been a good deal of fighting, 'for it is an established maxim that all old grudges and back reckonings are to be cleared up: all of which can be done with impunity'.[43] At Workington the Easter Tuesday football match was between two occupational groups, the seamen and the colliers, and the day was usually closed 'with a fight or two, as all disagreements during the past year are put off

---

[37] There are some illuminating ideas on this general point in Erving Goffman, *Encounters: Two Studies in the Sociology of Interaction* (Indianapolis and New York, 1961), especially the essay on 'Role Distance'.

[38] *Transactions of the Devonshire Association*, LX (1928), 129–30.

[39] Couch (ed.), *History of Polperro*, p. 159.

[40] Adolphus Ballard, *Chronicles of the Royal Borough of Woodstock* (Oxford, 1896), p. 138; and 'Dedication of Churches, With some Notes as to Village feasts and Old Customs in the Deaneries of Woodstock, Deddington, and Witney', *Oxfordshire Archaeological Society*, Transactions No. 47 (1904), 26. Irreverent and licentious behaviour had, for the most part, no serious radical implications: they were the acts of people who, since they could hold out little hope for any fundamental social change, sought some temporary satisfaction in ritual occasions which momentarily augmented their sense of power.

[41] Bamford, *Early Days*, pp. 144–5. A similar licence was observed on the 1st of May in Bury. (Barton, *History of Bury*, p. 12.) Further references to 'Mischief-Night Customs' may be found in Wright, *Calendar Customs*, II, 196–8.

[42] Sybil Marshall, *Fenland Chronicle* (Cambridge, 1967), p. 199.

[43] *Stamford Mercury*, 10 January 1840.

until this night to settle'.[44] The Shrovetide game at Hampton-on-Thames was also followed by a 'general settlement of the year's grievances'.[45] A special licence was sometimes pleaded in order to sanction such hostilities: on Easter Tuesday at Workington 'the town is almost considered in a state of siege, as the lower class think whatever wrong they do on that day the law cannot lay hold of them'; a similar assumption was held about the annual football match at Sancton in the East Riding: 'The carnival was supposed to be of such ancient date that the law had no power to stop it, even if a person was killed.'[46]

Hostilities between social groups were also channelled into certain recreational events. There was a pronounced clannishness and suspicion of outsiders in many English communities, and communal solidarity was partly a product of this prejudice against 'foreigners'. The world of the village was small and intimate, and unity was highly regarded. 'Betwixt those of the same parish', wrote William Borlase of Cornwall, 'there is a natural connexion supposed, from which . . . no one member can depart without forfeiting all esteem.'[47] Outsiders, who fitted awkwardly into this sort of constricted moral culture, were commonly perceived as enemies, as threats to the community. Joseph Lawson, for instance, emphasized the hostility felt by people in Pudsey in the early nineteenth century towards nearby villages, a feeling which might be revealed in the harsh treatment which was sometimes accorded to an outside courter of a local girl.[48] This aggressiveness and pride which arose from social separateness were often expressed in sporting competitions. 'At the Seasons of Football and Cock-fighting' many parishes were reported by the *Spectator* to 'reassume their national Hatred to each other. My Tenant in the Country is verily perswaded, that the Parish of the Enemy hath not one honest Man in it.'[49] When Cornish villages competed in hurling it was said that 'each parish looks upon itself as obliged to contend for its own fame, and oppose the pretensions, and superiority of its neighbours'.[50] In Keighley football play 'was sometimes carried to a riotous and dangerous extent, township being arrayed against township and village against village. Much excitement and alarm were often created by the great set matches between the Town and Parish of Keighley.'[51] The annual football match at Sancton 'often ended in much fighting and bloodshed, each party contending for the

---

[44] William Whellan, *The History and Topography of the Counties of Cumberland and West-moreland* (Pontefract, 1860), p. 479.

[45] Henry Ripley, *The History and Topography of Hampton-on-Thames* (London, 1884), p. 108.

[46] Whellan, *Cumberland and Westmoreland*, p. 479; William Smith (ed.), *Old Yorkshire*, III (1883), 11. At Exeter it was widely believed 'that the statutes . . . take no cognizance of any misdemeanours and breaches of the peace, short of downright rioting,' during the festivities of May the 29th. (Hone, *Year Book*, cols. 636–8.)

[47] Borlase, *Cornwall*, p. 300.

[48] Lawson, *Progress in Pudsey*, pp. 11 and 55–6; cf. Blakeborough, *North Riding of Yorkshire*, p. 98.

[49] *Spectator*, No. 432, 16 July 1712.

[50] Borlase, *Cornwall*, p. 300; cf. Douch, *Old Cornish Inns*, pp. 49–50.

[51] Robert Holmes, *Keighley, Past and Present* (London, 1858), p. 61.

honour of taking the ball home'.[52] A similar competitive spirit was observed
during the Haxey Hood game: 'the inhabitants of several villages adjacent
. . . contend for the mastery [of the hood], each little party striving to get
it to the village in which they reside'.[53] By the late seventeenth century the
bull-running at Tutbury was being used as a trial of strength between the
men of Staffordshire and Derbyshire, with each side attempting to drive
the bull into its own territory.[54] Wakes could also function as occasions
for the expression of inter-group hostilities. During the early nineteenth
century in Shropshire, for example, 'Wrekin Wakes' was highlighted by a
traditional battle between the colliers and the country people for the
possession of the hill on which the feast was held.[55]

As well as functioning as outlets for hostile feelings, popular recreations
also served to foster social cohesiveness and group unity. Competitive
team sports, for instance, often reinforced the sense of solidarity of the
communities from which the opposing players were drawn. One observer
said of the traditional sports of the people, no doubt with some exaggeration, that 'the victory obtained by their parish or hundred, served them
for the next half-year, till another holiday brought another trial of
strength'.[56] At times when a community's aggressiveness was externally
directed, its feeling of unity was likely to be enhanced. Moreover, when
internal conflicts were well modulated, there was often a binding force in
the competition itself, if only because the attention of many individuals
was concentrated on one widely-embracing social event. It was said of the
Derby football match that

> No public amusement is calculated to call forth so high a degree of
> public excitement. Horse races and white apron fairs must not be
> named in comparison with it. The aged and the young are drawn from
> their homes to witness the strife in which the robust and vigorous
> population of the town and immediate neighbourhood engage with
> all the energy of eager but amicable competition.[57]

The rituals which were observed on certain holidays – club day feasts,
Plough Monday processions, weavers' parades, Bishop Blaze festivities –
were affirmations of common interests and common sentiments, and always
helped to consolidate group pride. Parish feasts, as we have noticed,
encouraged social cohesiveness through their emphasis on fellowship,
hospitality, and good cheer. Indeed, most festive occasions which were
rooted in the small community served to articulate a vision of the social
harmony for which its members wished; festivities celebrated those ideals
which transcended self, they reinforced the individual's sense of his social
identity. 'Games and amusements', a French social historian has concluded,

---

[52] William Smith (ed.), Old Yorkshire, III (1883), 11.
[53] Stamford Mercury, 9 January 1846.
[54] Robert Plot, The Natural History of Staffordshire (Oxford, 1686), p. 440, and Thomas
Blount, Fragmenta Antiquitatis, p. 175.
[55] Burne (ed.), Shropshire Folk-Lore, pp. 362–3; cf. Bamford, Early Days, pp. 147–8, and
Porter, Cambridgeshire Customs, p. 145.
[56] Robert A. Slaney, Essay on the Beneficial Direction of Rural Expenditure (London, 1824),
pp. 199–200; cf. Moor, Suffolk Words and Phrases, p. 65.
[57] Derby Mercury, 20 February 1827.

4 *Bowling Outside an Alehouse* (English School)

5 Fight between John Jackson and Daniel Mendoza at Hornchurch in 1795 (English School)

'extended far beyond the furtive moments we allow them: they formed one of the principal means employed by a society to draw its collective bonds closer, to feel united.'[58]

Another function of popular recreations was that they provided realistic opportunities for the common people to acquire prestige and self-respect. Through them the people were able to create, as one writer has aptly put it, 'small-scale success systems of their own'.[59] Even a critical observer of Derby's Shrovetide football match could reveal some of this rationale for the game's popularity: 'I have seen this coarse sport carried to the barbarous height of an election contest; nay, I have known a foot-ball hero chaired through the streets like a successful member, although his utmost elevation of character was no more than that of a butcher's apprentice.'[60] A clergyman complained in 1830 of the Stamford bull-running that 'he who is the most daring, in facing the enraged animal, gains a sort of enviable notoriety among his fellows, which urges him on to fresh feats of adventure'.[61] It was said that during games of camping 'the spirit of emulation prevails, not only between the adverse sides, but [also] among the individuals on the same side, who shall excel his fellows'.[62] John Clare had a similar competitive mood in mind when he wrote of the wrestling at a village wake:

> For ploughmen would not wish for higher fame
> Than be the champion all the rest to throw
> And thus to add such honours to his name
> He kicks and tugs and bleeds to win the glorious game[63]

Football, cricket, boxing, running, wrestling, cudgelling: all these sports provided channels for gaining personal recognition. In fact, they were among the few kinds of opportunities which labouring men had to perform publicly for the esteem of their peers.

It is clear, then, that one of the important implications of many recreations was that the accomplishments on the playground, and the ritual displays at a festival, provided substantial raw material for status evaluations. Persons were accorded criticism or applause, respect or shame, as a consequence of their success or failure in certain well established recreational roles. We have noticed that festive events were often regarded as occasions for sexual display. Moreover, they could also serve as a test of a person's organizational abilities and canons of taste. At Middleton extensive preparations for the wake were made well in advance (elsewhere too this was the custom: special food was prepared, amusements were

---

[58] Phillipe Ariès, *Centuries of Childhood: A Social History of Family Life* (New York, 1965), p. 73.

[59] The phrase is used in a more general context by John Foster, 'Nineteenth-Century Towns – A Class Dimension', in H. J. Dyos (ed.), *The Study of Urban History* (London, 1968), p. 294.

[60] William Hutton, *The History of Derby* (London, 1791), p. 218.

[61] *Voice of Humanity*, I (1830–1), 69.

[62] Robert Forby, *The Vocabulary of East Anglia* (2 vols.; London, 1830), II, 53.

[63] Clare, *Village Minstrel*, stanza 83 (punctuation omitted); cf. Withers, *Poems*, I, 3, and J. N. Brewer, *Some Thoughts on the Present State of the English Peasantry* (London, 1807), p. 5.

planned, and the house was fully cleaned), and much effort was put into

> the arrangements and setting forth of 'the sheet'. This was exclusively the work of the girls and women; and in proportion as it was happily designed and fitly put together or otherwise, was their praise or disparagement meted out by the public: a point on which they would probably be not a little sensitive. The sheet was a piece of very white linen, generally a good bed sheet, and on it was arrayed pretty rosettes, and quaint compartments and borderings of all colours and hues which either paper, tinsel, or ribbons, or natural flowers could supply. In these compartments were arrayed silver watches, trays, spoons, sugar-tongs, tea-pots, snuffers, or other fitting articles of ornament and value; and the more numerous and precious the articles were, the greater was the deference which the party which displayed them expected from the wondering crowd.[64]

Any public recreation usually left in its wake a reservoir of incidents which could be retrospectively enjoyed and discussed, and the memorable details could be incorporated into the community's changing assessments of its own members. The details of the annual football match between the students of the Bromfield free school were said to have been 'the general topics of conversation among the villagers'; another observer, writing in the mid-nineteenth century about Hornsea, found that although a noted game against Sigglesthorne, described by an elderly resident, was fifty years past, he 'seemed to remember every close and field that the ball went into, and various feats of skill and activity, disasters and hurts that occurred'.[65]

Prestige and honour were also acquired during those recreational occasions which assumed a display of fancy dress. 'Whoever takes delight in viewing the various Scenes of low Life,' observed Bernard Mandeville, 'may on Easter, Whitsun, and other great Holydays, meet with scores of People, especially Women, of almost the lowest Rank, that wear good and fashionable Cloaths.'[66] These were the plebeian occasions for cutting a figure: they catered to basic desires for personal display, for an indulgence in finery, for an escape from the customary drabness. At the parish feast in John Clare's *The Village Minstreal* (stanza 71) –

> villagers put on their bran-new clothes
> And milk-maids drest like any ladies gay
> Threw cotton drabs and worsted hose away . . .

It was noted that the girls who attended the annual fair in Turton, near Bolton, were 'Deck'd in the gayest fashion of the year'.[67] In the ballad on 'Wrekington Hiring' the pleasures of self-display were warmly applauded:

[64] Bamford, *Early Days*, pp. 149–50.
[65] Hutchinson, *Cumberland*, II, 322n–23n; Bedell, *Account of Hornsea*, p. 88.
[66] Bernard Mandeville, *The Fable of the Bees*, ed. Phillip Harth (Penguin edn, 1970), p. 152; cf. Edward Ward, *The Dancing-School. With the Adventures of the Easter Holy-Days* (London, 1700).
[67] Sheldrake, *Turton Fair*, p. 15.

> An' Bess put on that bonny gown,
> Thy mother bought thou at the town,
> That straw hat wi' the ribbons brown,
> They'll a' be buss'd that's comin-O;
> Put that reed ribbon round thy waist,
> It myeks thou look se full of grace,
> Then up the lonnen come in haste,
> They'll think thou's cum'd frae Lunnen-O.[68]

A cottage woman's recollections of the late nineteenth century in the Huntingdonshire fens were explicit about the motives and deeply-rooted norms which underlay these dress-up affairs. On the Sunday School anniversary at the Primitive Methodist chapel, she recalled,

> Every mother, however poor she was, had to get her child'en looking smart for the anniversary, and if they couldn't buy new clothes for their families every child had to have one thing new. Among the girls, the secret o' what they were going to wear were kept as if their lives depended on it, and many a mother has dragged out to work for weeks in the field to be able to buy the new things for the anni. This were the part we loved best, because although we were as poor as anybody there, we knowed we could trust our mam to get us the prettiest frocks as well as better quality ones than anybody else's there.[69]

Dressing up and spending freely for a holiday were relatively accessible means of winning approval, and consequently they were much emphasized as social norms; many other channels through which status might theoretically have been achieved, especially those which the middle class favoured, were in practice blocked off by the completely unrealistic economic capabilities which they assumed. And on this issue there was a clear clash between popular and middle class norms. What seemed rational from the people's point of view was regarded by middle class observers as criminally extravagant and irresponsible. One writer, for instance, in discussing the hiring fairs in the North during the mid-nineteenth century, complained of

> the passion for dress and dancing, which prevails to an extraordinary extent among the canny daughters of the North ... The young ladies themselves carry their savings on their backs; and the result of a year's pinching is seen at the 'statty' ball, when a girl, whose ordinary attire is wooden clogs and a serge petticoat, turns out in white muslin, a wreath of flowers, and white kid boots and gloves.[70]

The labourers in the Turton area were said to be often indolent:

> Yet for some weeks before this horrid fair,
> They ply their treadles with assiduous care,

---

[68] 'A Collection of Broadsides and Ballads', B.M., 1875.d.13; cf. 'The Fair,' in C. J. D. Ingledew, *The Ballads and Songs of Yorkshire* (London, 1860), pp. 226–7.
[69] Marshall, *Fenland Chronicle*, pp. 205–6.
[70] T. E. Kebbel, *The Agricultural Labourer* (London, 1870), pp. 125–6.

Weave all night long, nor will their pains forego,
To make a splendid and triumphant show.[71]

It can be seen, then, that popular recreations may only be properly understood when account is taken of the overall complex of social relations and
norms in which they were rooted. The hostilities which arose at festive
gatherings were closely related to established, everyday antagonisms;
revelry and self-indulgence were counterparts to the inhibitions of normal
routine – the norms which strictly regulated personal relations, the tedium,
fatigue and dependence of the working man's (or woman's) daily labour;
certain customs were shaped by the perception of social privilege, preten-
sion, and authority; active sports could be opportunities for legitimate
aggressiveness; some gatherings were soaked in ritual and helped to draw
men more closely together, others emphasized group differences and reinforced the dislike of outsiders; dances, processions, ceremonials, festive
displays, individual and team sports – all these were occasions when
reputation was at stake. Popular diversions were not simply ephemera in
a play-world of little consequence; they were fundamental social activities
which were inseparable from the full range of social reality. Recreation was
one major dimension of an established culture – here rooted in exclusively
plebeian experiences, there overlapping with the culture of gentility – and
it was woven into, and derived its meanings from, the total social fabric.

[71] Sheldrake, *Turton Fair*, p. 8.

6

The undermining of popular recreations

Many of the recreational activities which existed in the eighteenth century were, by the time of the First World War, either almost completely unknown or of much diminished importance; others which survived had been drastically altered, both in their modes of conduct and their social implications. Most of the traditional patterns of recreation had disintegrated during the previous century and a half. Indeed, the decline of these recreations was well advanced by the early years of Victoria's reign; sports and pastimes and festive occasions which had been widespread in 1750 were, by 1850 in many localities, either of negligible significance or obviously on the wane. On this point there is abundant testimony from contemporary sources. Although the details of the pace and geographical scope of these developments remain only partially revealed, the direction of the change is clear: as Robert Southey remarked, with pardonable exaggeration, 'All persons . . . speak of old ceremonies and old festivities as things which are obsolete.'[1]

Some observers lamented the decline of traditional recreations, but most men of property seem to have applauded their demise as a sign of progress and national improvement. Genteel attitudes towards many aspects of popular culture had become increasingly unsympathetic since at least the last quarter of the eighteenth century; customs which had once been tolerated came to be questioned and sometimes heartily condemned. This hostile outlook could hardly fail to have a significant impact on the customary practices of plebeian society, especially when the strictures stemmed from legislators and magistrates, employers and zealous clergymen. But what were some of the principal dimensions of these changes in disposition and sentiment? And how did these altering attitudes and circumstances affect the status and practice of traditional recreations?

Underlying much of the growing hostility towards popular recreation was the concern for effective labour discipline. To men who especially valued industriousness, frugality, and prudence, many of the traditional diversions were apt to appear scandalously self-indulgent and dissipated – wasteful of time, energy and money. 'All sports are unlawful which take up any part of the Time, which we should spend in greater works', advised Richard Baxter; and though it was admitted that in some circumstances recreation might be justified, he was at pains to emphasize the dangers which were frequently involved: idleness, loss of precious time, worldliness, sensual pleasures.[2] The stress on labour discipline was particularly derived

[1] Robert Southey, *Letters from England: by Don Manuel Alvarez Espriella* (3 vols., London, 1807), III, 102–3; cf. Litt, *Wrestliana*, p. 110.
[2] Baxter, *Christian Directory*, Book I, pp. 388 and 244–5.

from the puritan tradition of the century before the Restoration,[3] and though much of the religious and political edifice of puritanism was destroyed after the Interregnum, many of its attitudes towards work and recreation survived into what was officially a non-puritan world and were gradually incorporated into the orthodox thinking of educated society. 'Much of the social content of puritan doctrine', suggests Christopher Hill, 'was ultimately accepted outside the ranks of the nonconformists and even by the apparently triumphant Church of England.'[4] The puritan emphasis on regularity, orderliness, sobriety, providence, and dutifulness in one's calling were reflections of a general regard for individual and social discipline. Thriftlessness, pleasure-seeking, levity, and idleness were among the enemies to be overcome, and it was easy for serious men to associate such ungodly qualities with the fabric of popular diversions as customarily observed. Although religious enthusiasm in England subsided after 1660, many of the puritans' social values persisted, at first with diminished strength and diluted by the revived traditionalism of the Restoration, but by the next century in a consolidated, more rigorous, and more widely accepted form: the Charity School Movement, proposals for the reform of poor relief, the campaign for the reformation of manners, many of the influential writings on economic and social matters – these were some of the later expressions, though more secular in tone, of the social morality of seventeenth-century puritanism.[5] This tradition, in all its various strands, posed one of the most powerful threats to the established customs of popular culture, and it significantly aggravated that widening rift between high and low society which was to emerge fully developed by the early nineteenth century.

One of the social virtues which was passed on to the eighteenth century, there to enjoy a position of prominence, was industry. Industry was thought to be the linchpin of English progress; it was the motive power of those remarkable advances which had so recently carried the nation to new heights of prosperity and world influence. 'It is our Industry that changed the Face of this Country from what it was,' thought one observer, 'and proved thereby the Source of our Liberty and Property; it is our Industry that is the Basis of domestick and foreign Trade, and consequently the

---

[3] See Christopher Hill's essay on 'The Industrious sort of People' in his *Society and Puritanism*, chap. 4; and Michael Walzer's chapter on 'The New World of Discipline and Work' in his *Revolution of the Saints*, especially pp. 210–19.

[4] Hill, *Society and Puritanism*, p. 506.

[5] For discussions of these topics, see Dudley W. R. Bahlman, *The Moral Revolution of 1688* (New Haven, Conn., 1957); M. G. Jones, *The Charity School Movement: A Study of Eighteenth Century Puritanism in Action* (Cambridge, 1938); Dorothy Marshall, *The English Poor in the Eighteenth Century: A Study in Social and Administrative History* (London, 1926); Edgar S. Furniss, *The Position of the Laborer in a System of Nationalism: A Study in the Labor Theories of the Later English Mercantilists* (New York, 1920; repr. 1965); and Edward A. Bloom and Lillian D. Bloom, *Joseph Addison's Sociable Animal* (Providence, Rhode Island, 1971), pp. 30–6. One illustration of this connection between piety and discipline may be found in a charity school tract of 1708, *A Discourse Concerning the Lawfulness and Right Manner of keeping Christmas, and other Christian Holy-days*, especially p. 24, where advice is given on the proper use of time during the Christmas season.

sole Fountain of our Riches; in short, it is our Industry that must maintain us, enable us to do Justice to others, and to live happily ourselves; for without it we can do neither.' It was only natural to conclude that 'Industry ought to be as much encouraged as possible, and that every thing capable of lessening it, ought to be the object of Censure.'[6] Industry was the spring from which progress flowed, and some contemporaries were prone to rhapsodize on its behalf:

> What a variety of blessings follow in thy train, O *Industry*! By thee our poor would be made happy, our riches would increase, more employments would be created for our shipping, our naval power would be extended, and our riches and power would either secure to us the quiet possession of our properties, or enable us to repel the united effort of our encroaching enemies.[7]

Industry was seen as a virtue with religious backing, a quality which was sanctioned as much by God as by the state. 'The Rules of Religion, and the Rules of social Industry do perfectly harmonize', opined Josiah Tucker, and 'all things hurtful to the latter, are indeed a Violation of the former. In short, the same good Being who formed the religious System, formed also the commercial.'[8] Jonas Hanway thought that 'honest industry is an essential part of religion, and the ways of it [are] a reward of virtue, and an earnest of happiness after death'.[9] Industry was very much a duty, not only to one's society, but also to the God who created it and supervised the public good. It is industry 'which makes the artificer and the labourer as useful and valuable as any members in society', suggested one contemporary:

> And as God hath allotted to men very different stations and condi-
> tions of life, and assigned them different gifts and talents to profit
> withal, different occupations and employments for the good of the
> whole; therefore to be diligent in the several provinces in which he
> hath placed us, is a duty we owe to him as well as to our neighbour
> and ourselves. It is our proper business, and a sort of trust reposed
> in us by the governor or the world: and therefore it is not only an
> offence against society, but a breach of our duty to heaven to desert
> or neglect it. And on the other hand, a diligent discharge of this
> duty from a principle of conscience towards God, is in its proper
> time and place an act of religious obedience; and will surely be as
> well accepted of by God, as any act of piety which may be thought
> more immediately addressed to his honour.[10]

[6] *London Magazine*, xvi (1747), 221.

[7] *Considerations on Taxes, as they are supposed to affect the Price of Labour in our Manu-factories* (London, 1765), pp. 53–4. On the authorship of this work and two other relevant tracts which are sometimes attributed to William Temple, see J. de L. Mann, 'Clothiers and Weavers in Wiltshire during the Eighteenth Century', in L. S. Pressnell (ed.), *Studies in the Industrial Revolution* (London, 1960), pp. 77–8.

[8] 'Instructions for Travellers' (1757), in R. L. Schuyler (ed.), *Josiah Tucker: A Selection from his Economic and Political Writings* (New York, 1931), p. 266.

[9] Jonas Hanway, *Letters on the Importance of the Rising Generation of the Laboring Part of our Fellow-Subjects* (2 vols.; London, 1767), ii, 214.

[10] William Adams, *The Duties of Industry, Frugality and Sobriety. A Sermon Preached before a Society of Tradesmen and Artificers, in the Parish Church of St. Chad, Salop, on Easter-*

If industry was to be established as one of the cardinal virtues, it was only natural that idleness would have to be regarded as a major vice. 'Indeed, an idle Person,' according to John Clayton, ' . . . who trifles away that Time unaccountably, which ought to be employ'd in honest Trades for necessary Uses, betrays such an inconsiderate Mind, such a Deadness of Heart, as absolutely disqualifies for every Duty; and is as truly inconsistent with the Spirit of the Gospel, as with the Dictates of natural Affection.'[11] Warnings against the dangers of idle habits were sometimes delivered in verse:

> In Works of Labour or of Skill
> I would be busy too:
> For Satan finds some Mischief still
> For idle Hands to do.[12]

Idleness was regarded by one observer (and this was a common sentiment) as 'the fruitful root of every vice'.[13] It involved a neglect of one's social and religious duty, a shameful avoidance of productive labour, and a vulnerability to diverse temptations. Idleness was a sin which bred, facilitated, and accentuated other sins: for many observers it was the main source of immoral behaviour, and it was a vice which ran rampant among the labouring people. (Although idleness might be construed as a personal failing of a gentleman, it was generally agreed that among the populace it was a fault of a different order: 'The Time of People of Fashion may be indeed of very little Value,' admitted an essayist in 1743, 'but, in a trading Country, the Time of the meanest Man ought to be of some Worth to himself, and to the Community.')[14] Most of the social and economic writers of the period had a low opinion of the moral standards of the common people. One critic, for instance, spoke of the 'manufacturing poor' as 'very depraved and wicked'; a preacher, thinking particularly of London, was of the opinion that 'the debauchery of these days among the lowest of the people is beyond all example of former times'.[15] This sort of disapproval varied in intensity, but there was clearly a widespread agreement on the need for improvement. Josiah Tucker was putting the case strongly, but not in an unrepresentative spirit, when he argued in 1746 that

> the lower class of people are at this day so far degenerated from what
> they were in former times, as to become a matter of astonishment,

Monday, 1766 (Shrewsbury, 3rd edn, 1770), pp. 16–17; cf. John Clayton, *Friendly Advice to the Poor* (Manchester, 1755), pp. 8–9.

[11] *Ibid.* pp. 12–13. Cf. Richard Mayo, *A Present for Servants* (London, 1693), p. 30; Thomas Cooke, *Work-houses the best Charity: A Sermon, Preacht at the Cathedral Church of Worcester, February 2nd 1702* (London, n.d.), *passim*; and James C. Scholes, *Memoir of the Rev. Edward Whitehead, M.A., Vicar of Bolton from 1737 to 1789* (Bolton, 1889), p. 19.

[12] Isaac Watts, 'Against Idleness and Mischief', in David Nichol Smith, *The Oxford Book of Eighteenth Century Verse* (Oxford, 1926), p. 57.

[13] Edward Barry, *A Letter on the Practice of Boxing* (London, 1789), p. 31.

[14] *Gentleman's Magazine*, XIII (1743), 486.

[15] *Considerations on Taxes*, p. 17; Robert Drew, *A Sermon Preached to the Societies for Reformation of Manners, at St. Mary-le-Bow, on Monday, January 27th, 1734* (London, 1735), p. 16.

and a proverb of reproach. And if we take the judgment of strangers, and foreigners of every other country, who are certainly the most unexceptionable judges in this respect, we shall find them all agreed, in pronouncing the common people of our populous cities, to be the most abandoned, and licentious wretches on earth. Such brutality and insolence, such debauchery and extravagence, such idleness, irreligion, cursing and swearing, and contempt of all rule and authority, human and divine, do not reign so triumphantly among the poor in any other country, as in ours: Nor did they ever in ours, 'till of late, in any degree to what they do at present.

> And the reason of this is, alas! but too easily assigned: Our people are *drunk with the cup of liberty*.[16]

This school of writers looked upon any signs of popular indulgence with intense misgivings. One observer criticized the 'beggarly Pride' of those poor men who insisted on keeping a dog; another attacked their weakness for 'Trifling Niceties' and their tendency to congregate in public places 'upon every Occasion of public Solemnity', such as at marriages and funerals.[17] The disapproval of the luxurious living of the poor – tobacco, finery, tea in particular – is amply documented and well known. Recreation was also an indulgence which could easily pass beyond the limits of social acceptability; if industry was to be kept up, it would have to be strictly controlled. 'Is it not melancholy', asked one writer, 'often to see what has been purchased by painful industry and labour squandered away in unprofitable and foolish recreations?'[18] It was pointed out by one tract, in a very moderate spirit, that

> the first Thing commonly thought on by Youth is Recreation and Pleasure: A Degree of which (if the Recreation be lawful) cannot reasonably be objected to; but Care must be taken that the Pursuit of Pleasure may not too much contract, or quite exclude any necessary Duty, and that it indispose not for the Returns of Labour ... A frequent Taste of any kind of Diversions is apt to grow upon the Palate, and give too strong a Relish for them; and when the Inclination is turn'd strongly towards them, and the Mind runs perpetually upon them, the Shop or the Work-room is like the Confinement of a Prison, and labour like a Weight that goes up Hill.[19]

Another observer expressed his concern just as temperately when he suggested that 'all Diversions, all Exercises, have certain Bounds as to Expence, and when they exceed this, it is an Evil in itself, and justly liable to Censure'.[20]

The nature of these bounds was, of course, very much open to debate, but it seems that the dominant inclination was to interpret them as narrowly

[16] Josiah Tucker, *Six Sermons on Important Subjects* (Bristol, 1772), pp. 70–1; from a sermon of 18 March 1746.

[17] Hilman, *Tusser Redivivus*, 'November', p. 4; Clayton, *Friendly Advice*, pp. 30 and 13.

[18] Adams, *Duties of Industry*, pp. 21–2.

[19] *The Servants Calling: With Some Advice to the Apprentice* (London, 1725), pp. 80–1.

[20] *Gentleman's Magazine*, xiii (1743), 485.

as possible. Work and recreation were commonly polarized, and the over-riding concern was to give the former the maximum of encouragement, the latter continual discouragement. One writer, commenting on the views of John Clayton, declared that

> The Way of Wealth, the certain, known, and beaten Track, is thro' Carefulness, Diligence, and Sobriety: This Road, always brings the assiduous Traveller to the wish'd-for End of his Journey; whilst a Desire in Men to spend their Time in Play or Pleasure, is sure, not only to stop them in their Road, but by enervating their Bodies, and their Minds, effectually to check their Progress, thereby prevent-ing them from advancing their Children . . . [21]

Recreation was commonly seen as an impediment, a threat of substantial proportions, to steady and productive labour. 'How often do we see the inhabitants of a country village drawn from their harvest-work, to see a cudgel-playing, or a cricket match!' complained an essay of 1764.[22] The characteristic attitude was to view most, if not all, traditional diversions with suspicion and irritation. Dorning Rasbotham of Farnworth, Lancashire, for instance, recalled that in July 1783, when provisions were dear, 'one evening I met a very large procession of young men and women, with fiddles, garlands, and every ostentation of rural finery, dancing Morris dances in the highway, merely to celebrate an idle anniversary, or what they had been pleased to call for a year or two a fair, at a paltry thatched alehouse upon the neighbouring common.'[23] Recreation, it was suspected, might not be in harmony with the scheme of the national economy; its legitimacy would have to be seriously questioned.

The customary holidays received particular criticism, for they were held to be most responsible for the loss of working time. 'Common Custom has established so many Holy-days,' remarked John Clayton, 'that few of our Manufacturing Work-folks are closely and regularly employed above two third Parts of their Time.' Such a situation was clearly insupportable: 'The Commandment of God is positive *six Days shalt thou labour, and do all that thou hast to do*; and enjoineth constant Diligence in the Pursuit of that Work which he hath given us to do; such solemn Occasions only being excepted from the Injunction, as are peculiarly dedicated to his immediate Service, by that Authority which he hath imparted to Rulers, whether Spiritual or Civil, for the edifying his Church, and the due Government of his People.'[24] Around 1739 Thomas Tonkin, a Cornish gentleman, was complaining that because of the large number of holidays the tin miners 'loiter away their time' and 'do not work one half of their month for their owners and employers'.[25] It was notorious that artisans and domestic

---

[21] Joseph Stot, *A Sequel to the Friendly Advice to the Poor of Manchester* (Manchester, 1756), pp. 19–20.

[22] *London Chronicle*, 4–6 October 1764.

[23] Quoted in B. T. Barton, *Historical Gleanings of Bolton and District* (Bolton, 1881–3), 1st series, pp. 262–3.

[24] Clayton, *Friendly Advice*, pp. 13 and 8.

[25] *Carew's Survey of Cornwall: To which are Added, Notes Illustrative of its History and Antiquities, by the late Thomas Tonkin*, compiled by Francis Lord de Dunstanville (London, 1811), p. 35.

outworkers were in the habit of observing a weekly cycle of only five, and sometimes even four, working days; Saint Monday was a common observance and among some workers the licence was extended to Tuesday. 'Every body knows', observed Bernard Mandeville, 'that there is a vast number of Journymen Weavers, Taylors, Clothworkers, and twenty other Handicrafts; who, if by four Days Labour in a Week they can maintain themselves, will hardly be perswaded to work the fifth.'[26] Moreover, the annual holidays, it was thought, were unnecessarily numerous and a heavy drain on the economy: in 1697 John Pollexfen reckoned that each holiday cost the nation £50,000; two generations later the loss was being put at £200,000.[27] By the late eighteenth century it was even being suggested that all (or virtually all) occasions of popular diversion might be better dispensed with, in the interests of industry, morality, and public order. 'It is . . . found by long experience,' argued Henry Zouch in 1786,

> that when the common people are drawn together upon any public occasion, a variety of mischiefs are certain to ensue: allured by unlawful pastimes, or even by vulgar amusements only, they wantonly waste their time and money, to their own great loss and that of their employers. Nay a whole neighbourhood becomes thereby unhinged in such a manner, that there is a general stagnation of labour for many days: the young and inexperienced, are here initiated in every species of immorality, and prophaneness: quarrels and disturbances are too often promoted, and of course, a great deal of irksome business is thrown upon Justices of the Peace.[28]

Given these attitudes to work and recreation and to popular behaviour, it was only to be expected that such writers would be entirely agreed on the need for more severe and effective labour discipline. 'The reins have been held with a loose hand', complained Joseph Townsend in 1786, 'at a time when the idleness and extravagance, the drunkenness and dissipation, with the consequent crimes and vices of the lower classes of the people, called for the most strenuous exertions of the magistrate, and the most strict execution of the laws.'[29] One writer in 1787 regretted that 'the lower order of civil polity in this kingdom is so little attended to' and 'so laxly administered'.[30] The common people had an inordinate fondness for independence; they waved the flag of liberty, claiming 'that as Englishmen they enjoy a birthright privilege of being more free and independent than in any country in Europe', and in so doing they undermined the

---

[26] *Fable of the Bees*, p. 208. Cf. John Houghton, *A Collection of Letters for the Improvement of Husbandry and Trade* (2 vols.; London, 1681–3), II, 176–7; Clayton, *Friendly Advice*, p. 29; and Mastin, *History of Naseby*, pp. 51–2. For a recent discussion of this popular tradition, see E. P. Thompson, 'Time, Work-Discipline, and Industrial Capitalism', *Past & Present*, No. 38 (December 1967), 72–9.

[27] John Pollexfen, *A Discourse of Trade and Coyn* (London, 1697), p. 50; *London Chronicle*, 4–6 October 1764, citing an unnamed author.

[28] Henry Zouch, *Hints Respecting the Public Police* (London, 1786), pp. 6–7.

[29] Joseph Townsend, *A Dissertation on the Poor Laws* (Berkeley and Los Angeles, 1971; 1st publ. 1786), p. 67.

[30] William M. Godschall, *A General Plan of Parochial and Provincial Police* (London, 1787), p. 1.

interests of their employers and the state. Such freedom – or more properly, licence – could only be tolerated at the risk of national ruin. 'The labouring people should never think themselves independant of their superiors; for, if a proper subordination is not kept up, riot and confusion will take [the] place of sobriety and order.'[31] The working people were seen as a sluggish, recalcitrant, insubordinate multitude, and the overriding problem was to control and regulate them, both for their own best interests and the interest of the public good. 'Unless a speedy reformation takes place among our manufacturing poor,' it was thought, 'unless some scheme be form'd to extirpate idleness, restrain excess and debauchery, prevent vagrancy, enforce industry, keep the poor constantly employed, and ease the lands of the heavy burthen of poor rates, real liberty will still be very precarious, for liberty without property is merely chimerical.'[32]

What, then, were the means recommended to achieve this greater degree of social discipline? How was efficient and regular industry to be effectively enforced, idleness to be punished? The basis for such labour discipline, it was generally agreed, had to be 'necessity'; if economic circumstances were such that men had to work continually in order to satisfy their basic needs, maximum productivity could be achieved and personal indulgence would be discouraged under pain of severe penalties. This would be the best way of deterring inclinations to idleness. 'When Men shew such an extraordinary proclivity to Idleness and Pleasure', remarked Bernard Mandeville, 'what reason have we to think that they would ever work, unless they were obliged to it by immediate Necessity?'[33] The preference of labouring people for leisure over increased income when times were good was a fault which had to be eradicated. Wages, it was thought, should be kept low and prices high; scarcity was conducive to industriousness whereas abundance allowed men to be idle, self-indulgent, and insubordinate. This was one of the essential messages of the economic writers and has been discussed by E. S. Furniss as 'the doctrine of the utility of poverty'.[34] Subsistent poverty was the greatest incentive to labour for it meant that men had to work with regularity in order to survive; if the poor were allowed any surplus they would probably spend it on nonproductive activities ('as they ought to be kept from starving,' said Mandeville, 'so they should receive nothing worth saving').[35] Necessity was one of the fundamental planks of social control. 'When provisions are dear, so that virtually wages are less,' said William Temple, 'industry and sobriety assume their seat among the manufactures . . . Great wages and certainty of employment render the inhabitants of cities insolent and debauched. Low wages and uncertainty of employment near at hand, if discharged, make the husbandman temperate and humble.'[36] Although

---

[31] *An Essay on Trade and Commerce* (London, 1770), pp. 56–8.
[32] *Ibid.* pp. 51–2.
[33] *Fable of the Bees*, pp. 208–9.
[34] Furniss, *Position of the Laborer*, chap. 6.
[35] *Fable of the Bees*, p. 209.
[36] [William Temple], *A Vindication of Commerce and the Arts* (London, 1758), pp. 57–8; cf. Houghton, *Collection of Letters*, II, 174–86.

this was not the only attitude to labour efficiency, it seems to have been the most highly regarded; only a few commentators were prepared to consider the case for higher wages. William Temple was a candid advocate for the disciplinarians: 'The only way to make them temperate and industrious,' he said of the labouring people, 'is to lay them under a necessity of labouring all the time they can spare from meals and sleep, in order to procure the common necessaries of life.'[37]

The most direct (and the traditional) means to encourage labour discipline was through the application of state power, and this kind of control continued to be generally applauded. Government was to back up the workings of the free market, to complement the discipline which was inherent, though not always entirely effective, in the market economy. Industry was a social duty, and where economic necessity failed to enforce it fully, the responsibility for assistance fell to the state. The market and the state were mutual help-mates. One commentator, speaking in support of such restraining laws, suggested that 'to hold the lower Orders to Industry, and guard the Morals of the Poor, on whom all Nations must rely for Increase and Defence, is the truest Patriotism'.[38] Joseph Townsend thought that 'it will be necessary for magistrates to pay more than common attention to the police, till industry and subordination shall be once more restored'.[39] The whole problem of popular behaviour was commended as a suitable topic for the attention of the nation's leaders. 'A good police must be established, a good set of laws, relative to the employment of the poor, must be framed, and their execution be properly enforced, so that constant labour may grow into habit', and 'our manufacturing poor are contented to labour six days for the same sum which they now earn in four days'. 'What can be more worthy the attention of the legislature,' this author exclaimed, 'than the framing of laws which would tend to make several millions of poor labouring people sober, industrious, frugal, temperate, virtuous, and happy, and the state, in consequence of this, the richest and most powerful in the world?' He warned, though, that one had to be discreet in applying such laws if work of good quality was to be expected, for 'the lower sort of people in England, from a romantic notion of liberty, generally reject and oppose every thing that is forced upon them'. Labour which was provided under conditions of quasi-slavery, he realized, was apt to suffer a decline in efficiency. It was better to regulate labour with greater subtlety: 'If possible, the effects of such laws should be produced, almost insensibly, and without the appearance of force: for force will hardly ever answer the end proposed in this land of liberty.'[40]

An important prerequisite of such labour discipline was the regulation

[37] *Vindication of Commerce*, pp. 56–7. Some of the more sympathetic attitudes towards labour are discussed in A. W. Coats, 'Changing Attitudes to Labour in the Mid-Eighteenth Century', *Economic History Review*, 2nd series, xi (1958–9), 35–51.

[38] *Reflections on Various Subjects Relating to Arts and Commerce* (London, 1752), pp. 62–3.

[39] Townsend, *Dissertation on the Poor Laws*, p. 67.

[40] *Essays on Trade*, pp. 69, 71, and 92–3, cf. pp. 211 6. For a general discussion of attitudes concerning 'the enforcement of the duty to labor', see Furniss, *Position of the Laborer*, chap. 5.

of all means of diversion, for these were among the most damaging of the many temptations which distracted the populace from work. We will examine in the following chapter some of the opinions on this issue: the view that annual holidays must be kept to a minimum; that unnecessary festivities – wakes, pleasure fairs, archaic rituals – should be reformed or eliminated; that boxing matches and other large assemblies should be curtailed; that public houses ought to be strictly regulated and prevented from offering recreational attractions.[41] 'A Journeyman can no more afford to lose, give or throw away his Time, than the Tradesman can his Commodity', wrote an essayist in the *Public Advertiser* on 2 September 1757; 'and the best way of preventing this useful Body of Men from this Species of Extravagancy is, to remove from their Sight all Temptations to Idleness; and however Diversions may be necessary to fill up those dismal Chasms of burdensome Time among People of Fortune, too frequent Relaxations of this kind among the Populace enervate Industry.' Josiah Tucker suggested that taxes be levied on various forms of recreation with the intention of 'preventing Idleness, promoting Industry, and checking Extravagance'. They ought to be laid, he thought,

> on all Places of public Resort and Diversion, such as public Rooms, Music-Gardens, Play-Houses, etc. also on Booths and Stands for Country Wakes, Cricket Matches, and Horse Racing, Stages for Mountebanks, Cudgel Playing, etc. moreover on Fives Places, and Ball Courts, Billiard Tables, Shuffle Boards, Skittle Alleys, Bowling Greens, and Cock Pits: Also Capitation Taxes should be levied on itinerant Players, Lottery-men, Shew-men, Jugglers, Ballad Singers, and indeed on all others of whatever Class or Denomination, whose very Trades and Profession have a natural Tendency, and whose Personal Interest it is to make other People profuse, extravagant, and idle.[42]

The more popular diversion could be controlled and restrained, the more would the national economy be strengthened and expanded; habits of leisure had to be brought in line with the requirements of efficient and orderly production.

   This general outlook on labour discipline was certainly influential and probably growing in strength, but during at least the first half of the eighteenth century it was offset to a considerable degree by the tolerance and conservatism of the tradition of paternalism.[43] It is likely that the practical

[41] On the regulation of public houses, see Sidney and Beatrice Webb, *The History of Liquor Licensing* (London, 1903), especially chap. 3 and the Appendix. For a few of the contemporary criticisms of the recreational functions of public houses, see *An Enquiry into the Causes of the Encrease and Miseries of the Poor of England* (London, 1738), pp. 50–1; *Propositions for Improving the Manufactures, Agriculture and Commerce, of Great Britain* (London, 1763), p. 61; an essay in the *London Chronicle*, 4–6 October 1764; [John Powell], *A View of Real Grievances, with Remedies Proposed for redressing them* (London, 1772), pp. 16–17; Zouch, *Public Police*, pp. 4–5; *A Principal Cause of the Miseries of the Poor* (London, 1787), 6–7; and *Reports of the Society for Bettering the Condition and Increasing the Comforts of the Poor* (5 vols.; London, 1798–1808), ii, 189n–90n.

[42] Schuyler (ed.), *Josiah Tucker*, p. 261.

[43] For a discussion of the relation between these two traditions, see below, pp. 158–70.

impact of the ideas we have outlined was only widely felt from the latter part of the eighteenth century, in part because of population growth (and the consequent abundant supply of labour) and the rising cost of living; these economic and demographic circumstances, very different from those which prevailed during the first half of the century, made for that state of 'necessity' (low wages/high prices) which many of the economic writers regarded as the foundation for effective labour discipline. Moreover, with the increasing sophistication of industrial organization in some regions, most dramatically represented by the factories in parts of the Midlands and the North, the curtailment of many traditional customs of popular leisure, and the effective regulation of those pastimes which remained, became basic ingredients in the employers' codes of industrial discipline. The irregularity of the pre-industrial employment of time, and the premium which the people put on leisure, were found to be inconsistent with the necessity of making full use of the substantial investments in fixed capital (large buildings, new machinery, and the like): the older habits had to be attacked and hopefully undermined in order that the economic advantages of larger and more complex manufacturing units could be fully realized. The erosion of the traditional patterns of recreation among the Cornish miners as a result of such demands has been fully explored in a recent study.[44] By the second quarter of the nineteenth century most of the former holidays of the miners had been regulated or completely suppressed. But the disciplining of popular traditions was no easy matter: it often met with bitter resistance and was only achieved after a long period of opposition. Josiah Wedgwood, one of the most vigorous of the early industrial entrepreneurs, was complaining in 1772 of how his workmen 'keep wake after wake in summer when it is their own good will and pleasure', and despite his threats and admonishments, absenteeism at the times of local holidays (as well as during the normal week) remained a persistent problem.[45] On occasion legal deterrents were utilized in order to encourage the desired forms of behaviour: in 1836, for example, two Birmingham apprentices 'who for some time past had been in the habit of keeping St. Monday at their masters' expense' were given a month of hard labour in a House of Correction.[46]

The tension between popular and propertied interests, between independence and dependence, was certainly accentuated from the later eighteenth century, and historians have recently been examining the various ways in which this process of labour discipline accompanied industrialization.[47] Such tension, of course, was not a novel phenomenon: labour

---

[44] Rule, 'Labouring Miner in Cornwall', pp. 72ff.
[45] [Katherine E. Farrer, ed.], Letters of Josiah Wedgwood 1762–1780 (2 vols.; London, 1903), II, 14; Sidney Pollard, 'Factory Discipline in the Industrial Revolution', Economic History Review, 2nd series, XVI (1963–4), 256; and Neil McKendrick, 'Josiah Wedgwood and Factory Discipline', Historical Journal, IV (1961), 38–42, 46, and 51.
[46] Philanthropist, 1 September 1836.
[47] As well as the articles by Pollard and McKendrick referred to above, see Keith Thomas, 'Work and Leisure in Pre-industrial Society', Past & Present, no. 29 (December 1964), 50–62; Thompson, 'Time, Work-Discipline, and Industrial Capitalism'; and Sidney Pollard, The Genesis of Modern Management (London, 1965), chap. 5.

discipline was a long-standing concern, and accelerating social change only heightened conflicts which earlier generations had already tasted. For example, a letter of 8 July 1702 to William Blathwayt, a country gentleman, dwelt on some of the labour difficulties which were hindering progress on the construction of his new house at Dyrham, Gloucestershire:

> Honorable Sir,
>
> I begin to despair of getting Things in any good order agt. you come down, such a pack of People you have here that there is no depending upon them. Sunday last was this Town and Cullern [Colerne] Wake or Revell, and between them a great part of the Workmen have been Revelling and drunkening ever since till this Morning, particularly Richard Broad and his Partner, who will hardly have finisht the Rail and Ballisters before you come, neither can we prevail upon them to send in the Coving Stones for the New Chimneys, and several other Things that are much wanted.[48]

A few days later the same correspondent was noting that 'I misst some of the Workmen this day, particularly Ri. Broad and his People, and upon Enquiry find it to be Box Revel, so must not expect them before to Morrow.'[49] Similarly, on 22 July 1765 the steward at Nocton, Lincolnshire was finding that 'these two feasts at (Potter) Hanworth and Dunston have so turned our labourers' heads from work that we have not been able to get all our hay mown last week'; and a week later he reported that 'this last week has been our horse race, which has been another help to keep our heads turned from minding business, and this week is our Assizes. I hope when they are all over we shall fall to business again.'[50] Popular habits and business efficiency were, it is clear, often at loggerheads, and the proponents of the latter became increasingly intent on enforcing the acceptance of behaviour which was consistent with their most deeply felt social values.

Another powerful influence which helped to weaken the customs of popular recreation, and often worked in tandem with the emphasis on labour discipline, was the evangelical movement. Beginning from a variety of sources in the 1730s, it grew so markedly that within a century it was a force of great weight in English society, both within and without the Established Church. Evangelical sentiment was almost always at odds with the traditions of popular diversion. It was forward-looking, morally 'reformist', profoundly concerned with sin and salvation and the need for social and self-discipline, interested more in the individual's private life than in the affairs of the community (though the former assumed attention to the latter),[51] suspicious of worldly pleasures (though nicely discriminat-

---

[48] Gloucestershire R.O., D. 1799/E 242.
[49] *Ibid.* letter of 13 July 1702.
[50] Quoted in Sir Francis Hill, *Georgian Lincoln* (Cambridge, 1966), p. 54.
[51] William Wilberforce thought that 'the great distinction between our constitution and that of the ancient republics is, that with them the general advantage was the object, without particular regard to individual comfort: whereas in England individual comfort has been the object, and the general advantage has been sought through it.' (Robert

ing in its suspicions), and contemptuous of much of the culture of earlier generations (especially that of its immediate predecessors); on most counts its morality was completely inconsistent with the conservative, gregarious, and ritualistic morality which was represented in the pastimes of the common people. Evangelicalism could not accommodate itself to the traditions of popular leisure without abandoning its basic presuppositions; indeed, there was virtually no room for compromise. The standards of morality and propriety which were advanced by evangelicalism established more rigorous criteria for the evaluation of diverse forms of social behaviour, and as the limits of tolerance contracted, as new norms were opposed to old, the consensus which underlay the traditional practices was whittled away and replaced by an atmosphere of open hostilities. Moral enlightenment became engaged in warfare with the forces of unregeneracy. Customs which had previously been relatively unquestioned came to be seriously challenged, and the disposition of public opinion gradually shifted from a qualified leaning towards traditionalism to a sympathy for progressivism and reform.

What, then, were the main areas of tension? Which elements of evangelicalism were especially opposed to recreational practices?

The starting point for the evangelicals' antipathy to recreation was their suspicion of 'the world' and many of its activities. Evangelicalism posited a fundamental opposition between the life of service to God, a life of holiness, and the life of worldliness, of self-dedication to secular concerns. The ways of the world were essentially wicked, and the moral person had to be acutely aware of the temptations which constantly impinged upon his life and threatened to cast him into an abyss of darkness; a state of grace was extremely difficult to sustain and only continual vigilance could shield him from the forces of evil which surrounded mortal existence. Salvation was won through repentance and a subsequent devotion to spiritual concerns; damnation went to those who neglected their souls and instead concentrated their attention on worldly affairs. True religion, said Hannah More, involved 'a turning of the whole mind to God'.[52] The evils which were most clearly opposed to such a state of holiness were those of the flesh. The struggle between divine and demonic forces was always at work – within the individual, in the society where God had placed him. In an admirable representation of the basic evangelical structure of belief, G. M. Young has emphasized the theological foundations of the faith and suggested some of the ways in which their consequences were discerned in the operation of social reality. 'Evangelical theology', he writes,

> rests on a profound apprehension of the contrary states: of Nature and of Grace; one meriting eternal wrath, the other intended for

Isaac Wilberforce and Samuel Wilberforce, *The Life of William Wilberforce* (5 vols.; London, 1838), v, 214.)

[52] Quoted in Asa Briggs, *The Age of Improvement 1783–1867* (London, 1959), p. 71. 'I declare my greatest cause of difference with the democrats', wrote Wilberforce in 1819, 'is their laying, and causing the people to lay, so great a stress on the concerns of this world, as to occupy their whole minds and hearts, and to leave a few scanty and lukewarm thoughts for the heavenly treasure'. (Quoted in Ford K. Brown, *Fathers of the Victorians: The Age of Wilberforce* (Cambridge, 1961), p. 113n.)

eternal happiness. Naked and helpless, the soul acknowledges its worthlessness before God and the justice of God's infinite displeasure, and then, taking hold of salvation in Christ, passes from darkness into a light which makes more fearful the destiny of those unhappy beings who remain without. This is Vital Religion. But the power of Evangelicalism as a directing force lay less in the hopes and terrors it inspired, than in its rigorous logic, 'the eternal microscope' with which it pursued its argument into the recesses of the heart, and the details of daily life, giving to every action its individual value in this life, and its infinite consequences in the next . . . The world is very evil. An unguarded look, a word, a gesture, a picture, or a novel, might plant a seed of corruption in the most innocent heart, and the same word or gesture might betray a lingering affinity with the class below.[53]

Recreation, being so much a part of the world, had always to be held at arm's length, to be closely scrutinized before being welcomed. And under such scrutiny it was frequently found to be a dangerous fruit – a distraction from things holy, a temptation to immoral indulgence. 'That Christian is the most prudent and most honourable,' declared one observer, 'who keeps at the greatest distance from the ensnaring and polluting vanities of the world'; 'real Christians, who diligently discharge the duties of their stations, and conscientiously fill up their places in their families, in their callings, and in the church, will find but little opportunity or occasion for amusement'; 'when the love of God in Christ Jesus is shed abroad in the heart, the believer will feel no desire for carnal amusements, nor could he relish them'.[54] 'Can you, who love the Lord Jesus Christ,' it was asked, 'have any inclination to associate yourselves with idle and vicious pastimes? Impossible! Your heart, your treasure, your home, is not on earth – neither can you be delighted with earthly things; much less with things sensual and polluting.'[55] 'The Christian's conversation is in heaven, his affections are set upon things above', argued another clergyman in a sermon against the conventional observance of village wakes:

> What spirit, then, can draw you thither to these scenes of frivolity and vice? Is it *there* you can meditate upon the themes in unison with your renewed soul? Is it *there* you can contemplate the mysteries of redeeming love? Is it *there* you would think of CHRIST, His incarnation, agony, and bloody sweat, His cross and passion, His precious death and burial, His glorious resurrection and ascension? Is it *there* you would desire to live? Is it *there* you would wish to die?[56]

[53] G. M. Young, *Victorian England: Portrait of an Age* (London, 2nd edn, 1953), pp. 1–2.

[54] George Burder, *Lawful Amusements; A Sermon* (London, 2nd edn, 1805), pp. 36 and 34.

[55] Francis Close, *The Evil Consequences of Attending the Race Course Exposed, in a Sermon* (Cheltenham, 2nd edn, 1827), p. 15.

[56] William J. Kidd, *Village Wakes; Their Origin, Design and Abuse* (Manchester, 1841), p. 11 (I am indebted to Mr Brian Harrison for this reference). An early evangelical attack on wakes may be found in John Fletcher, *An Appeal to Matter of Fact and Common Sense* (Bristol, 1772), p. 117 (I am indebted to Mr Barrie Trinder for drawing my attention to Fletcher's writings).

Such advice gave little encouragement to notions about 'innocent amusement'. Indeed, many evangelicals were at pains to point out that what others saw as innocent was often a snare for the unwary, a catalyst for the evil passions of human nature, 'the inherent depravity of man'. Permissiveness on this point could not be excused; corruption was too liable to take root if the moral defences were relaxed. 'But again and again is the question put to us, – "What harm can there be in *once* complying with the wishes of our children, and letting them go, at least once, to a place of public amusement? We take them merely to gratify a natural and innocent curiosity." Brethren, the curiosity is too natural to be innocent.'[57] Even when some degree of recreation was theoretically accepted, it was usually so hedged in with restrictions that few of the traditional diversions would have been able to qualify. Hannah More laid down that 'the amusements of a Christian must have nothing in them to excite the passions which it is his duty to subdue; they must not obstruct spiritual-mindedness, nor inflame "the lust of the flesh, lust of the eye and pride of life"'.[58] 'In estimating the propriety or rather the lawfulness of a given amusement,' advised one writer, 'it may safely be laid down, that none is lawful of which the aggregate consequences are injurious to morals: nor if its effects upon the immediate agents are, in general, morally bad: nor if it occasions needless pain and misery to men or to animals: nor, lastly, if it occupies much time or is attended with much expense.'[59] Amusement, to the extent that it is necessary, should be morally constructive and uplifting, and for the most part it should be sought only in order to refresh the spirits for higher tasks.

Public assemblies for diversion were particularly suspect, for it was in these settings that the temptations were most intense, the chances of contamination most likely, the sensual indulgences most extreme. Morality was always vulnerable in crowds, and since large gatherings were commonly associated with traditional recreation, the grounds for disapproval were seen to be almost overwhelming. 'There are occasions', declared one clergyman (he was thinking especially of pleasure fairs), 'when this dangerous world is even made *more* dangerous; when the disobedient and rebellious subjects of God countenance and strengthen one another in the ways of sin – draw their destructive forces to one common arena – and transgress in troops and bands. And then it is that the Christian Watchman is to sound the alarm of impending danger.'[60] Public gatherings generated vices which otherwise might not be encountered; they corrupted the innocent through exposure, and they encouraged the unregenerate to cast off all restraint. 'At an age when evil passions are beginning to assert their power, when friendly counsel and brotherly aid are most of all necessary,

---

[57] R. C. Dillon, *A Sermon on the Evils of Fairs in General and of Bartholomew Fair in Particular* (London, 1830), p. 132.

[58] Quoted in Muriel Jaeger, *Before Victoria: Changing Standards and Behaviour 1787–1837* (Penguin edn, 1967), p. 28.

[59] Jonathan Dymond, *Essays on the Principles of Morality, and on the Private and Political Rights and Obligations of Mankind* (2 vols ; London, 1829), I, 446; cf. Brown, *Fathers of the Victorians*, pp. 442–3.

[60] Dillon, *Evils of Fairs*, p. 118.

when the armour for the life-long contest against the devil, the world, and the flesh, ought to be buckled on in earnest, these young persons are thrown into the way of manifold and fiery temptations, to which they only too often yield': this was one of the main objections to hiring servants at statute fairs.[61] The licence which so commonly characterized public diversions was widely acknowledged and much deplored. An observer of the 1829 bull-running at Stamford complained that 'Many young women too were among the number, whose conduct was anything but modest. Indeed all classes seemed as if they had, on that day, license to cast off all appearance of decency and order, and plunge into every excess of riot, without shame or restraint.'[62]

The only safe course was to avoid such assemblies and to confine one's recreation, so much as it was necessary, to domestic pleasures. The home was a refuge from the world; here amusement could be 'rational', regulated, uplifting, and subservient to the laws of religion. 'It is happily and kindly provided', wrote one moralist, 'that the greatest sum of enjoyment is that which is quietly and constantly induced. No men understand the nature of pleasure so well or possess it so much as those who find it within their own doors.'[63] This was a view which came to be widely held, and in so doing one of the basic features of many popular practices lost much of its public sanction. Popular tastes, which were closely associated with public gatherings and displayed a strong liking for crowds, were very much in conflict with middle class values of privacy and family autonomy. As the home was elevated in status, the value of the public realm came to be depreciated, and evangelical criticism was significantly responsible for putting it on the defensive.

Evangelicalism also acted as a restraint on recreation as a result of its solicitude for a strict observance of the Sabbath. A Sabbatarian tradition was, of course, already established, but it was very much strengthened and revitalized by a whole battery of evangelical influences –Wilberforce, Hannah More, the Society for the Suppression of Vice, Methodism, the *Evangelical Magazine*, the cheap Repository Tracts, the wide range of literature for moral improvement. For the evangelicals Sabbath observance was a matter of the first importance – 'As Mrs More pointed out at the beginning of the campaign, Sunday observance is the Christian Palladium; when it is lost, everything is lost' – and they were repeatedly pointing to it as one of the surest signs of a true believer.[64] Indifference to the Sabbath

---

[61] Greville J. Chester, *Statute Fairs. A Sermon Preached at the Parish Churches of Farndish and Puddington, Beds.* (London, 1858), pp. 4–5.

[62] Winks, *Bull Running at Stamford*, p. 16.

[63] Dymond, *Principles of Morality*, I, 455. Answering William Windham's defence of bull-baiting in 1802, Wilberforce pointed out that 'Great writers had placed the summit of human happiness, not in picnics, but in the cottage of the peasant, surrounded with his smiling family. This was the happiness, and this the recreation, varied and combined with manly exercises abroad, which belonged naturally to the people of England.' (*Parliamentary History*, XXXVI, p. 847.)

[64] Brown, *Fathers of the Victorians*, p. 441; George Mark Ellis, 'The Evangelicals and the Sunday Question, 1830–1860: Organized Sabbatarianism as an Aspect of the Evangelical Movement' (unpubl. Ph.D. thesis, Harvard University, 1951), pp. 6–13.

was a clear indication of profligacy, and this crime, it was thought, often marked the opening of the floodgate for a profusion of vice. A Select Committee of 1832 referred to the Sabbath, in moderate evangelical spirit, as 'this most important institution of the Christian Religion, the more or less decorous observance of which may be considered, at any given time, to afford the safest test of the greater or less degree of Moral and Religious feeling pervading the Community'.[65]

Evangelicalism was probably the main moving force behind the appreciating regard for a disciplined Sunday which became so deeply rooted in nineteenth-century society. Recreation on the Sabbath was thoroughly unacceptable: it was widely regarded as one of the worst types of desecration. 'Private, and especially public amusements on this day, are clearly wrong', advised one essayist; Wilberforce argued that 'the people could only innocently recreate themselves on that day by attending to their religious duties'.[66] From the later eighteenth century attitudes were hardening, and the kinds of Sunday relaxation which had formerly been tolerated gradually succumbed to the pressures of respectable disapproval, retiring completely from public view and seeking their consolation in the partial sanctuary of the alehouse. A resident of a hamlet in Buckinghamshire explained how in her locality Sunday proprieties came to be enforced, and active recreation restrained:

> For several years after I first settled in East Burnham, cricket was regularly played during the summer on Sunday afternoons, by all the men and lads of the vicinity. The common, indeed, presented a lively and pleasing aspect, dotted with parties of cheerful lookers-on, with many women and children and old persons, among whom we ourselves, and our servants, not unfrequently mingled. But about the year 1842–3, some boys of our hamlet having been taken up and carried before the Beaconsfield Bench, for playing cricket on a Sunday, and fined 'fifteen shillings each, or six weeks of Aylesbury gaol', the practice of playing cricket was effectually checked in East Burnham. The young men and boys, having thenceforth no recreative pastime, spent their afternoons in the beershops, or played at skittles in public-houses, or prowled about the lanes looking for birds'-nests, game-haunts, hare 'runs', and the like; while the common was left lonely and empty of loungers.[67]

Evangelicalism had a profound impact on English society. Its voice is to be heard time and time again in the sources of the several decades after the 1790s – in the press, in parliamentary debates, in tracts and pamphlets, in serious works of enquiry, in the appeals of social reformers; it was a voice which spoke in earnest tones, which was acutely sensitive to issues of morality (as well as propriety), preoccupied with the tension between

---

[65] 'Report from the Select Committee on the Observance of the Sabbath Day', *Parliamentary Papers*, 1831–2, VII, p. 261.
[66] Dymond, *Principles of Morality*, I, 171–2; *Parliamentary History*, XXXIV, p. 1,008 (debate of 30 May 1799).
[67] *Some Account of the Hamlet of East Burnham, Co. Bucks.*, by a Late Resident (London, 1858), p. 45n. Cf. Mary Mitford, *Our Village*, I, 148, and Litt, *Wrestliana*, pp. 21–2.

virtue and vice, bearing its sense of righteousness with directness and intense self-consciousness. Evangelical attitudes became common currency, entering the thinking and discourse of many who might not have considered themselves members of the movement; on many issues there was an impressive cross-fertilization between evangelicalism and the cult of respectability. Evangelicalism was not the only important voice of the period – there were nostalgic Tories, High Churchmen, gentlemen of pleasure, Utilitarians, Romantics, working class radicals – but it was certainly one of the most powerful of the competing systems of belief. Men found themselves, as G. M. Young has remarked, 'at every turn controlled, and animated, by the imponderable pressure of the Evangelical discipline', and closely associated with it, 'the almost universal faith in progress'.[68]

It should be noted as well that some of the evangelical impetus for reform arose from the working people's own religious associations: not all of it was promoted by parson, gentleman-reformer, or employer. Wesleyan Methodism, a socially mixed (though increasingly respectable) denomination, helped to weaken the plebeian attachment to traditional diversions; Wesley himself had spoken against recreational indulgences, and this hostility was energetically maintained by his successors.[69] One writer, for instance, explained in some detail why Methodists should not conform to the conventional practice of observing parish feasts. 'Wherever any of the Methodists give into the custom,' he said, 'the result is, that they suffer such loss in their souls by it, as they seldom recover for many months'.[70] In 1784 the Methodist Conference at Leeds had considered the problem of wakes: 'Let none of our brethren make any wake or feast,' it was advised, 'neither go to any on Sunday, but bear a public testimony against them.'[71] Methodism, by urging men to abandon their customary forms of diversion, had a substantial impact on the patterns of recreational life in those regions where it became firmly rooted: this was the case, for example, in numerous mining communities in Cornwall and the northern Pennines.[72] William Howitt was of the opinion that 'in the manufacturing districts, where the Methodists have gained most influence . . . they have helped to expel an immense quantity of dog-fighting, cock-fighting, bull-baiting, badger-baiting, boxing, and such blackguard amusements', though

[68] Portrait of an Age, p. 1.
[69] The Works of John Wesley (14 vols.; London, 1872), VII, 506, and VIII, 270; Fletcher, Appeal to Matter of Fact, pp. 114–21; and E. P. Stigant, 'Methodism and the Working Class, 1760–1821: A Study in Social and Political Conflict' (unpubl. M.A. thesis, University of Keele, 1968), pp. 197–200.
[70] James Wood, An Address to the Members of the Methodist Societies, on Several interesting Subjects (London, 1799), p. 9; cf. E. P. Thompson, The Making of the English Working Class (Penguin edn, 1968), pp. 449–50.
[71] Quoted in W. B. Whitaker, The Eighteenth-Century English Sunday: A Study of Sunday Observance from 1677 to 1837 (London, 1940), p. 178. A similar warning was given by Thomas Cocking, The History of Wesleyan Methodism, in Grantham and Its Vicinity (London, 1836), pp. 179–80.
[72] Rule, 'Labouring Miner in Cornwall', pp. 304ff.; Hunt, Lead Miners of the Northern Pennines, chap. 11.

he added that 'Maying, guising, plough-bullocking, morris-dancing, were gone before, or would have gone, had not Methodism appeared'.[73]

During the generation after the end of the Napoleonic Wars the Primitive Methodists were particularly active in campaigning against the worldliness of popular culture. 'No person shall be continued a member of our society,' they declared, 'who visits public or worldly amusements; nor those who waste their time at public-houses.'[74] They frequently conducted camp meetings at the times of wakes in order to counteract, and hopefully to undermine, the influence of profane festivity;[75] in August 1820 a camp meeting was held on the Sunday of the annual football contest between Preston and Hedon in the East Riding, and at Ashbourne in 1845 the local congregation organized a tea party as a counter-attraction to the Shrovetide football match.[76] Many working men found themselves converted to Primitive Methodism and their modes of life appropriately reformed. It was said, for instance, that Filey in the East Riding was 'a place noted for vice and wickedness of almost every description. Drunkenness, swearing, sabbath-breaking, cock-fighting, card-playing, and dancing, have been the favourite diversions of this place for many years; but which, through the mighty power of God, have received such a shock as will not soon be forgotten; and such as I hope they will never recover.'[77]

There were more subtle ways too in which changing outlooks and values served to undermine the practice of traditional recreation. The waning of these diversions cannot be entirely explained by reference to the outright attacks which were levelled against them (some of which are examined in the following chapter), or the appreciating concern for moral improvement and a strict labour discipline; their decline, it is clear, was partly a consequence of other social transformations, changes of a more general sort, which carried significant implications for leisure activities. Vigorous opposition to recreational customs was only the most visible indication of the tenuousness of their standing, for underlying these explicit tensions were a number of central, long-term social changes which accompanied the whole process of 'modernization'.

One of these important causes of recreational losses was the enclosure movement. Many outdoor recreations depended on an open field as the place for their exercise, and if the field became enclosed it was often difficult to find any alternative playing place. In 1824 Robert Slaney wrote of how in rural areas, 'owing to the inclosure of open lands and commons,

---

[73] Howitt, Rural Life (1840), p. 415.

[74] Primitive Methodist Magazine, i (1819), 218.

[75] Primitive Methodist Magazine, i (1819), 7–8, 56–7, 132–3, and ii (1821), 12 and 14; John Petty, The History of the Primitive Methodist Connexion (London, 2nd edn, 1864), pp. 18–19; H. B. Kendall, The Origin and History of the Primitive Methodist Church (2 vols.; London, n.d.), i, 61–2 and 287–90.

[76] Petty, Primitive Methodist Connexion, pp. 131–3; Derby and Chesterfield Reporter, 7 February 1845.

[77] William Howcroft, 'On the Work of God at Filey', Primitive Methodist Magazine, iv (1823), 255; cf. B. S. Trinder, 'The Memoir of William Smith', Shropshire Archaeological Society Transactions, lviii (1966), part ii, 178–85.

the poor have no place in which they may amuse themselves in summer evenings, when the labour of the day is over, or when a holiday occurs'.[78] This was a familiar, though certainly not universal, problem. The *Derby and Chesterfield Reporter* of 8 March 1844 admitted to 'a feeling of regret, when we have seen those pieces of common land, near to small towns and villages, on which the rural sports of generations have been followed, enclosed'. William Howitt claimed that football 'seems to have almost gone out of use with the enclosure of wastes and commons, requiring [as it does] a wide space for its exercise'.[79] This was an exaggeration, but the trend was undeniable. Enclosure militated against popular recreation since it involved the imposition of absolute rights of private property on land which had previously been accessible to the people at large, at least during certain seasons of the year, for the exercise of sports and pastimes. The sense of social responsibility which was felt by a landlord in Berkshire suggested that the usual consequences of enclosure were clearly not to the advantage of popular recreations. 'Since the enclosures have been made,' he said, 'I think some place should be provided for the exercise and recreation of the working-classes, and especially for their children. I have set out four acres at Oldworth as a play-ground for the children, or whoever likes to play. They have now their cricket-matches, their quoit-playing, and their revels there.'[80] The 1845 Enclosure Act, in providing for the preservation of surviving village greens for popular diversions and in recommending the provision of a playing field in certain cases of the enclosure of waste land, explicitly acknowledged the losses which had often accompanied previous Acts of Enclosure.[81]

There were numerous localities in which enclosure had a direct influence on the practice of a traditional recreation. After the enclosure at Hornsea in 1809, for instance, it was said that 'the sport of foot-ball, which was much practiced up to that time, has necessarily been disused . . . Matches were sometimes made between different villages, the play being from village to village, two or three miles apart.'[82] The enclosure at Pudsey forced the feast from the nearby moor; and at Ratby, Leicestershire, the sports which were associated with the annual 'meadow mowing' – dancing, 'wrestlings, footballs, cudgel-playing, and other athletic exercises' – were terminated with the enclosure of the parish's fields.[83] Enclosure did away with a similar custom near Bicester:

> At the mowing of *Revel-mede*, a meadow between Bicester and Wendlebury, most of the different kinds of rural sports were usually practised; and in such repute was the holiday, that booths and stalls were erected as if it had been a fair . . . The amusements took place at

[78] Slaney, *Rural Expenditure*, p. 200.
[79] Howitt, *Rural Life* (1840), p. 527.
[80] Quoted by Edwin Chadwick in M. W. Flinn's edition of Chadwick's 1842 *Report on the Sanitary Condition of the Labouring Population of Great Britain* (Edinburgh, 1965), p. 338.
[81] 8 & 9 Victoria c. 118, especially sections 15 and 30.
[82] Bedell, *Account of Hornsea*, p. 88.
[83] Lawson, *Progress in Pudsey*, p. 13; Throsby, *Views in Leicestershire*, II, 83–4.

the time when the meadow became subject to commonage . . . These sports entirely ceased on the enclosure of Chesterton field.[84] At one time the working people in Coventry played such games as football, quoits, bandy, bowls, and cricket on a nearby open space of several hundred acres, but it was subsequently enclosed and the former sports were no longer allowed.[85] The official who investigated the living conditions in Portsmouth and its environs for the 1845 Inquiry into the State of Large Towns found that 'formerly an open space, known as the "Laboratory Field", was much used by the inhabitants of Portsea for the purpose of exercise and recreation; but by its enclosure, by order of the Board of Ordnance, as well as by a similar curtailment of another open space . . . hardly any space is left within easy reach but the ramparts of the surrounding fortifications'.[86]

By the middle of the nineteenth century any kind of open space for recreation was very much at a premium. The custom of playing games on public thoroughfares was no longer tolerated; enclosure usually eliminated any public use of agricultural land; and the rapid growth of cities involved the appropriation of much open space, some of which had served as customary playgrounds, for commercial building. The consequences for traditional recreation of urbanization were often acknowledged. In 1833, for example, the Select Committee on Public Walks concluded from its investigations that during the previous fifty years, 'from the increased value of Property and extension of Buildings, many inclosures of open spaces in the vicinity of towns have taken place, and little or no provision has been made for Public Walks or Open Spaces, fitted to afford means of exercise or amusement to the middle or humbler classes'.[87] Equally gloomy conclusions emerged from subsequent investigations which gave some attention to the provision of recreation grounds: the 1840 Select Committee on the Health of Towns, Edwin Chadwick's 1842 Report on the Sanitary Condition of the Labouring Population of Great Britain, and the two Reports from 1844–5 of the Commissioners for Inquiring into the State of Large Towns and Populous Districts.[88] The evidence presented by these reports told a dismal tale of speculative building, land expropriations, and civic indifference marching hand in hand to restrict the opportunities for popular recreation.

The problem of adequate playing space was to be found in varying degrees in many parts of the country. With one or two exceptions, very few industrial towns in the Midlands or the North had any public playing

[84] John Dunkin, *The History and Antiquities of Bicester* (London, 1816), p. 269.

[85] 'Report from the Select Committee on the Health of Towns', *Parliamentary Papers*, 1840, xi, pp. 369–70.

[86] 'Second Report of the Commissioners for Inquiring into the State of Large Towns and Populous Districts', *Parliamentary Papers*, 1845, xviii, p. 651.

[87] 'Report from the Select Committee on Public Walks', *Parliamentary Papers*, 1833, xv, p. 339. This report contains much information concerning the lack of recreational facilities in cities.

[88] *Parliamentary Papers*, 1840, xi; Chadwick's *Report*, ed. Flinn, pp. 335–9; and *Parliamentary Papers*, 1844, xvii, and 1845, xviii (especially the evidence relating to point no. 24 of the Commission's questionnaire).

fields worth speaking of, though some might have access to a nearby field or moor on the sufferance of a landlord. In most places there were only very limited outlets for athletic exercises. In 1833 a Middlesex magistrate reported that previously in the vicinity of London, 'Wherever there was an open place to which people could have access they would play, but they are now driven from all . . . On sufferance formerly they were allowed to play, and they are now expelled from all . . . I have witnessed their dissatisfaction at being expelled from field to field, and being deprived of all play-places.'[89] At Basford, a suburb of Nottingham, it was found that

> There is nothing in the shape of open ground for recreation in or around the village, and this want has been very much complained of. The school-boys are consequently driven into the streets, to their own injury, and to the general annoyance of the inhabitants. The want here complained of is likewise a fruitful source of bickering and recriminations between the young men of the parish and the owners and occupiers of lands, trespasses on the part of the young men, for the purposes of cricket-playing and other games, being very common.
>
> There are now no common lands belonging to the parish. Formerly there were very extensive grounds of this class; but in 1793 these rights were resumed and the grounds enclosed, but without leaving a single acre for the use of the public.[90]

This was a common sort of situation: customary playing spaces were nullified, no new alternatives were available. The weight of the evidence points strongly to the conclusion that prior to the mid-nineteenth century, as cities were extending over the landscape and as land was being taken in for a variety of commercial purposes, many traditional playing grounds were eliminated, and that compensation, in the form of public recreation fields, was almost everywhere negligible. It was only in the second half of the century that parks and playgrounds were widely established and came to be generally regarded as essential amenities of urban life.[91]

It is also important to appreciate the ways in which the changing attitudes towards 'custom', some of which were revealed in disputes over enclosure, were so closely associated with the decline of popular diversions. Many of the common people's activities were imbedded in traditions of customary practice. These customs were sustained and sanctioned by certain expectations about social behaviour for which there was a widespread, though increasingly fragile, consensus. The customary rights which the people claimed arose from fundamental assumptions about the reciprocity of social relations; they were based on presuppositions concerning the rights and obligations which were felt to be associated with the different ranks of the social hierarchy. The essence of a custom was that persons who exercised authority were expected to make particular concessions in the interest

---

[89] *Parliamentary Papers*, 1833, xv, p. 354; cf. p. 398.
[90] *Parliamentary Papers*, 1845, xviii, p. 618.
[91] For a general discussion of playgrounds during the mid-nineteenth century, see J. L. Hammond and Barbara Hammond, *The Age of the Chartists 1832–1854: A Study of Discontent* (London, 1930), chaps. 7 and 8, and pp. 343–6.

of the labouring people. A custom, then, involved the assertion and recognition of a popular privilege. In the late seventeenth century, for example, the Dymokes of Scrivelsby, Lincolnshire, were holding 'certain lands by exhibiting on a certain day every year a milk-white bull with black ears to the people who are to run it down, and then it is cutt in pieces and given amongst the poor'.[92] Whatever their legal standing may have been, all customs had the same basic social significance: they imposed certain requirements on the more powerful people to patronize or tolerate specific activities which were of especial benefit to popular interests. These standards and traditional ideals may have been diluted during the seventeenth century, but they certainly did not disappear. Many communities, it seems, preserved into the eighteenth century an accepted fabric of traditional rights and customs – the custom of gleaning in the fields, the right to gather fuel, the tradition of a rural feast which assumed the squire's patronage, the right to solicit (and obtain) donations on some annual holiday, the custom of sporting in a field at certain times of the year; such popular privileges were sanctioned (as the people usually claimed) by usage 'from time immemorial' and upheld through the value system of an oral tradition.

The language of custom and privilege is a recurrent feature in contemporary sources. It was reported that on the Shrove Tuesday of 1636 at Penkridge, Staffordshire, 'the apprentices, and servants, and young boyes of the town . . . were sporting themselves according to the accustomed manner and liberty of that day'.[93] At Randwick, Gloucestershire, the people justified their annual revel by pleading 'the prescriptive right of antient custom for the licence of the day'.[94] The farm labourers, said Robert Bloomfield, 'are guests by right of custom' at the annual harvest dinner.[95] When the R.S.P.C.A. was lobbying for the suppression of Stamford's bull-running in 1830, the magistrates expressed a reluctance to interfere, 'alleging that the populace looked to it as a privilege which they had a right to claim, as a privilege which had been granted them for many centuries, as a privilege which could not now be refused to them without very serious disturbances'.[96] The people regarded it as a 'lawful ancient custom' which, though it could not be validated by a legal document, was sanctioned by the usage (it was claimed) of some 600 years. A similar view was taken of some of the Shrovetide football matches. For the most part it would appear that such customs remained relatively unchallenged during at least the first half of the eighteenth century; the gentry accepted them as legitimate, or at least harmless, traditional practices, and few were seriously inclined to question their continuance.

---

[92] *Diary of Abraham de la Pryme*, p. 109. The custom appears to have been a kind of bull-running.
[93] Staffordshire R.O., Quarter Sessions Rolls, Epiphany 1636, no. 19 (I am indebted to Mr Farr of the Warwickshire Record Office for this reference).
[94] Rudder, *Gloucestershire*, p. 619.
[95] Robert Bloomfield, *The Farmer's Boy, A Rural Poem* (London, 4th edn, 1801), p. 44 (from 'Summer', l. 303).
[96] *Voice of Humanity*, I (1830–1), 72.

Among the customs which helped to support recreational life were those which provided that a specific field in a parish was to be made available, at least during certain times of the year, for sports and festivities; and the changing status of these special customs nicely illustrates the essential character of those long-term alterations which were influencing most customary rights. In many places the village green would have been the normal location for outdoor recreations, but in other communities the customary playground existed as a result of different circumstances. A case which was heard in the King's Bench in 1665 dealt with a disputed field of just this kind: in answer to the charge of trespassing in the plaintiff's close (in order to dance there), the defendant pleaded 'that all the inhabitants of the vill, time out of memory, etc. had used to dance there at all times of the year at their own free will, for their recreation', and consequently were justified in continuing to do so.[97] It was expected that the privilege claimed would be recognized and accepted by everyone in the community. A document which survives from Great Tey in Essex provides a more detailed illustration of the use of this sort of field and the norms which authorized its existence. At the Quarter Sessions of January 1728 several parishioners were indicted by a copyhold tenant, John Lay, for breaking into his close to play some games and thereby destroying his oats. The defendants, pleading not guilty, claimed that Lay had only been admitted to the feeding and pasturage of the close and had no right to cultivate the land. The core of their case was that

> The Close of Land here mentioned is a Common playing place and has been used as Such out of mind where the memory of man hath not been the contrary and hath been always used on particular days of Rejoyceing for the making bonfires therein. The young people of Tey and the neighbouring parishes have been known to play at football and other games there constantly from time to time and particularly on every Trinity Monday which is the Time of the fair at Tey – and we prove this for upwards of 70 years and the old wittnesses who prove the Same which Boys say they have heard their fathers say they did play there and make Bonfires and no where Else in the said Town . . . [98]

Similarly, in an action argued in the Court of Common Pleas in 1795 the defendants were charged with breaking into the plaintiff's close at Steeple Bumpstead in Essex and 'playing there . . . at a certain game called cricket, and other games, sports, and pastimes'. One defendant pleaded

> That there now is and from time whereof, etc. hath been a certain antient and laudable custom used and approved of in the said parish . . . that all the inhabitants . . . [have] used and been accustomed to have, and of right ought to have had, and still of right ought to have the liberty and privilege of exercising and playing at

[97] 'Abbot v. Weekly', *English Reports*, LXXXIII, p. 357. Judgement was given for the defendant.
[98] Essex R.O., D/DBm T5B, document no 84.

all kinds of lawful games, sports and pastimes, in and upon the said close . . . at all seasonable times of the year at their free will and pleasure . . . [99]

There are numerous references to such playing grounds. At Dorrington, Lincolnshire, a piece of land called the 'Play Garths' had been 'left by an inhabitant for the young men and women of the village to play in' and was still being used in the early nineteenth century for dancing, 'foot-ball, wrestling, and other athletic exercises'.[100] Camping, the East Anglian version of football, was often played in a field specifically known as a 'camping close'; this in fact was the name of the playing field in Steeple Bumpstead. A camping close seems to have been a familiar feature in many villages of East Anglia. One was still being used for recreations at Landbeach, Cambridgeshire, in 1727 and at Burgh Castle, Suffolk, during the early nineteenth century.[101] It is clear as well that at some time or other many other parishes had a camping close: Shepreth in Cambridgeshire; Buxhall, Fressingfield, Ashfield, Needham Market, and Harleston in Suffolk; Elsing, Hevingham, Mattishall, Denver, Garboldisham, and Swaffham in Norfolk.[102] There was a 'football close' in North Leverton, Nottinghamshire, in Baldock, Hertfordshire, and in Skelton near Richmond; at least two Bedfordshire parishes, Felmersham and Wyboston, had a field of the same name.[103] Kirkleatham in the North Riding had a 'football garth' and Stock Harvard, Essex, a 'Football Field'.[104] However, in all these cases it is not known whether or not the fields were still being used for recreational purposes during the eighteenth century.

It is evident that many of these customary rights were being undermined by the eighteenth and early nineteenth centuries. Indeed, some of them may have been terminated during the seventeenth century: the camping close at Milton, Cambridgeshire, for instance, had been annexed to the rectory in 1653.[105] In individual cases the particular circumstances behind the loss of such rights are often obscure, but the long-term trend is

[99] 'Fitch v. Rawling, Fitch and Chatteris', *English Reports*, cxxvi, pp. 614–17; cf. *Chelmsford Chronicle*, 13 February 1795.

[100] Hone, *Year Book*, col. 984.

[101] William K. Clay, 'A History of the Parish of Landbeach in the County of Cambridge', *Publications of the Cambridge Antiquarian Society*, vi (1861), 60; William A. Dutt, *Highways and Byways in East Anglia* (London, 1901), pp. 151–2.

[102] *East Anglian*, New Series, viii (1899–1900), 128; W. A. Copinger, *History of the Parish of Buxhall in the County of Suffolk* (London, 1902), p. 194n; and Charles Chandler, 'On the Significance of some East Anglian Field-Names', *Norfolk Archaeology*, xi (1892), 149; cf. Porter, *Cambridgeshire Customs*, p. 230.

[103] Nottinghamshire R.O., DP 37/2 (land conveyance of 1659); W. Branch Johnson, *The Hertfordshire Pepys: John Carrington, of Bramfield, and his Diary from 1797 to 1810* (Letchworth, n.d.), p. 19 (reference from 1703); North Riding County R.O., ZFY (estate survey of 1775); and Bedfordshire R.O., G.A. 1341, X. 202/193, and X. 202/201 (references from the mid-seventeenth century).

[104] North Riding County R.O., ZK 499–500, 681–2, 813, and 946 (land conveyances of 1628–68); F. W. Austen, *Rectors of Two Essex Parishes and Their Times* (Colchester, 1943), p. 141 (will of 1668).

[105] William K. Clay, 'A History of the Parish of Milton in the County of Cambridge', *Transactions of the Cambridge Antiquarian Society*, xi (1869), 25.

reasonably clear. As economic change accelerated, and as the market economy established a firmer grip on social thinking and behaviour, many customary practices came to be ignored or abrogated, with the result that the recreations they supported, their defences weakened, were increasingly restrained or forced into disuse. The Great Tey case of 1728 throws some light on how such a conflict might develop. The tenant of the playing field had apparently tried to dispense with the customary restrictions which were imposed on him by turning the close into arable, presumably because it was more profitable to do so – the defendants alleged that he 'did break up and sow the said Close with oates . . purely (as he said) to make the Land his own and hinder the publick Rejoyceings there'. They went on to offer their version of the details of the dispute:

> The time the Defendants Entered in to the said Close or playing place was on his present Majestyes proclamation, at Gunpowder or Treason, and at his said Majesteys Coronation, at all which times Bonfires were then made as usually have been for these ages past. The said Defendants and others of the parishioners of Tey aforesaid told the said Lay that he must not sow or break up the ground for it was a Common playing place and if he did that they would notwithstanding play there. All this was told him before he sowed the ground and the Defendants accordingly did play when the oats were in the Grass and made Bonfires at the time aforesaid which indeed spoiled part of them, there being but very few . . .
>
> The former Tenants of the Close were so farr from pretending a right or to hinder the Youths playing and making Bonfires at publick Rejoyceings that John Hills a Tenant or occupier thereof on a day when the youth were going to play there (The Grass being pretty good he desired them to go into another of his fields and play there and spare the Close or playing place and gave the young men then present a large quantity of strong beer for their soe doing) and they accordingly played in his other Close.

Moreover, 'To show how farr the Defendants intended no malice or willfull destruction of the oates they offered John Lay after he had sown the Close to play in another of his fields if he'd give them leave on Condition he'd noe more sow the said Close.' It was also claimed that the custom enjoyed the landlord's approval:

> If it be said that the Ground is the Lord of the Mannors Then it's plain the Defendants have his leave for he holds his Court on every Trinity Monday and is usually present there – and in particular the Court after Lay had sown the oats, Lay desired Sir William Holton (Deputy Lord of the Mannor) to Grant his Warrant against the Youth then playing and he refused it. The said John Lay also applyed to Mr. Tuffnell one of his Majestyes Justices who was at the Court and he also denied the said Lay a Warrant.

Although John Lay's efforts failed on this occasion, it seems that the playing rights were lost – we do not know how – sometime before the end of the century.[106]

The Great Tey document is unusual in its richness of detail. For the most part the evidence concerning the manner in which such rights might have been lost is very sparse, though what exists is suggestive. In 1724, for instance, a dispute arose between the parish clerk of White Roding, Essex, and a number of other parishioners: the latter, it was said, 'pretend a right or claim for their playing att football and using other sports att all times when they shall think fit in a certain close or croft of Land called Grass croft part of the Glebe belonging to the parsonage of White Rooding aforesaid'. The disputants agreed to have two Justices of the Peace consider the case, and if the parishioners could not produce 'some Will Deed or other instrument in Writeing whereby to manifest and legally make appear the right title and claim of the said Inhabitants of White Rooding for their playing and sporting in the said croft called Grass Croft as aforesaid that then they the said Inhabitants . . . should and would sink and drop all their pretensions and claim of right and title to the said Croft for ever here-after'. No title could be presented and consequently the recreational rights were abandoned.[107] (In most such cases strong legal proof would not have existed, and as a result the customs involved were particularly vulnerable to the challenges of property rights; their principal defence – and one which was falling out of favour – was usage 'from time im-memorial'.) In 1746 a similar kind of dispute was carried to greater judicial heights, the Court of Common Pleas. On this occasion the defendants, who were charged with trespass, pleaded a custom for 'all the inhabitants of the town of Coleshill for the time being to have and enjoy the liberty and privilege of playing at any rural sports or games in the said close every year at all times of the year at their will and pleasure'; but the Court found for the plaintiff on the grounds 'that the custom as laid extending to any rural sports was too general and uncertain'.[108]

One would be inclined to suspect that in many places where such customs lapsed some measure of force, subtle or direct, may have been applied in order to effect their dissolution. It is not likely that these rights would often have been readily abandoned or indifferently neglected by the common people. Sometimes a tenant or landlord may have decided unilaterally to disregard a customary practice, and in many cases little could be done about it. At times certainly a community would have organ-ized resistance – in the early nineteenth century, for instance, a farmer in Purton, Wiltshire, attempted to incorporate into his orchard a portion of the close which served as a playground, and he was vigorously (and success-fully) opposed by the villagers[109] – but normally such resistance must

[106] Essex R.O., D/DBm T5B, document no. 84; and *An Account of the Tenures, Customs, etc. of the Manor of Great Tey, . . . in a Letter from Thomas Astle, Esq. to the Right Honourable the Earl of Leicester* (London, 1795), pp. 13–15.
[107] Essex R.O., D/P 304/1/1, a note at the end of the parish register.
[108] 'Millechamp v. Johnson and Others', *English Reports*, cxxv, pp. 1,133n–1,134n.
[109] Hone, *Every-Day Book*, ii, col. 1207; cf. Burne (ed.), *Shropshire Folk-Lore*, p. 366.

have been difficult to sustain, especially in rural parishes with an un-sympathetic resident squire. Few labouring men could have afforded to carry a dispute to the courts. Perhaps many disputed rights were lost by default. Others may have been settled in the vestry, or at a manorial court, or in the study of a local magistrate, in many cases, we might suppose, to the advantage of the man of property.

But whatever the circumstances of conflict may have been, it is evident that these kinds of recreational rights were widely in retreat. In East Bilney, Norfolk, there was a field near the church called the 'camping-land', and it was said in 1830 that 'though that use of it has long ago ceased, the old inhabitants well remember the time when the lads of the village regularly repaired thither, after evening service on Sundays, to play foot-ball and other games'.[110] Similarly, it was reported in 1890 that a close known as 'Butts Field' in Coggeshall, Essex, 'has not been used as a playground within the memory of the oldest inhabitants, yet some of them heard their parents say that it was formerly so used'.[111] The right of access to a field called the 'Foot Ball Garth' in Harewood in the West Riding may have been lost during the same period.[112] In 1844 the rector of Hitcham, Suffolk, was complaining of 'how entirely the labourers seem to be without innocent and manly amusements . . . They have no village green, or common, for active sports. Some thirty years ago, I am told, they had a right to a play-ground in a particular field, at certain seasons of the year, and were then celebrated for their foot-ball; but somehow or other, this right has been lost to them, and the field is now under the plough'.[113] By the 1830s the 'camping close' at Boxted, Essex, was being leased out as an arable field and part of it served as a gravel pit.[114] Indeed, the loss of such customary rights seems to have been a widespread phenomenon. Commenting on public walks, the investigator of the north-east for the 1845 Inquiry into the State of Large Towns reported that 'in Sunderland, as in other towns visited, a strong impression was conveyed to me that the public are deprived of varied rights which at former periods they have been accustomed to enjoy'.[115] The undermining of these kinds of custo-mary rights was a source of bitterness among some of the labouring people. 'It is the abolition of the old custom', thought Hitcham's parson, 'that is looked upon as a grievance almost too heavy to be borne with patience, and which is not unlikely to be stored up in the memories of the three generations of the families offended; who look upon it as an actual infringe-ment upon the rights of the poor.'[116]

Customary practices declined for other reasons too. Custom is parti-cularly the mark of the small, closely-knit community, and it tends to

---

[110] Forby, *Vocabulary of East Anglia*, II, 53.
[111] George F. Beaumont, *A History of Coggeshall, in Essex* (Coggeshall, 1890), p. 250.
[112] Jones, *History of Harewood*, p. 168.
[113] J. S. Henslow, *Suggestions Towards an Enquiry into the Present Condition of the Labouring Population of Suffolk* (Hadleigh, 1844), pp. 24–5.
[114] 'Thirty-Second Report of the Charity Commissioners, Part I', *Parliamentary Papers*, 1837–8, xxv, p. 628.
[115] *Parliamentary Papers*, 1845, xviii, p. 557.
[116] Henslow, *Labouring Population of Suffolk*, p. 29.

6 *The Cockpit* (1759) by William Hogarth

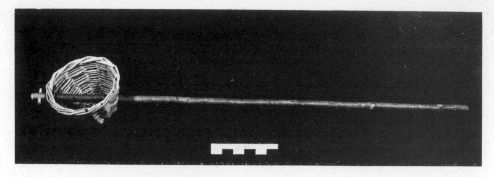

7 A singlestick

8 Bull-baiting, c. 1800 (from *Country Life*, 14 November 1941)

lose its force in a larger, more mobile, and more impersonal world; for here the impact of a clear-cut and rigid public opinion is considerably lessened, and the free market very much dilutes the strength of traditional habits. In the more diversified and anonymous urban world there are, as a rule, fewer possibilities for the imposition of custom and more for the exercise of free choice – though in practice the range of choice for the labouring people may be exceedingly limited. In the course of any process of 'modernization' customary practices take a severe beating. But it still must be emphasized that many customary rights were forcibly undermined, and that their dissolution was often effected by men of property in order to enhance their own interests. Custom was one of the people's basic defences; it was one of the normative weapons of the weak against the strong, one of the ways in which power was disciplined and concessions enjoyed. Custom was a constraint on the behaviour of the propertied classes; it restricted their freedom of action (especially their freedom to dispose of property), imposed on them certain obligations, and in many cases limited their profits. In a society which was putting increasing emphasis on the sanctity of the individual, customary rights could easily come to be regarded as insupportable burdens.

In addition, it must be acknowledged that the growth of cities, as well as eliminating playing spaces and hastening the demise of customary norms, also posed a major challenge to the survival of all those recreational experiences which were imbedded in rural culture. Harvest feasts, sheep-shearing dinners, and Plough Monday celebrations obviously had little meaning for urban workers; similarly, many of the usual rituals of May Day assumed a rural setting. More generally, the seasonal cycles of agriculture, which served as the foundation of the traditional holiday calendar, very much declined in importance for labouring people as a growing proportion of the work force became involved in factories and other urban enterprises where patterns of employment, and the concepts of time, were quite different from those in rural areas. The conditions of urban-industrial life usually emphasized a regularity of labour which was incompatible with the cyclical rhythms of the countryside. Consequently, as people migrated to the cities they were obliged to abandon those habits and practices which could not be transplanted into a radically different environment. Much of the rural past had to be set aside, and most of the migrants discovered that the expanding urban centres had, as yet, only an extremely raw and restricted recreational culture to put in its place.

7

Popular recreations under attack

From around the middle of the eighteenth century there are many signs of an increasing willingness among people of authority to intervene against the customary practices of popular recreation. Recreational customs were subjected to a multitude of direct attacks, many of which were initiated and organized at the local level, though they were usually related to some of the more general changes in attitudes and circumstances which we have already discussed. Attacks of this kind were always intended to achieve the outright suppression of some particular practice, and their objectives, at least in the long run, were normally fulfilled. Efforts to eliminate some long-standing custom – a blood sport in one place, a fair, a wake, or a football match in another – were taking place in all parts of the country, and some of the campaigns for reform resulted in passionate controversy, and occasionally even physical confrontations.

The traditional blood sports, along with most of the common people's pastimes, had been sometimes condemned and vigorously attacked during the Tudor and Stuart periods, but it was not until the eighteenth and early nineteenth centuries that they were subjected to a systematic and sustained attack. Prior to the mid-eighteenth century they still retained a degree of favour, or at least sufferance, from the governing class, and many gentlemen, as we have seen, actively patronized cock-fighting and sometimes even bull-baiting. Blood sports had not yet come to be widely regarded as cruel or disreputable. When Prince Lewis of Baden was being entertained by William III in January 1694 it was reported that 'there was bear's baiting, bulls' sport, and cock fighting instituted for his diversion and recreation'.[1] With time, however, the mood of public opinion altered. One of the early statements of dissatisfaction with such amusements appeared in the *Craftsman* of 1 July 1738:

> I am a profess'd Enemy to Persecution of all Kinds, whether against Man or Beast; though I am not so much a Pythagorean as to extend my Philosophy to those Creatures, which are manifestly design'd for our Food and Nourishment; but We ought to make the Manner of their Deaths as easy to Them as possible, and not destroy or torment Them out of Wantonness. Upon this principle I abhor Cock-fighting, and throwing at Cocks, as well as Bull-baiting, Bear-baiting, Ass-baiting, and all the other butcherly Diversions of Hockley in the Hole.

In later years criticisms of this sort were voiced with greater warmth, and by the early nineteenth century the opposition to blood sports was

---

[1] *Diary of Abraham de la Pryme*, p. 33.

vehement and intense. A tract of 1833 by a Birmingham school master, for example, expressed this concern with particular fervour:

Staffordshire, for ages, has been notoriously distinguished for Bull-baiting, and the numerous collieries of Tipton and its vicinity, have produced thousands of beings, who being trained in their infancy to the love and practice of Bull-baiting, possess nothing human, (when arrived at man's estate) but the form. Ignorant, vulgar, and wicked to excess, their ferocious rage for this bloody and barbarous amusement, knew no bounds, would brook no controul. Against these, the Rev. John Howells, the clergyman of that parish for twenty years, with unceasing zeal, 'warred a good warfare', and so successful were his exertions to rescue the poor suffering Bull from these demons in human shape, that the year 1827 was gloriously distinguished by the total extirpation of the bloody sport. Not a Bull was to be found in the whole parish, kept for the purpose of being baited at the wake. Thus he gave most convincing proof what great things may be accomplished by zealously persevering in the cause of God . . .[2]

The movement against popular blood sports was at its peak during the first forty years of the nineteenth century; by the 1840s most of them had been almost entirely eliminated.

Throwing at cocks was the first of the blood sports to be seriously attacked and the first to be generally suppressed. Periodic attempts may have been made to curtail the sport during the Stuart period, but it was not until the middle of the eighteenth century that a sustained and widespread campaign was directed against the custom. The earliest condemnation of the amusement in the *Gentleman's Magazine* appeared in 1737, and between 1750 and 1762 there were six pieces in the journal which criticized the pastime, five of them letters to the editor.[3] In 1739 the Rev. Joseph Greene of Stratford-upon-Avon included some severe comments on the sport in a letter to his brother, and in 1767 he submitted a letter on the subject to the editor of *Jackson's Oxford Journal*.[4] Attacks on the custom were also published in the *Sheffield Weekly Journal* (17 February 1756) and *Aris's Birmingham Gazette* (5 March 1764 and 10 February 1777).[5] Around the middle of the century the prominent clergyman and writer,

[2] Abraham Smith, *A Scriptural and Moral Catechism, Designed Chiefly to Lead the Minds of the Rising Generation to the Love and Practice of Mercy, and to Expose the Horrid Nature and Exceeding Sinfulness of Cruelty to the Dumb Creation* (Birmingham, 1833), p. xx.

[3] *Gentleman's Magazine*, VII (1737), 6–8; xx (1750), 18–19; xxi (1751), 8; xxiii (1753), 5; xxvi (1756), 17–18; xxxi (1761), 201–2; and xxxii (1762), 6–7. The last two of these contributions made reference to a recent publication entitled *Clemency to Brutes: The Substance of two Sermons preached on a Shrove-Sunday, With a particular View to dissuade from that Species of Cruelty annually practised in England, The Throwing at Cocks* (London, 1761).

[4] Levi Fox (ed.), *Correspondence of the Reverend Joseph Greene 1712–1790* (London, 1965), pp. 42–3 and 101–2; *Jackson's Oxford Journal*, 28 February 1767.

[5] G. A. Cranfield, *The Development of the Provincial Newspaper Press 1700–1760* (Oxford, 1962), p. 267; John A. Langford, *A Century of Birmingham Life: or, a Chronicle of Local Events, from 1741 to 1841* (2 vols.; Birmingham, 1868), I, 143 and 257.

Josiah Tucker, produced a short tract against cock-throwing, a public service which was applauded on at least one occasion by a contributor to the *Gentleman's Magazine*.[6] One of the letters in the *Gentleman's Magazine*, a representative expression of these critical sentiments, begged permission, 'on behalf of these guiltless, useful animals, to intreat all in authority, magistrates, peace-officers, parents, and masters of families, to exert themselves with the utmost vigour, in the suppression of the infamous and iniquitous custom, a custom which conduces to promote idleness, gaming, cruelty, and almost every species of wickedness'.[7]

The opinions of such critics did not go unheeded. As early as 1753 it was suggested that 'a progress towards the suppression of this evil, is already made in some places'.[8] In February 1755 it was said by one newspaper that at Aylesbury in Buckinghamshire 'there never were fewer cocks thrown at than on last Shrove Tuesday'.[9] Widespread efforts were apparently being made to suppress the amusement. In 1752 measures were taken to arrest people participating in Shrovetide sports in London, Reading, Bristol, and Northampton, and one of the specifically condemned pastimes was throwing at cocks.[10] At Newbury in 1750 the amusement was presented as a nuisance, and at Wakefield the bellman was paid 6d. 'for crying down throwing at cocks' in 1755 and 1758.[11] In 1753 at Nottingham the chamberlain was requested to 'pay to John Gunthorpe Ten Shillings allowed to the Constables for parading ye Town to prevent throwing at Cocks and all Mobbing and other Disorders on Shrove Tuesday', and at Castor, Northamptonshire, the constables' accounts for February 1759 included a charge of one shilling 'for returning a warrant to prevent ye Cox being holled at on Shrove Tuesday'.[12] At Norwich in 1753 one man was fined 3s. 4d. for engaging in the sport, and on 17 February 1759 the city's Court of Mayoralty, 'in just abhorrence of the cruel practice of throwing at cocks in this season of the year, and to prevent such disorders as usually arise therefrom', ordered the constables to patrol the streets and actively enforce a ban on the sport; a similar type of order was issued by the Essex Quarter Sessions every year between 1758 and 1761.[13] Active means were also being employed to eliminate the diversion at Sheffield in the

[6] Josiah Tucker, *An Earnest and Affectionate Address to the Common People of England, Concerning their Usual Recreations on Shrove Tuesday* (London, n.d.); *Gentleman's Magazine*, LI (1781), 72; cf. *The Country Clergyman's Shrovetide Gift to His Parishioners* (Sherborne, 3rd edn, n.d.), pp. 12–14.

[7] *Gentleman's Magazine*, XXI (1751), 8.

[8] *Gentleman's Magazine*, XXIII (1753), 5.

[9] Quoted in Robert Gibbs, *A History of Aylesbury* (Aylesbury, 1885), p. 554.

[10] *Gentleman's Magazine*, XXII (1752), 89.

[11] V. C. H. *Berkshire*, II, 297; quoted in J. W. Walker, *Wakefield, Its History and People* (2 vols.; Wakefield, 2nd edn, 1939), I, 115.

[12] *Records of the Borough of Nottingham*, VI, 253; W. D. Sweeting, *Historical and Architectural Notes on the Parish Churches in and Around Peterborough* (London and Peterborough, 1868), p. 12.

[13] *Norwich Mercury*, 10 March 1753; quoted in *Norfolk and Norwich Notes and Queries*, Series 2 (1896–9), 396; Essex R.O., Q/SO 10, pp. 98–9, 150, 208, and 254.

1750s, High Wycombe in 1774, and Manchester in the third quarter of the century.[14]

Throwing at cocks was not immediately suppressed. Like many of the people's diversions, its long history and deeply-rooted practice armed it with a certain short-run resilience, and in many cases it was only put down after repeated exertions. Orders against the sport were sometimes reissued several times by local authorities. The *Northampton Mercury* of 1 March 1762 reported that on Shrove Tuesday 'our Mayor and Justices, attended by their proper Officers, perambulated the Precincts of this Town, to prevent the scandalous and inhuman Practice of Throwing at Cocks,' adding that 'we hope the same will be no more used'; but as late as 1788 a warning against the practice was still felt to be necessary: 'We cannot but express our Wishes,' the paper observed, 'that Persons in Power, as well as Parents and Masters of Families, would exert their authority in suppressing a Practice too common at this Season – throwing at Cocks.' In the same breath, however, it was acknowledged that the pastime, 'to the Credit of a civilized People, is annually declining'.[15] Indeed, towards the end of the century it was generally agreed that the custom was very much on the wane, if not already completely eliminated. In 1777 John Brand reported that in Newcastle-upon-Tyne the pastime 'is now laid aside'; by the last quarter of the century it was seldom found in East Sussex, and in the early 1780s James Spershott of Chichester claimed that 'this cruel practice is almost over in these parts'.[16] In 1781 a contributor to the *Gentleman's Magazine* was of the opinion that throwing at cocks 'is in many places abolished', and a letter in the *Monthly Magazine* of 1797 suggested that 'cock-throwing is . . . nearly extinct'.[17] 'The magistrates,' wrote Joseph Strutt, 'greatly to their credit, have for some years past put a stop to this wicked custom, and at present it is nearly, if not entirely, discontinued in every part of the kingdom.'[18] A few residues managed to survive into the nineteenth century. The magistrates in Warwickshire were taking steps to suppress the sport in 1814, and a decade later the mayor of Warwick was obliged to issue a request that 'so disgraceful a Practice', a custom which was thought to have been completely abandoned, would not be revived by any of the inhabitants.[19] In 1825 William Hone said that the diversion 'is still conspicuous in several parts of the kingdom', and at Quainton in Buckinghamshire it was said to have continued until as late as 1844.[20] However, it would appear that these were only the last remnants of the amusement. For most of the common people in most parts of the

---

[14] Robert E. Leader, *Sheffield in the Eighteenth Century* (Sheffield, 1901), p. 45; Gibbs, *Aylesbury*, p. 554; and J. P. Earwaker (ed.), *The Constables' Accounts of the Manor of Manchester* (3 vols.; Manchester, 1891–2), III, 66, 132, 178, 249, and 342.

[15] *Northampton Mercury*, 2 February 1788.

[16] Brand, *Popular Antiquities*, p. 234 (cf. p. 377n); F. E. Sawyer, 'Sussex Folk-Lore and Customs Connected with the Seasons', *Sussex Archaeological Collections*, XXXIII (1883), 239; and *Memoirs of James Spershott*, p. 14.

[17] *Gentleman's Magazine*, LI (1781), 72; *Monthly Magazine*, IV (1797), 198.

[18] Strutt, *Sports and Pastimes*, p. 212; cf. *Gentleman's Magazine*, LXXII (1802), part II, 998.

[19] *Warwick and Warwickshire General Advertiser*, 19 February 1814 and 6 March 1824.

[20] Hone, *Every-Day Book*, I, col. 252; Gibbs, *Aylesbury*, pp. 554–5.

country throwing at cocks was a forbidden and neglected recreation by the end of the eighteenth century.

The relatively early demise of throwing at cocks seems to have stemmed from a number of circumstances. For one thing, it was widely regarded as exceptionally unsporting; it was thought to be lacking even the elementary features of fair competition. 'What a Noble Entertainment is it', wrote one critic, 'for a Rational Soul, to fasten an innocent weak defenceless Animal to ye ground, and then dash his bones to pieces with a Club? I can compare it to nothing but the behaviour of that silly Fellow, who boasted of his Activity, because he had tripp'd up a Beggar who had a pair of Wooden Leggs!'[21] Throwing at cocks, argued the *Warwick and Warwickshire Advertiser* of 6 March 1824, 'is far more barbarous than . . . cock-fighting; the poor sufferer has no rival bird to inflame his jealousy, and call forth his powers, but, fastened to a stake, he is compelled to endure the battering of stocks and other missiles'. This fact of unfairness, the fact that the cock was put in such a weak competitive position, was mentioned by many of the critics, and it probably served to draw the attention of people with doubts about animal sports in general to cock-throwing first, and to the other sports, those with one or two extenuating features, not until later. In addition, since cock-throwing was more a game for small groups than a major community activity, it lacked the underlying strength of a broadly-based social support (the more a community was united en masse behind a festive event, the more difficult it was to suppress the event); consequently, it was relatively vulnerable to any organized attacks. Moreover, the suppression of cock-throwing did not imply a really drastic curtailment of the people's recreational life, for its elimination involved not the complete loss of a holiday, but only one of the holiday's diversions. Finally, it was of some importance that throwing at cocks was almost exclusively a plebeian sport, for it was always easier to suppress a recreation when there was little risk of encroaching on the interests of gentlemen. Several critics condemned with equal fervour both of the Shrovetide blood sports, cock-fighting as well as cock-throwing, but in almost all cases it was only the distinctly popular pastime which was actually prohibited.

Bull-baiting, which drew more controversial attention than any of the other blood sports, may have already been in decline by around 1800, at least in certain parts of the country. 'This custom of baiting the bull,' claimed the *Sporting Magazine* in 1793, 'has of late years been almost laid aside in the north of England'; at Lincoln it was said in 1789 to be 'in a dwindling state'.[22] In 1797 a contributor to the *Monthly Magazine* referred to the sport as 'greatly diminished', and Joseph Strutt was of the same opinion.[23] In Nottingham and at Hornsea in the East Riding bull-baiting seems to have died out by the beginning of the nineteenth century.[24] The

[21] *Correspondence of Joseph Greene*, pp. 42–3; cf. Tucker, *Earnest and Affectionate Address*, p. 4.

[22] *Sporting Magazine*, iii (1793), 77; *Stamford Mercury*, 13 November 1789.

[23] *Monthly Magazine*, iv (1797), 198; Strutt, *Sports and Pastimes*, p. 193.

[24] Roy A. Church, *Economic and Social Change in a Midland Town: Victorian Nottingham 1815–1900* (London, 1966), p. 15; Bedell, *Account of Hornsea*, p. 88.

reasons for this apparent decline are not at all clear. There is little evidence of outright suppressions of bull-baiting during the eighteenth century. Perhaps the growing hostility of genteel opinion discouraged its survival in areas where the authority of such views could not be easily ignored. The sport was particularly dependent on some form of outside assistance – patronge, sponsorship, or promotion – and it is likely that such assistance was increasingly difficult to obtain. By the late eighteenth century butchers were no longer providing bulls for baiting, as they had often done in the past; gentlemen had in almost all cases given up their patronage of the sport; and many publicans must have become increasingly reluctant to act as promoters, especially when such involvement might put their licences in jeopardy.

But whatever the reasons may have been for this eighteenth-century decline (and some contemporaries may have overstated their case), it is clear that bull-baiting was still being practised in many places during the first forty years of the nineteenth century. It continued to be a popular 5th of November diversion at Lincoln, Bury St Edmunds, and at Axbridge, Somerset.[25] At Norwich it survived through at least the first two decades of the century and at Bristol until the 1830s.[26] It persisted in many Derbyshire towns (for instance, Chesterfield, Wirksworth, Chapel en le Frith, Bakewell, Ashbourne) and in parts of Buckinghamshire and Oxfordshire (Oakley, Thame, Wheatley).[27] It was a customary practice at Wokingham, Berkshire (on December 21st), until at least 1823 and at Beverley (on the annual swearing-in of the mayor) it continued during the first two decades of the century.[28] Bull-baiting remained widespread in south Lancashire, and it was particularly prevalent in Shropshire, Staffordshire, and the Birmingham area.[29]

The persistence of bull-baiting (along with other blood sports) was a cause for considerable concern in respectable society, especially among the increasingly influential evangelicals, and this concern was frequently voiced during the first third of the century in the political arena. The legal

[25] *Stamford Mercury*, 9 November 1821; *Bury and Norwich Post*, 18 November 1801 and 10 November 1802, and *Monthly Magazine*, XII (1801), 464; *Gentleman's Magazine*, LXXV (1805), part I, 203–4.

[26] *Norfolk Chronicle*, 14 March 1807, 21 January 1815, and 23 May 1818; Latimer, *Bristol in the Nineteenth Century*, p. 68; K. Backhouse, *Memoir of Samuel Capper* (London, 1855), p. 31; *Animals' Friend*, No. 5 (1837), 18.

[27] *V. C. H. Derbyshire*, II, 304; *The History and Topography of Ashbourn* (Ashbourn, 1839), pp. 94–5; *Derby Mercury*, 2 September 1829; Gibbs, *Aylesbury*, 559–60; Oxfordshire R.O., Quarter Sessions Rolls, 1827, Epiphany No. 5, and 1828, Epiphany Nos. 1–4; W. O. Hassall (ed.), *Wheatley Records 956–1956* (Oxfordshire Record Society, XXXVII, 1956), pp. 90–1.

[28] H. Edwards, *A Collection of Old English Customs* (London, 1842), pp. 63–4; Arthur T. Heelas, 'The Old Workhouse at Wokingham', *Berks, Bucks and Oxon Archaeological Journal*, XXXI (1927), 170–1; *Hull Advertiser*, 11 October 1817 and 13 October 1820.

[29] On Lancashire: *Parliamentary History*, XXXVI, p. 840 (a remark of William Windham in a debate of 1802); *Northampton Mercury*, 18 November 1820 (on Rochdale); and *Voice of Humanity*, I (1830–1), 50–1; on the West Midlands: Burne (ed.), *Shropshire Folk-Lore*, p. 447; Trinder, 'Memoir of William Smith', pp. 181–2; *Voice of Humanity*, I (1830–1), 49–52; *Animals' Friend*, No. 3 (1835), 6, *Christian Advocate*, 22 November 1830; and Abraham Smith, *Scriptural and Moral Catechism*, part ii, pp. 5–6.

standing of blood sports remained ambiguous: cruelty to animals could be dealt with under the common law (usually as a common nuisance), but the lack of any statute on the subject tended to militate against prosecutions. Reformers were well aware of the limitations of the law and attempted to rectify the situation: between 1800 and 1835 Parliament considered eleven bills on cruelty to animals, most of which were explicitly or indirectly concerned with blood sports. Bills against bull-baiting were introduced in 1800 and 1802; both were lost by narrow margins, principally because of the vigorous opposition and eloquence of William Windham.[30] Bills generally dealing with cruelty to animals were debated in 1809 and 1810, and again both efforts failed.[31] An Act of 1822 to 'Prevent the Cruel Treatment of Cattle' was interpreted by some magistrates to apply to bull-baiting, though this had probably not been Parliament's intention (in fact, in a decision of 1827 the King's Bench declared that the bull, which was not referred to in the Act, was not included in the genus of 'cattle').[32] Efforts to outlaw blood sports were continued after 1822: bills to this purpose were introduced in 1823, 1824, 1825, 1826, and 1829, on each occasion without success.[33] Finally, in 1835, a Cruelty to Animals Act unequivocally established the illegality of all blood sports which involved the baiting of animals.[34]

There were other indications of the growing revulsion against blood sports. A large number of essays dealing in part or entirely with blood sports (all of them critically) were published during the later eighteenth century and the first half of the next century. In 1800–2 at least three tracts appeared which were specifically directed against bull-baiting.[35] Sermons on the theme of humanity to animals were often delivered, sometimes as a result of special endowments. Newspapers and journals periodically included condemnations of some blood sport, commonly in the form of a letter to the editor. By the second quarter of the century genteel concern was substantial enough to support the formation of several reform societies, all of which drew some of their strength from the sentiments against blood sports: the Society for the Prevention of Cruelty to Animals

[30] *Parliamentary History*, xxxv, pp. 202–14, and xxxvi, pp. 829–54.

[31] *Cobbett's Parliamentary Debates*, xiv, pp. 851–3, 989–90, 1,029–41, and 1,071; and xvi, pp. 726 and 845–6.

[32] 3 George IV c. 71; *Parliamentary Debates*, New series, xix, pp. 1,121–2 (6 June 1828); F. A. Carrington and J. Payne, *Reports of Cases Argued and Ruled at Nisi Prius* (9 vols.; London, 1823–41), iii, 225–8; and *Voice of Humanity*, i (1830–1), 49. The one unequivocal statute on the subject was the 121st section of 3 George IV c. 126, which made illegal bull-baiting on the public highways.

[33] *Parliamentary Debates*, New Series, ix, pp. 433–5; x, pp. 130–4, 368–9, and 486–96; xii, pp. 657–61 and 1,002–13; xiv, pp. 647–52; and xxi, pp. 1,319–20.

[34] 5 & 6 William IV c. 59. An Act of 1849 'for the more effectual Prevention of Cruelty to Animals', 12 & 13 Victoria c. 92, was similar to the Act of 1835, though it was more explicit about the illegality of cock-fighting (the earlier Act had only outlawed the keeping of cockpits).

[35] [Sir Richard Hill], *A Letter to the Right Hon. William Windham, on his late Opposition to the Bill to Prevent Bull-Baiting* (London, 2nd edn, n.d.), 1st publ. in 1800; Percival Stockdale, *A Remonstrance Against Inhumanity to Animals; and Particularly Against the Savage Practice of Bull-Baiting* (Alnwick, 1802); Edward Barry, *Bull-Baiting! A Sermon on Barbarity to God's Dumb Creation* (Reading, 1802).

(established in 1824); the Association for Promoting Rational Humanity Towards the Animal Creation (1830–3); the Animals' Friend Society (1832–c.1852); the Ladies' Society for the Suppression of Cruelty to Animals (the 1830s); and in a region where blood sports were especially prevalent, the South Staffordshire Association for the Suppression of Bull-baiting (established in 1824). Some of these societies sponsored tracts and periodicals (for instance, the *Voice of Humanity* and the *Animals' Friend*), and during the 1830s they were active in investigating and carrying to court many cases of animal sports.[36]

As the nineteenth century advanced bull-baiting was gradually overpowered. Clergymen were especially active in preaching and informing against bull-baiting and in organizing practical efforts of resistance. In early July 1796, for instance, the vicar of St Gluvias, Cornwall, noted in his diary: 'Wrote a few pages in the morning, and snatched some moments in the evening and on Sunday before prayers, of a Sermon respecting inhumanity to animals, induced by a Bull-baiting in the parish: a brutal amusement.'[37] Aside from a small body of Tories, genteel opinion had become almost solidly hostile. At Tutbury the sport was 'at length suppressed by the humane interference of the surrounding gentry', and at Stone, also in Staffordshire, it was eliminated in 1838.[38] It was suppressed at Aylesbury in 1821–2, at Beverley in 1822–3, and at Wheatley by 1837.[39] At Lincoln bull-baiting had been put down by the mid-1820s, and it was reported that on the 5th of November 1826 'the bullwards, notwithstanding much threats and boasting, did not venture to revive their barbarous diversion, which has been happily declining in public favor for some years past'.[40] In 1837 it was said that 'Thame is no longer the scene of that brutality which once cast a blemish over its inhabitants; the bull-baiting is now done away with, and in its place we had a really good and efficient band of music parading the town'.[41] By the early 1840s bull-baiting had been eliminated in Ashbourne, Derbyshire, during the wakes week and some of the residents were thinking of introducing steeplechase races as a substitute.[42]

Such suppressions were often only effected after years of opposition and numerous failures, for in many places the people were keen in their resistance and capitulated only under persistent and determined pressure. In the Birmingham-Black Country area a vigorous campaign against bull-baiting was continued through the first third of the century – there were prosecutions, convictions, sermons, journalistic attacks, personal interventions by clergymen and magistrates; and during the 1830s, especially

---

[36] For a brief account of these reform societies, see the Appendix.

[37] Lewis Bettany (ed.), *Diaries of William Johnston Temple 1780–1796* (Oxford, 1929), p. 187.

[38] Mosley, *History of Tutbury*, p. 90; R.S.P.C.A. MS Minute Book no. 3, pp. 14 and 24–6.

[39] Gibbs, *Aylesbury*, p. 559; Oliver, *History of Beverley*, p. 422; R.S.P.C.A. MS Minute Book no. 2, pp. 93–4 and 202–4, and *Twelfth Annual Report of the S.P.C.A.*, 1838, pp. 81–2.

[40] *Stamford Mercury*, 10 November 1826.   [41] *Jackson's Oxford Journal*, 21 October 1837.

[42] *Derby Mercury*, 10 August 1842.

after a strong legal leverage was provided through the Cruelty to Animals Act of 1835, there was a final wave of charges (and normally convictions) against bull-baiters, many of which were actively supported or initiated by the Animals' Friend Society.[43] The reformers' determination and zeal were fully satisfied: within a few years bull-baiting was completely eliminated from the area. On 30 September 1839 it was reported by *Aris's Birmingham Gazette* that 'at the annual wake at Brierly Hill and Wordesley on Monday last, the cruel and barbarous practice of bull-baiting was entirely abandoned'. The Animals' Friend Society was noticing a definite decline in bull-baiting after 1835, and by 1841 it was able to point,

> with great satisfaction to the chief late bull baiting districts, at the happy results which have followed the exertions of this Society in those districts. From Birmingham a letter of Mr Chapman, Hon. Sec. to the Birmingham Branch Animals' Friend Society, of the 4th of July 1840, says that bull baiting at Handsworth (where the Society last year distributed its bills) is now at an end, and that a police force was established there, which there is now every reason to hope entirely prohibits it. At Birmingham, Mr. Yewen, on arriving there this year, found the happy effects of his former exertions; bull baiting having, as far as he was able to ascertain, disappeared from there and the vicinities.[44]

The demise of bull-baiting was complete by the early years of Victoria's reign. 'Happily', reported a tract of 1838 on bull-baiting and running, 'they are now nearly every where abandoned.' 'After many a hard contest,' said William Howitt, bull-baiting '[has] been eventually put down'. 'The appeal of good sense and of humanity has been listened to in almost every part of the United Kingdom', rejoiced a reformer in 1839, 'and this useful animal is no longer tortured amidst the exulting yells of those who are a disgrace to our common form and nature.'[45]

During the generations from the later eighteenth century until the 1840s, there was a persistent tension between the growing sentiments for reform and the popular conservatism which underlay the sometimes vigorous resilience of traditional blood sports. Active confrontations often arose when practical efforts were taken to suppress a particular sport, for the people could be determined in the defence of what they regarded as one of their rights; in some instances their resistance was effective enough to prolong the diversion for several decades. In almost all of these cases the custom was eventually abolished, though only to the accompaniment of considerable social friction, and not without the application of substantial legal or physical pressure.

One of the lengthiest and most spirited of these clashes emerged during

---

[43] *Animals' Friend*, no. 4 (1836), 4–5; no. 5 (1837), 16–18; no. 6 (1838), 31–2; no. 7 (1839), 27; and *Aris's Birmingham Gazette*, 20 November 1837.

[44] *Animals' Friend*, no. 9 (1841), 41–2.

[45] William H. Drummond, *The Rights of Animals, and Man's Obligation to Treat them with Humanity* (London, 1838), p. 104; Howitt, *Rural Life*, p. 525; and William Youatt, *The Obligation and Extent of Humanity to Brutes* (London, 1839), p. 159.

the last fifty years of the observance of the annual bull-running at Stamford. The bull-running had existed for generations without any significant opposition; although a few earlier observers had disapproved of the practice, it was not until 1788 that an attempt was actually made to effect its suppression. At the Borough Quarter Sessions in January an order was delivered prohibiting the custom in the future, and from early October a vigorous campaign was directed by the magistrates against the approaching holiday, which fell on November 13th. (The principal instigator of the prohibition seems to have been the Earl of Exeter, the town's aristocratic overseer.) At the Sessions of October 6th the sport was forbidden on the grounds that it had been 'productive of Vice, Prophaneness, Immorality, Disorder, Riot, Drunkenness, and Mischief, amongst many People, Inhabitants of this Borough, and the Neighbourhood thereof; of every Species of Inhumanity, by the lower Order of People, to an unhappy Animal; and of great Annoyance, Danger, and Delay, to all Travellers passing and repassing upon the King's Highway in this Borough'.[46] No obstructions were to be placed in any of the streets, and to facilitate the enforcement of the orders forty-eight special constables were sworn in to assist the twelve regular constables. Publicans were ordered not to let persons linger in their houses on the 13th, and tradesmen were advised to keep their shops open and follow their usual business. At the end of the month, in response to the many expressions of discontent and the rumours that a subscription was on foot to purchase a bull, a further notice was issued threatening prosecutions under the Riot Act against any resisters. There were disturbances outside the Mayor's residence on November 8th: a request for assistance was sent to the War Office and on the 12th a troop of dragoons arrived from Newark. Excitement was at a high pitch on the 13th, and for a few hours it seemed that the authorities were going to be completely successful. Around noon, however, while the soldiers and constables were watching a suspicious looking bull to the south of town, another was brought in from the west and run freely through several streets.[47] When the authorities caught up with this development a minor scuffle broke out and Lord Exeter and Sir Samuel Fludyer were 'roughly treated' by the populace; the bull was confiscated, several arrests were made, and the crowd gradually dispersed.[48] The next day the *Stamford Mercury* applauded the magistrates' firmness and reported that 'last night and this morning the populace were very quiet, and we trust there is now an end to a custom which has too long disgraced the town of Stamford'. In January four of the participants in the disturbance of November 8th received jail terms of two weeks to three months.[49]

In 1789 the magistrates repeated the prohibitions and precautions of

[46] *Stamford Mercury*, 10 October 1788.
[47] MS. notes by the Rev. John Swann in Harrod's *History of Stamford*, transcribed in a book of cuttings and miscellaneous notes on the bull-running, no. 183 in the Phillips Collection, Stamford Town Hall. The pages of this volume are not numbered but the items are arranged in a rough chronological order and are readily found.
[48] Excerpt from the MS diary of Maurice Pollard of St Martin's parish, Phillips Collection no. 183.
[49] *Stamford Mercury*, 16 January 1789.

the previous year. But despite the strong warnings and the attendance of dragoons, this year's holiday was said (by the Rev. John Swann) to have 'exhibited the same scene with rather more daring spirit in the populace who broke open a lock and let out a Bull from a Croft in Scotgate of Farmer Wright's and . . . actually run it for several hours through every part of the Town and with the most consummate audacity bid defiance to the Mayor, Aldermen, [and] the Recorder Lord Exeter for which several were the next day committed to jail'.[50] An obese woman named Ann Blades, dressed in a bright blue frock, had led the bull and his followers into the town; the crowd was met by the Mayor, the constables and the military, but the captain of the dragoons, apparently more impressed by the orderliness of the bullards than the wishes of the Mayor, declined to offer any resistance and dismissed his men, who promptly joined the bull-running.[51] In January three men were sentenced for riot, one to six months' imprisonment and the others to one month.[52]

It seems that the magistrates were now becoming discouraged and less confident of success. In 1790 dragoons were again summoned but left the town without being called into service. On November 13th, according to Swann, 'the populace persevered in their designs with the most determined resolution and brought a bull from Ryhall and ran him several times through all parts of the Town without any opposition of the Mayor etc. who wisely left them to their own will thinking it the most likely method of suppressing this savage diversion by taking no notice thereof'.[53]

The authorities had been defeated and popular feeling revelled in the victory. Several broadsides and ballads glorified the success and predicted similar results in the event of future encounters. One broadside skit, entitled 'Bull Running Reviv'd', presented a Lord Wing (alias the Earl of Exeter) vexed and murmuring to himself when a bull was found to be loose:

> Ye Gods! how wretched my exalted State,
> I thought I rul'd, I thought I once was great:
> The other Day I cou'd command the Waves,
> To cease their Course, and bid all Men be Slaves;
> The Beggars' humble Hut, the Prisoners' Cell,
> Suits their mean Pride, and all within is well:
> These Wretches find more pleasure in their Sport,
> Then I can find in B – r – gh's gilded Court . . . [54]

Similar sentiments persisted well into the next century. John Drakard's *Stamford News* of 11 November 1825 included an irreverent contribution from an anonymous poet:

> Said Martin, of Galway,[55] to Justice Conant,
> To stop the Bull-running at Stamford I want:

[50] Phillips Collection no. 183; *Stamford Mercury*, 20 November 1789.
[51] Phillips Collection no. 183 (MS diary of Pollard); Burton, *Chronology of Stamford*, p. 52.
[52] *Stamford Mercury*, 15 January 1790.
[53] Phillips Collection no. 183; cf. Burton, *Chronology of Stamford*, p. 53.
[54] Phillips Collection no. 183.
[55] Richard Martin of Galway, M.P., the principal sponsor of the 1822 Cruel Treatment of Cattle Bill, persistently introduced legislation against blood sports during the 1820s.

So do I, Mr. Martin, the big-wig replied,
But the Bullards of Stamford your law have defied;
They bid us not meddle, and swear, if we do,
That the dogs shall pin me, and the bull shall toss you.
Now, this pinning to earth, and this tossing in air,
You'll confess, my dear friend, is no laughing affair,
So we'd better be quiet, and stay where we are.

A minor culture of popular self-expression grew up around the bull-running. Some of the local mugs were enscribed with the patriotic slogan 'Bull For Ever', and enterprising boys made water-colour sketches of particular bull-running incidents and sold them for a few pennies to local enthusiasts.[56] The opposition subsided and seems to have maintained a discreet silence. Periodic sermons and letters to one of the newspapers continued to condemn the custom, but during the first thirty years of the nineteenth century the holiday was subjected to no serious challenges.

Some observers during the 1820s and early 1830s thought that the bull-running was declining in popularity. Changing tastes and interests and more refined manners were cited as the reasons for this trend. A fortnight before the 1833 holiday the bullards were said to be having difficulty raising enough money to promote the run. But this creeping apathy was soon checked when it was reported in early November that the Society for the Prevention of Cruelty to Animals was intending to intervene in that year's bull-running. This announcement prompted such a generous subscription for the holiday that it was rumoured sufficient funds had been collected to finance the diversion for another two or three years. One Charles Wheeler, supposedly an agent for the R.S.P.C.A. but in fact an imposter (he was, though, a bona fide if devious campaigner against blood sports),[57] arrived in Stamford to press the issue with the magistrates, but he was so ill-received by the inhabitants that he found it expedient to remove himself from town. According to the *Lincolnshire Chronicle* of 15 November, the 13th saw 'a savage kind of *esprit du corps* [sic] amongst the "bullards", and ... the present year's "sport" ... received a degree of *éclat* of which no recent anniversary affords an example'. Clubs were actually formed expressly to perpetuate the amusement. Recalling the lessons of 1788–90, the local press remarked on the worthy motives but indiscretion of the intervention from London. A proverb was cited from the bullards' own lore in support of moderation, that 'the bull may die, but he cannot be killed'. In an indignant letter Wheeler talked of 'riot, confusion, plunder, and bloodshed', and concluded by complaining that 'for my humble endeavours to prevent the bull-bait [sic] I was threatened with personal violence and the most horrid imprecations [were] uttered against me by the ferocious and blood-thirsty bull-baiters of Stamford'.[58]

---

[56] Burton (ed.), *Old Lincolnshire*, p. 165; Phillips Collection no. 183.
[57] For a brief note on Wheeler, see the Appendix. Although the R.S.P.C.A. did not actually obtain official royal patronage until 1840, its more familiar initials will be used consistently in our discussion.
[58] This paragraph relies principally on the reports in the *Lincolnshire Chronicle*, 15 and 22 November 1833, and the *Stamford Mercury*, 15 November 1833.

Although the intervention of 1833 was in itself a very inconsiderable threat, there was a real and growing possibility of effective interference from some of the more influential London reformers. In 1830 a reporter from the *Christian Adovcate* and an agent from the R.S.P.C.A. had been sent to Stamford, the one to publicize the bull-running and the other to seek the support of the magistracy.[59] The R.S.P.C.A. maintained its interest in Stamford: replying to a letter in the spring of 1834, its Committee reaffirmed its opposition to the bull-running but admitted that 'they are fearful that the Laws now in force, are not sufficiently strong to suppress it . . . and they regret to say also, that the limited Funds at present at their disposal, do not justify them in incurring the expence of . . . a proceeding [against the sport]'.[60] During the next two years these disabilities were largely removed: the 1835 Cruelty to Animals Act provided a solid foundation for prosecutions, and the receipt of a legacy of £1,000 in October 1836 encouraged the Society to pursue a more ambitious and aggressive policy.[61] (Its secretary and an inspector had returned from observing the 1835 bull-running with information concerning twenty-eight of the most active participants, but because of financial considerations the idea of legal action had to be dropped.)[62] Thereafter the Society was campaigning in earnest. In 1837 charges were laid against eight men for their involvement in the previous bull-running. At the summer Assizes in Lincoln five were acquitted and three were found guilty; the sentences were deferred in order to allow the bullards to reconsider the wisdom of their persistence.[63] By this time the R.S.P.C.A. had laid out on the Stamford case (its first on a considerable scale) at least £350, and in 1837 it accounted for almost a quarter of the Society's total expenditure.[64]

Prior to the 1837 bull-running the Stamford magistrates were being urged to action by the Home Office, which had itself been petitioned by the R.S.P.C.A.[65] A letter of November 2nd from the Home Office called for firm measures and enquired about the strength of the town's constabulary force. The magistrates' reply was full of doubt about the feasibility of putting down the festival:

> Their Worships do not think the [forty] special Constables already sworn in would act with effect to suppress or prevent a Bull running assemblage and they wish not to disguise that great difficulty would be found in organizing a force sufficient to prevent it. The Chief Constable [has] . . . offered to make oath that neither the regular

[59] *Christian Advocate*, 15 November 1830; R.S.P.C.A. MS Minute Book for 1824–32, pp. 128–30; *Voice of Humanity*, I (1830–1), 14–23 and 67–75.

[60] R.S.P.C.A. MS Minute Book no. 1, pp. 131–2.

[61] R.S.P.C.A. MS Minute Book no. 2, pp. 92–3.

[62] *Ibid.* pp. 19–26 and 34; *Tenth Annual Report of the S.P.C.A.*, 1836.

[63] *Stamford Bull-Running, Report of a Criminal Prosecution (Rex v. Richardson and Others), Trial at Lincoln Summer Assizes, July 18, 1837* (Stamford, 1837), a copy of which is held in the Stamford Town Hall; Burton, *Chronology of Stamford*, p. 55; RS.P.C.A. MS Minute Book no. 2, pp. 124 and 179–80.

[64] *Twelfth Annual Report of the S.P.C.A.*, 1838, pp. 14ff.

[65] *Stamford Mercury*, 10 November 1837; R.S.P.C.A. MS Minute Book no. 2, pp. 89–92, 98–101, and 196–9.

Police nor the special Constables can be depended upon for that purpose . . . [66]

The lukewarm spirit of the magistrates was sharply challenged in the next Home Office letter, and their resolve was stiffened to the extent that they published notices promising severe punishments for bull-running and enlisted another 240 special constables, 'generally of the most able and many of the most opulent Inhabitants of the Town'.[67] At the same time the publisher of the *Stamford Mercury*, Richard Newcomb, was offering an insider's version of the local circumstances in a private letter to the R.S.P.C.A.:

> I am one of the Magistrates of the Borough; and I regret to say the only one not favourable to the continuance of the Bull Running. Through my suggestion in a letter to London a correspondence has arisen and is at present carrying on between the Secretary of State . . . and the Magistrates of Stamford . . . The correspondence has produced a collision between my brother magistrates and myself; and the exhibition on their part of an odious system of delusion calculated to get over the coming anniversary without a direct inter-position on the part of Government . . . Some of them (including the Mayor) will I verily believe do all they can to promote the contin-uance of the cruel custom, on the expressed persuasion by them that it is sanctioned by Charter and by Law and that Mr. Phillips (the learned Under Secretary of State) is wrong in calling it 'illegal'. They urge upon Lord John Russell the bringing in of a Bill to make the Sport of Bull Running unlawful ! ! ! and then they hint it might be stopped at Stamford but not otherwise.
>
> They also state that Special Constables . . . cannot be found amongst those who are to be depended on for respecting their oathes: a gross calumny on many respectable townsmen who will willingly be sworn into office on that day, provided the Magistracy show a purpose to protect them from being murdered . . . [68]

Newcomb's representation of the other magistrates' sentiments was confirmed during an interview which the R.S.P.C.A.'s secretary had with the town's authorities on 12 November 1837. They were found to be un-sympathetic to any of his proposals: 'It was evident to all', he reported later, 'that the majority of the Magistrates did not wish to do anything either to prevent the Bull Running or to apprehend the offenders.'[69] At 9 a.m. on the 13th nearly 300 constables assembled at the Town Hall, but (according to the magistrates) 'the general expression and determination manifested by them in favour of a Bull running (though they declared a readiness to protect property, etc.) was such as to amount at once, to a convincing proof that no reliance could be placed on them'.[70] The

[66] P.R.O., H.O. 52/34, Lincolnshire bundle, letter of 4 November 1837.

[67] Phillips Collection no. 183, letter of 21 November 1837.

[68] R.S.P.C.A. MS Minute Book no. 2, pp. 200–1. Newcomb wrote similar letters to the Home Office; two of his fellow magistrates resigned in protest against these clandestine activities. (P.R.O., H.O. 52/34, Lincolnshire bundle.)

[69] R.S.P.C.A. MS Minute Book no. 2, p. 217.

[70] Phillips Collection no. 183, letter of 21 November 1837.

R.S.P.C.A.'s officers reported that 'the Special Constables were . . . called up to the Magistrates, and in a very short space of time they came running and stamping down [the] Stairs shouting and yelling Bull for Ever! Yahoo Yahoo'.[71] By midday bull and bullards were running freely about the town. In the afternoon the bull was paraded through the streets and displayed in front of the Town Hall as the people 'shouted, yelled and groaned several times in defiance'.[72] On November 25th six men were tried in a very crowded Town Hall under the 1835 Cruelty to Animals Act. Four were acquitted and two were convicted and fined; one of the fines was paid immediately from a collection taken up right in the court.[73]

The attack became more consolidated and better grounded in 1838. As a result of an appeal against the Assize convictions of 1837, the bull-running was explicitly declared illegal by the Court of Queen's Bench.[74] In early November the Home Office, under pressure from the R.S.P.C.A., ordered twelve London Police and thirty-five dragoons to Stamford; the magistrates decided on a firmer stand and commissioned sixty special constables.[75] Letters of the 2nd and 7th of November from Richard Newcomb to the R.S.P.C.A. were uncommonly optimistic: 'A wonderful change has taken place in the feeling of the Magistrates . . . [They] are quite converted and see now the peril of their position if they do not act as they ought to, in aid of the purpose of Government so clearly and energetically evinced'.[76] Until one o'clock on the 13th no bull appeared. Then, by coincidence, an apparently innocent farm servant was found to be leading through the town a herd of nine cows and one bull. Some of the people relieved him of the bull and succeeded in running it through much of the town before they were restrained by the police and the military. The bull was confiscated and the law enforcers were pelted with stones by a resentful crowd. Newcomb was satisfied with the day's efforts and thought that the tradition had been effectively broken.[77] At the January Quarter Sessions four persons were tried for rioting but all were acquitted by a sympathetic jury.[78]

The 1839 preparations took on minor siege proportions: 20 metropolitan police and 43 dragoons arrived in Stamford to assist the 90 local constables. On the 12th notices were distributed which summarized the duties and powers of the special constables and described in some detail the overall plan for maintaining order the next day (it included provisions for messen-

[71] P.R.O., H.O. 44/30, Lincolnshire bundle, p. 7 of a report on the 1837 proceedings; see also R.S.P.C.A. MS Minute Book no. 2, pp. 214–27, for a detailed account of this year's activities.

[72] R.S.P.C.A. MS Minute Book no. 2, p. 221; cf. Stamford Mercury, 17 November 1837.

[73] Stamford Mercury, 1 December 1837.

[74] Stamford Mercury, 9 November 1838; R.S.P.C.A. MS Minute Book no. 2, pp. 242ff.

[75] Thirteenth Annual Report of the S.P.C.A., 1839, p. 10; R.S.P.C.A. MS Minute Book no. 3, pp. 3, 11–12, and 18–22; Stamford Mercury, 9 November 1838; and P.R.O., H.O. 52/37, Lincolnshire bundle, especially the magistrates' report on the 1838 proceedings.

[76] R.S.P.C.A. MS Minute Book no. 3, pp. 33–4 and 36–7.

[77] Stamford Mercury, 16 November 1838; Lincolnshire Chronicle, 16 November 1838; The Times, 16–17 November 1838; and R.S.P.C.A. MS Minute Book no. 3, pp. 39–40.

[78] Lincolnshire Chronicle, 11 January 1839.

gers, lookouts at all the accesses, and procedures for safely escorting passing cattle).[79] Once again, though, the preventive measures failed. In the early afternoon a bull was surreptitiously introduced into town and pursued in the customary manner. The police attempted without success to confiscate the bull, so the dragoons had to be summoned to the scene; they arrived just in time to prevent the release of another bull.[80] At the next meeting of a disillusioned town council there was prolonged and confused debate on the bull-running. The main point of contention was the swelling cost of the attempts to put it down. Almost £150 had been expended in the previous year and this year's failure was expected to cost twice as much; an additional sixpence in the pound had to be levied on the ratepayers.[81] (Disgruntled Tories interpreted the pressure from the Home Office as Whig revenge on the borough for returning two Conservative Members.)[82]

In the end it was this financial pinch which induced a concerted assault on the bull-running. In early November 1840, 670 inhabitants signed a petition pledging to assist personally in its suppression and requesting that no outside force be invited to attend. The signatures must have represented the bulk of the borough's ratepayers. The pledge was accepted by the magistrates, the R.S.P.C.A., and the Home Secretary (Lord Normanby), and on the 13th this broadly-based application of pressure was effective.[83] A letter from a member of the R.S.P.C.A.'s committee who had observed the occasion reported

> that Lord Normanby's letter [warning against persisting in the sport] was in every shop window, that there appeared to be no meeting of the Magistrates, that there were here and there groups of the lower orders who occasionally called out 'A Bull, A Bull', out of fun and that all the respectable people to whom he spoke were desirous that there should be no more Bull Running; he said that about six o'clock . . . a party of boys drove a Steer thro' the streets but that it was soon housed and one of the Boys taken into custody. There is no doubt that this was by way of keeping up the charter and to have to say that there has been no interruption of the custom. It is altogether a great triumph for the Society.[84]

Thereafter no serious attempt was made to revive the holiday. The amusement was finished but its pleasures and traditions lingered on in the popular mind. The 'Bull-Running Song', almost a local anthem, was often sung on public occasions in later years and was still remembered and sometimes introduced as late as the 1880s.[85]

[79] Phillips Collection no. 183.
[80] Stamford Mercury, 15 November 1839; P.R.O., H.O. 52/43, bundle 'S', file on Stamford for 1839.
[81] Stamford Mercury, 22 November 1839 and 17 January 1840; Stamford Town Hall, MS Minute Book vol. vi, Council meeting of 16 November 1839.
[82] Lincolnshire Chronicle, 22 November 1839.
[83] R.S.P.C.A. MS Minute Book no. 4, pp. 51–6; Stamford Mercury, 6, 13 and 20 November 1840; Lincolnshire Chronicle, 20 November 1840.
[84] R.S.P.C.A. MS Minute Book no. 4, p. 60.
[85] Burton, Chronology of Stamford, p. 66; and Burton (ed.), Old Lincolnshire, p. 133n.

Although the resistance to the attacks against Stamford's bull-running was exceptional in the extent and vigour of its determination and popular support, it was a representative expression of the sort of ardent conservatism which was evident on a smaller scale in many of the instances when blood sports were directly threatened. In the West Midlands, for instance, the people clung almost as tenaciously to their bull-baiting practices. The particular resilience of the bull-running seems to have stemmed from a number of relatively atypical circumstances. Because of the very large crowds which the event attracted – it drew support not only from a sizeable market town, but also from much of the surrounding countryside – the difficulties of enforcing a prohibition were unusually formidable. In such conditions popular resistance had a better chance of overpowering official directives. 'The annual Bull-running at Stamford', observed the town clerk in 1837, 'is attended by a large and powerful assemblage of persons of the lower orders of society, many from the country, strongly impressed with the idea that their practise is a lawful ancient custom, warranted by an exercise of 600 years . . . and which they ought not to be deprived of except by an express legislative enactment'.[86] Indeed, local enthusiasm for the holiday does appear to have been uncommonly intense. Around 1730 William Stukeley had spoken of the citizens' 'lov'd bull-runnings', and in 1809 the *Stamford Mercury* referred to 'the extraordinary devotion of the people of this town to their far-famed bull-running'.[87] Moreover, it was not only the common people who patronized the holiday. 'So strong was the prejudice in favor of this barbarous custom,' reported the R.S.P.C.A. in 1836, 'that even the Mayor himself, as well as several of the Aldermen, were subscribers to the annual *sport* as it was termed; and [it is said] that it would be dangerous to any persons to appear publicly in any endeavour to prevent or suppress it.'[88] Some of the aldermen's sons were active participants in the diversion.[89] 'Persons of *respectability* follow the bull at Stamford,' complained the *Stamford Mercury* of 20 November 1812, 'who would be affronted with the imputation of doing any thing else on a parity with such a proceeding.' This was a circumstance which on several occasions the reformers noted with regret – many of the participants in the 1835 bull-running, the R.S.P.C.A.'s inspector reported, were 'very respectable in their appearance, the rest of the lowest grade' – and in 1830 it was noticed that 'the windows which afforded a good view of the sport were

---

[86] P.R.O., H.O. 52/34, Lincolnshire bundle, letter of 4 November 1837; cf. *Stamford Mercury*, 18 November 1836.

[87] *The Family Memoirs of the Rev. William Stukely* (3 vols.; Publications of the Surtees Society, LXXIII, LXXVI, and LXXX, 1882–7), LXXIII, 118; *Stamford Mercury*, 3 March 1809; cf. *Stamford Mercury*, 18 November 1836. In a rough hand-bill, apparently dating from the 1790s, it was asked: 'Shall it be said in after ages that we have been cowards, and given up what our ancestors have so often delighted with . . . ? No, our children shall not say we are afraid, but we'll set them an example to keep it up, and be true Stamfordians.' (Phillips Collection no. 183.)

[88] *Tenth Annual Report of the S.P.C.A.*, 1836, p. 64.

[89] *Christian Advocate*, 15 November 1830; *Voice of Humanity*, I (1830–1), 67, 73, and 74; R.S.P.C.A. MS Minute Book no. 2, p. 25.

filled with well dressed persons'.[90] The special constables, though they were drawn from the town's more substantial citizens, were for the most part supporters of the holiday. Indeed, the 'respectable' attitude towards the bull-running was remarkably sympathetic, and it helped significantly to strengthen the resilience of the custom and to provide it with a degree of legitimacy which few of the other sports so effectively retained.

The other blood sports retreated more gradually and their decline was accompanied by considerably less controversy and social conflict. Badger-baiting and dog-fighting, both of which were secondary amusements, were under attack during the same period as bull-baiting; during the later 1830s the Animals' Friend Society was in the habit of investigating dog-fighting (and sometimes badger-baiting) as well as bull-baiting on the occasions of its annual missions into the Birmingham area. Neither sport, however, prompted much public outcry or heated discussion. They were both substantially reduced by the 1840s, probably to negligible proportions in the country as a whole. In a few areas, however, they survived into the later nineteenth century, mostly because of the difficulties of tracking them down: they could be more easily conducted in secrecy, in confined places away from the public gaze (such concealment was not possible with bull-baiting), and this also meant that their offensiveness was less immediately disturbing. It is likely that they are not unknown today.[91] Cock-fighting was even more resilient, partly for the same reasons, partly because of its considerable genteel following. Advertisements for gentlemen's cock-fights continued to appear in the provincial press during the first quarter of the nineteenth century, and though its support among all classes was certainly falling off in this period, it was not until the beginning of Victoria's reign, when the great majority of gentlemen had abandoned the sport, leaving it for the most part in the hands of lesser men, that an active campaign against the sport was actually mobilized. The R.S.P.C.A. began its attack in the late 1830s, and between 1838 and 1841 it prosecuted at least thirteen cases against cock-fighting, almost all of which were against men of little social standing. The sport still retains a small following today.

What were the main grounds for the complaints against blood sports? Why had they come to be so poorly regarded? Many of the criticisms arose from moral and religious considerations which can be easily appreciated: such diversions were 'barbarous', 'inhuman', 'uncivilized', and generally at odds with enlightened morality. They involved 'such scenes as degrade mankind beneath the barbarity of a savage, and which are totally inconsistent with the laws of nature, the laws of religion, and the laws of a civilized nation'.[92] 'Such a custom might comport with the barbarism and darkness of past ages,' conceded a critic of the Stamford bull-running,

[90] R.S.P.C.A. MS Minute Book no. 2, p. 23; *Voice of Humanity*, I (1830–1), 72–3; cf. Burton (ed.), *Old Lincolnshire*, p. 165, and Winks, *Bull Running at Stamford*, p. 16.
[91] For evidence concerning the practice of modified forms of badger-baiting, see the *Guardian*, 25 October 1967, p. 6.
[92] *Stamford Mercury*, 13 November 1789.

'might suit the genius of an uncivilized and warlike race; but surely, must be regarded as an indelible stain upon the history of an enlightened and professedly christian people.'[93] This was a familiar line of argument: the 'march of intellect' should be overpowering such primitive practices. Many of the common people regarded combat with animals as an inherent part of the 'natural' processes of life; the reformers, of course, had a quite different view of man's place in the order of nature. For them, the general framework of man's moral duties was to be found in the great chain of being: man had been granted the power to govern the animal world, but just as God benevolently oversaw the lives of humans, so man should not misuse his authority over subordinate creatures. There was a hierarchy of rights and duties, and man's obligations towards the dumb creation were not to be lightly neglected. As a clergyman put it in 1830: 'man was appointed the terrestrial sovereign of the brute creation. But did God, in entrusting the brute creation to the care of man, and in giving him the power of awing their brute force into submission and obedience, at the same time give him the power to put them to unnecessary torture, and to destroy them in mere wantonness'[94] 'Clemency to Brutes is a Natural Duty,' argued another reformer, 'and Natural Duties are of eternal and universal Obligation.'[95] The basic theological and ethical position was most precisely spelled out by Soame Jenyns in an essay of 1782:

> Man is that link of the chain of universal existence, by which spiritual and corporeal beings are united: as the numbers and variety of the latter his inferiors are almost infinite, so probably are those of the former his superiors; and as we see that the lives and happiness of those below us are dependent on our wills, we may reasonably conclude, that our lives, and happiness are equally dependent on the wills of those above us; accountable, like ourselves, for the use of this power, to the supreme Creator, and governor of all things. Should this analogy be well founded, how criminal will our account appear, when laid before that just and impartial judge! How will man, that sanguinary tyrant, be able to excuse himself from the charge of those innumerable cruelties inflicted on his unoffending subjects committed to his care, formed for his benefit, and placed under his authority by their common Father? whose mercy is over all his works, and who expects that this authority should be exercised not only with tenderness and mercy, but in conformity to the laws of justice and gratitude.[96]

It followed from these views that the mistreatment of animals should be regarded as a serious breach of divine injunctions. 'Cruelty towards Men is most confessedly an Offence against God, and can the same Disposition towards Brutes be otherwise? Did not the same Hand which made

---

[93] *Stamford Mercury*, 12 November 1814.
[94] *Voice of Humanity*, I (1830–1), 68–9. Cf. *ibid.* p. 20; Nehemiah Curnock (ed.), *The Journal of the Rev. John Wesley* (8 vols.; London, 1909–16), IV, 175–6; Stockdale, *Inhumanity to Animals*, p. 4; and Winks, *Bull Running at Stamford*, p. 4.
[95] *Clemency to Brutes*, p. 6.
[96] *Annual Register*, 1782, p. 166; from an essay 'On Cruelty to Inferior Animals', reprinted in full from Jenyns's *Disquisitions on Several Subjects* (London, 1782).

Them make Us?'[97] 'If we eagerly stimulate brutal fierceness', declared one reformer, 'we are guilty of a most barbarous impiety.'[98] An individual's position on this question would probably bear on his spiritual prospects. 'It does not appear to me extravagant', suggested an observer in 1801, 'to suppose that our conduct with respect to the brute creation will be taken into consideration at the day of retribution, and have considerable influence on our future state.'[99] Later writers were to advance the same fear with greater warmth. 'The cruelty with which they have treated the victims of their sport', claimed one writer of Stamford's bullards, 'will embitter their expiring moments, and plant on their dying pillow the thorn of remorse.'[100] Another critic of blood sports pointed to 'the inseparable connection between cruelty and impiety. In no other situation, under no other circumstances, can a person have an opportunity of witnessing impiety to such an extent . . . Who but must acknowledge that the promoters of them rank amongst the worst enemies of God and man, and are the most active agents the DEVIL has under his controul?'[101]

It was also argued that blood sports served to undermine social morality. 'Every act that sanctions cruelty to animals', observed the *Manchester Mercury* of 15 April 1800, 'must tend to destroy the morals of a people, and consequently every social duty.' Cruel sports, it was feared, would naturally give rise to cruel men:

> the greatest Unhappiness attending the rude Exercises of Cock-Throwing, Bull-baiting, Prize-fighting, and the like Bear-garden Diversions, (not to mention the more genteel Entertainment of Cock-fighting) . . . the greatest Misfortune arising from these Brutal Sports is, That they inspire the Minds of Children and young People with a savage Disposition and Ferity of Temper highly pleased with Acts of Barbarity and Cruelty. Good-nature, Compassion and Tenderness, will with great Difficulty afterwards gain Possession, if the Mind be first tinctured with Inhumanity and Blood.[102]

It was thought that 'all such trainings of the mind of a people to delight in scenes of cruelty, are as dangerous in their tendancy to the public peace and order, as they are corruptive of the young and uninstructed, whose most natural principles, (benevolence and compassion) they extinguish, and pervert their hearts to the contrary'.[103] The logical consequence of indulgence in such sports could be crime of the highest order: 'Whatever is morally bad cannot be politically right. The monster, who can wilfully persevere to torture the dumb creation, would feel little or no compunction, to serve a purpose, in aiming his bludgeon at the head, or ingulfing the murderous blade within the warm vitals of his fellow creature.'[104]

[97] *Clemency to Brutes*, p. 7.   [98] Stockdale, *Inhumanity to Animals*, p. 3.
[99] *Hull Advertiser*, 19 December 1801.
[100] *Voice of Humanity*, I (1830–1), 21.
[101] Abraham Smith, *Scriptural and Moral Catechism*, part II, p. 52.
[102] *Gentleman's Magazine*, VII (1737), 8; cf. Thomas Young, *An Essay on Humanity to Animals* (London, 1798), pp. 3–6.
[103] *Bury and Norwich Post*, 18 November 1801.
[104] Barry, *Bull Baiting*, p. 12.

One writer felt that 'much of the misery and crime of the English rural districts, is to be ascribed to the influence' of cock-fighting, 'which has trained many a victim for the gallows, and reduced many a family to want and beggary'.[105]

Blood sports, then, involved special dangers, but they also shared with other popular diversions a general tendency to undermine social discipline. They tempted men from productive labour; they disrupted the orderly routine of everyday life; they encouraged idleness, improvidence, and gambling; and sometimes they resulted in boisterous and tumultuous assemblies. Speaking in favour of the bull-baiting bill in 1800, Sir William Pulteney declared that the sport 'was cruel and inhuman; it drew together idle and disorderly persons; it drew also from their occupations many who ought to be earning subsistence for themselves and families; it created many disorderly and mischievous proceedings, and furnished examples of profligacy and cruelty'.[106] Similarly, Sir Richard Hill pointed out that 'men neglected their work and their families, and in great crowds spent whole days in witnessing those barbarous exhibitions. From the baiting-field they retired to the alehouse, and wasted the whole night in debauchery, as they had done the day in idleness.'[107] In short, the concern for cruelty and its consequences was strongly reinforced by the solicitude for public order and for labour discipline.

Many traditional football matches, especially the major holiday events, were increasingly condemned during this period, and some of them were successfully put down. Football, of course, had never enjoyed full approval from people of influence. From the fourteenth to the sixteenth century it had been frequently prohibited on the grounds that it distracted public attention from the much more useful recreation of archery. Thereafter other arguments began to be directed against the sport, in particular the inconvenience of its exercise in public thoroughfares. 'I would now make a safe retreat,' said a Parisian in a skit by Sir William Davenant, 'but that me-thinks I am stopt by one of your Heroick Games, call'd Foot-ball; which I conceive . . . not very conveniently civil in the streets; especially in such irregular and narrow Roads as *Crooked Lane*.'[108] An order of 1608 from the court leet of Manchester addressed itself to a grievance which was to persist for almost another three centuries:

> Whereas theire hath bene heretofore great disorder in our towne of Manchester, and the Inhabitants thereof greatelye wronged and charged with makinge and amendinge of theire glasse windowes broken yearelye and spoyled by a companye of lewde and disordered persons usinge that unlawfull exercise of playinge with the ffootebale in ye streets of the said towne, breakinge many mens windowes and

---

[105] James Macaulay, *Essay on Cruelty to Animals* (Edinburgh, 1839), p. 124; cf. Abraham Smith, *Scriptural and Moral Catechism*, part ii, p. 19.

[106] *Parliamentary History*, xxxv, p. 202.

[107] *Annual Register*, 1800, p. 148.

[108] Sir William Davenant, *The First Days Entertainment at Rutland-House* (London, 1657), p. 62.

glasse at theire plesures, and other greate inormyties, Therefore Wee of this Jurye doe order that no maner of persons hereafter shall playe or use the ffootebale in any streete within the said towne of Manchester . . . [109]

(For a number of years, 1610 to 1618, the court appointed annually three officers whose particular responsibility was to ensure that the order was effectively enforced, and in 1655–7 the constables were specifically desired to present everyone who was found playing football in the streets.)[110] In 1615 a similar order was issued banning street football in the area around the City of London, allegedly a source of 'great disorders and tumults'; and at Maidstone in 1656 a man was indicted for disturbing the public peace by kicking a football through the High Street 'in a violent and boisterous manner'.[111]

There is evidence from the next century of a number of attempts to prohibit football play. It was cried down at Louth in 1745 and 1754, and at Worcester in 1743 2s. 6d. was paid to 'the bellman, for crying down football kicking'.[112] At Derby there were several unsuccessful attempts to suppress the Shrovetide match in the eighteenth century; a prohibition of 1747 made particular reference to 'Tumults and Disorders' and 'breaking Windows, and doing other Mischief to the Persons and Properties of the Inhabitants of this Borough'.[113] A football game in the market place and through the streets of Bolton on 5 January 1790 was taken into consideration by the Lancashire Quarter Sessions as a disturbance of the peace.[114] At Kingston-upon-Thames the several efforts during the 1790s to put down the sport were successfully resisted. On 24 February 1799 three Kingston magistrates wrote to the Home Secretary concerning their difficulties in dealing with the annual custom:

> It having been a practice for the populace to kick foot ball in the Market Place and Streets of this Town on Shrove Tuesday to the great nuisance of the Inhabitants and of persons travelling through the Town and complaints having been made by several Gentlemen of the County to the Magistrates of the Town they previous to Shrove Tuesday 1797 gave public Notice by the distribution of hand bills of their determination to suppress the Practice which not having the desired effect several of the offenders were Indicted and at the last Assizes convicted but sentence was respited and has not yet been declared the Judge thinking that after having warn'd them of their situation that they would not attempt to kick again but we

[109] J. P. Earwaker (ed.), *The Court Leet Records of the Manor of Manchester* (12 vols.; Manchester, 1884–90), II, 239–40.

[110] *Ibid.* II, 256, and IV, 143, 171, and 209.

[111] J. C. Jeaffreson (ed.), *Middlesex County Records* (4 vols.; London, 1886–92), II, 107; quoted in L. O. Pike, *A History of Crime in England* (2 vols.; London, 1873–6), II, 188–9. I am indebted to Mr John Beattie for this latter reference.

[112] R. W. Goulding, *Louth Old Corporation Records* (Louth, 1891), p. 54; quoted in John Noake, *Worcester in Olden Times* (London, 1849), p. 197.

[113] *Derby Mercury*, 27 February 1747, 11 and 18 February 1796, 23 February 1797; Morris Marples, *A History of Football* (London, 1954), p. 84.

[114] Lancashire R.O., QSP May 1791.

the present Magistrates of the Town having been previously in-
formed it was their intention with others to kick again as on last
Shrove Tuesday some days before issued hand bills giving Notice
of our intention to prosecute any persons who should on that day
kick foot ball in the said Town and apprehending that we should
find great opposition two days previous thereto addressed a Letter
to the officer commanding the Cavalry at Hampton Court informing
him of the Circumstance and stating that if we found it necessary
we should call on him for the assistance of the Military.

On the Shrove Tuesday a great number of persons having assembled and begun to kick a ball in the market place we caused three
that seemed the most active to be taken into Custody hoping that
would induce the others to disperse but not having that effect we
then caused the Riot Act to be read and the Mob not then dispersing
but increasing in Number and threatening to Use violence in liberating those in Custody we addressed another Letter to the Officer on
Command at Hampton Court requiring him to send part of the
Cavalry to our assistance but not receiving an answer in a reasonable
time one of Us went to Hampton Court in search for the Officer
when it was said that Major Hawker was the Officer on Duty there
but was gone from home and not to be seen nor could any other be
found who could Act and the Men at the same time kicking foot
ball on Hampton Court Green.

Nor being able to obtain the assistance required the persons in
Custody were rescued by the mob as the Constables were conveying
them to Prison and the Keeper was violently assaulted and much
hurt. If the Military had attended we should have succeeded in
abolishing the nuisance without much difficulty but not having met
with such support the Game will be carried on to a greater height
than it ever has been the mob conceiving they have got the better
of Us and that the Military would not attend.[115]

Public thoroughfares had always been regarded as legitimate playing
places by the common people, but as the pace of urbanization accelerated,
and as the means of social control became increasingly sophisticated, the
clash between this popular point of view and the growing concern for
orderliness and property rights was very much accentuated. The sort of
conflict which must have been very common is illustrated by an incident
of 1818 in Hull: elaborating on a report concerning a man who had recently
been fined 40s. for playing football in the streets, a local newspaper pointed
out that 'the police of Sculcoates have strict orders to prevent any person
from playing at any games in the streets troublesome to the inhabitants
of the said parish, which have of late been so prevalent, to the great
annoyance and personal danger of the public' [116] In 1829 and 1836 the
vestry of Barnes, Surrey, complained of the nuisance of street football
and recommended its suppression to the officers of the peace.[117] The

---

[115] P.R.O., H.O. 42/46, fol. 128. I am indebted to Mr E. P. Thompson for this reference.
[116] *Hull Advertiser*, 25 April 1818.
[117] Surrey R.O., P 6/3/5, vestry meetings of 5 March 1829 and 10 February 1836.

Highways Act of 1835 made explicit reference to the sport (5 & 6 William IV c. 50, clause 72): it provided for a fine of up to 40s. for playing 'at Football or any other Game on any Part of the said Highways, to the Annoyance of any Passenger', and thereby afforded solid grounds for future prosecutions. In later years football in the streets was forcibly terminated at a number of towns in Surrey: at Richmond (1840), at East Mousley and Hampton Wick (1857), at Hampton (1864), and at Kingston-upon-Thames (1867).[118]

Shrovetide football in Derby was only put down after considerable controversy. During the early decades of the nineteenth century its practice had been periodically deplored, but no direct action was taken until 1845. In January a petition to end the match was presented to the Mayor; and at the same time a subscription was taken up to promote alternative sports on the customary holiday on the condition that football in the streets was abandoned, a bargain which was alleged to have the support of 'a large number of those who have heretofore been the leading players on both sides'.[119] There was a general concern among men of property to avoid giving the impression that they were callously crushing a favourite amusement without offering some sort of compensation. Surprisingly energetic efforts were made to win the support of the working people for the new arrangements: the Mayor met with many of the footballers and (it was said) found that his proposals were well received; notices were posted to publicize the new sports and the prizes they carried; and on Tuesday 'bands of music were engaged to perambulate the streets, preceded by banners' with 'suitable mottoes', and several thousand people collected to test the innovations. However, when it was learned a little later that a football was being kicked through the streets by a few dissidents (apparently only a fraction of the usual numbers), the new amusements were called off and the large crowd was left in the lurch, unoccupied and discontented.[120] Later that month the Town Council voted to re-establish the Derby races, and thereafter it was common to regard the races as a recreational substitute for the Shrovetide sports and a further justification for eliminating the older holiday.[121]

The next year, at a Town Council meeting of February 4th, the football question was again introduced.

> The mayor and others agreed that there ought to be no pudding exhibitions, no swarming greased poles, nor grinning through collars, as were proposed last year. (These remarks elicited much laughter.) For his own part he delighted to see the working classes enjoy a rational amusement; and he thought if they were denied one amusement, they ought to have some others provided. This had already been done. (Hear, hear.) The Races having been estab-

---

[118] Richmond Borough Library, Richmond Vestry Minute Book for 1829–42, pp. 466 and 468, and *Surrey Standard*, 6 March 1840; *Surrey Comet*, 28 February 1857, 13 February 1864, and 9 March 1867.
[119] *Derby Mercury*, 22 January 1845.
[120] *Derby Mercury*, 5 February 1845; *Derby and Chesterfield Reporter*, 7 February 1845.
[121] *Derby Mercury*, 26 February 1845.

lished, he thought that the irrational and disgraceful pastime to which Mr Pegg had called attention, ought now to be put down; and he should be happy to use what influence he possessed, in conjunction with his fellow magistrates, to effect its abolition. (Hear, hear.)[122]

An order prohibiting football was issued, several hundred 'respectable inhabitants' were sworn in as special constables, and (with the approval of the Home Secretary) two troops of dragoons were summoned from Nottingham. Some of the footballers acquiesced and on the evening before Shrove Tuesday formally surrendered the ball to the Mayor and promised to try to persuade their fellows to obey the ban. Others were less obliging. Precautions were taken to block off the market place, and one ball which appeared on Tuesday was quickly captured by the police and cut up, but in mid-afternoon another ball

> was thrown up and taken down the river as rapidly as possible, and a detachment of police and specials . . . proceeded to the Railway Bridge to intercept it, but were overpowered. The Mayor . . . and other Magistrates came up. Some ruffian threw a brick bat and bludgeon – one or both of which hit the Mayor upon the shoulder. The ruffian was seized . . . and [soon] rescued by considerable violence being offered to his capturer; other unmistakeable manifestations of the temper of the mob were given, and the civil power being found insufficient, the Riot Act was read and the military called out; but before they could reach the Railway Bridge the players had made all speed with the ball down the river out of the bounds of the borough.[123]

Under the direction of a County magistrate, the dragoons, specials, and regular police were soon in hot pursuit, and a later confrontation occurred around Normanton where the players and police skirmished for the ball. This, however, was the last time of resistance: during the next three years precautions were taken before each Shrove Tuesday and dragoons were posted nearby, but there was no further attempt to perpetuate a tradition which the magistrates had determined to suppress.

Many of these holiday football matches were particularly resilient, for they were fortified by a festival context, long-standing traditions, and large numbers of followers. The Nuneaton game was still extant in the late nineteenth century, and the Dorking and Workington matches survived into the twentieth century. Several games were able to continue by shifting their ground to more open spaces (though in so doing they sometimes lost much of their peculiar appeal). When steps were taken at Alnwick in 1827–8 to bar the Shrovetide game from the streets, the Duke of Northumberland provided a convenient meadow for its refuge.[124] At Twickenham in 1840 the magistrates prevented the Shrovetide football from 'taking place in the town, but it was most spiritedly carried on in a meadow belonging to Mr Cole, the brewer of that parish, under the

---

[122] *Derbyshire Advertiser and Journal*, 11 February 1846.
[123] *Derby and Chesterfield Reporter*, 27 February 1846.
[124] Marples, *History of Football*, pp. 101–2; Magoun, *History of Football*, p. 126.

superintendence of a man named Kirby, who has been ''master of the sports'' for the last 50 years'; 'formerly . . . the sport had been extended throughout every avenue of the place; but of late years, and more particularly since the passing of the new Highway Act, by which it has altogether been prohibited in any public thoroughfare . . . it has been confined to' the meadow of 'Mr. Cole, who kindly offered it for the purpose.'[125] There was periodic talk of putting down the annual football at Kingston-upon-Thames, but nothing came of it until 1867 when the corporation directed the players off the streets and onto a new playing field, an order which sparked off some angry protests and a little rioting but was generally accepted the following year.[126] The Ashbourne game, after weathering an attack in 1860–1, removed itself to the outskirts of town[127] and survived into the twentieth century to be condoned and patronized, not only by the common people, but by civic officials, the Church, and on one occasion (in 1927) by the Prince of Wales.

The main objections against popular football stemmed from the concern for public order. 'The Game of Football as practised in this Town on Shrove Tuesday', it was claimed in a motion introduced at the Kingston Town Council on 29 February 1840, 'is an obstruction to the passengers, a great annoyance to the peaceable Inhabitants, subversive of good order and prejudicial to the morality of the Town.'[128] Football in the streets obviously disturbed the normal routine of business, and such disruptions were no longer as readily tolerated.

> It is not so much with a wish to deprive the lovers of this sport of their enjoyment, that I advocate its abolition [wrote a Derby critic in 1832], but more particularly to condemn the fitness of the place of its competition for such a purpose; instead of emanating from the centre of the town, let them assemble in the Siddals, or some such place, so as not to interfere with the avocation of the industrious part of the community; it is not a trifling consideration that a suspension of business for nearly two days should be created to the inhabitants for the mere gratification of a sport at once so useless and barbarous.[129]

During a discussion of the Kingston game in 1857 one of the Town Councillors claimed that 'he knew what loss he sustained on that day by the diminution of trade, and no doubt his friend Mr. Jones knew too, and so did every grocer and draper'.[130] In 1845 Derby's Mayor was suggesting that

> In former times, when the town contained but few inhabitants, the game was not attended with its present evils, but it was now a well

[125] *The Times*, 2 and 6 March 1840.
[126] *Surrey Comet*, 2 and 9 March 1867, 29 February 1868.
[127] *Derby Mercury*, 15, 22 and 29 February and 7 March 1860, 20 February and 6 March 1861; 12 March 1862; *Derbyshire Advertiser*, 20 February 1863; cf. Magoun, *History of Football*, pp. 109–10, and Marples, *History of Football*, pp. 102–4.
[128] Kingston-upon-Thames Guildhall, Kingston Court of Assembly Book 1834–1859, D.I. 4.5.
[129] *Derby and Chesterfield Reporter*, 23 February 1832.
[130] *Surrey Comet*, 7 February 1857.

ascertained fact that many of the inhabitants suffered considerable injury, in person as well as property, from this annual exhibition; and he himself knew of instances where persons having an interest in houses, especially the larger ones, had experienced losses from want of occupiers, at adequate rents; parties who would otherwise have expended many thousands a year on the trade of the town, having left it, or declined to reside in it, because they did not like to bring up their families here, under the idea that Derby was one of the lowest and wickedest places in the kingdom.[131]

During the prosecution of some of the recalcitrant Derby footballers in 1846 it was argued that

in a town consisting of 40,000 inhabitants, one-third of whom were labouring population, persons must not assemble for such low and improper amusements at the present day in the public streets, whatever they might have done when football was originally practised – Derby being at that time a very small place; but at the present time the town had become very large. Persons from a distance occasionally residing in it, whose characters were unknown, availed themselves of this opportunity of injuring persons by destroying property, alarming the timid and well-disposed inhabitants, and putting a stop to all business for the greater part of two days.[132]

Although there was a definite element of moral opposition to the holiday matches (at Derby the game was variously spoken of as 'brutalizing', 'disgraceful', 'inhuman', 'filthy and disgusting'), it is clear that moral outrage was a much less prominent theme in the opposition to football than it was in the attacks against blood sports, or perhaps even pleasure fairs. There were fewer objective grounds for passionate denunciations: while many football games were undoubtedly rough and unregulated, serious injuries during the major holiday matches seem to have been uncommon; for the most part the crowds were relatively orderly, and the games were pursued in a reasonably sporting manner.[133] 'During these boisterous *Saturnalia*,' remarked one observer of the Kingston game, 'the inhabitants are reduced to the necessity of barricading their windows; and the trade of the town is somewhat impeded; yet the general good-humour with which the sport is carried on prevents any serious complaints; and the majority of the corporation are favourable to its continuance.'[134] Football was regarded by some gentlemen as a 'manly sport', rugged but character-building, and there was some feeling that it helped to sustain the Englishman's 'bull-dog courage'. Several matches enjoyed a considerable genteel following, a feature which was often remarked on. One writer, for instance, spoke of how at Derby 'the crowd is encouraged by respectable persons attached to each party . . . who take a surprising

[131] *Derby and Chesterfield Reporter*, 7 February 1845.
[132] *Derby Mercury*, 25 March 1846.
[133] For evidence in support of these points, see the *Derby Mercury*, 9 February 1815 and 29 January 1845; *Penny Magazine*, 6 April 1839; *Surrey Standard*, 20 February 1836 and 13 March 1840; *Surrey Comet*, 9 February 1856, 7 February 1857, and 13 February 1858.
[134] E. W. Brayley, *A Topographical History of Surrey* (5 vols.; London, 1841–8), III, 51–2.

interest in the result of the days' "sport"; urging on the players with shouts, and even handing to those who are exhausted, oranges and other refreshment.'[135] The circumstances at Kingston were much the same: many gentlemen were known to be favourably disposed towards the custom. An attempt to suppress the practice in 1840 was blocked by the Town Council, and at the same time a petition from the inhabitants was sent to the Commissioners of the Metropolitan Police requesting that they not interfere with the sport.[136] In 1860–1, when efforts were made to put down the Ashbourne game, its supporters included some of 'the most respectable citizens of the town'.[137] Indeed, the resilience of some of the holiday matches is partly explained by the fact that they received a reasonable degree of backing from respectable opinion, and when popular and genteel conservatism joined hands the attacks of the reformers were much less likely to succeed.

The only other athletic sport to be frequently criticized was boxing. From the later eighteenth century magistrates became increasingly prepared to prohibit the staging of prize-fights and to prosecute their principals whenever possible. In 1791, for instance, the Bedfordshire justices, 'being convinced of the ill Tendency of Stage fighting or Boxing Matches have resolved that publick notice be given that they are determined not to suffer them to take Place'.[138] Prize-fighting could be readily restrained under the law, either as a breach of the peace or an unlawful assembly, and though many matches were winked at – some were partly protected by their influential patrons, and others were accompanied by crowds too large for the resources of local constables – successful interventions against intended prize-fights were often reported in the newspapers of the first half of the nineteenth century. Boxing was not infrequently the cause of accidental deaths and serious maulings, a circumstance which incurred for it much public disfavour. 'These dreadul catastrophes', suggested one paper, 'bespeak it the duty of every magistrate, as well as every man, to use their utmost endeavours to repress so disgraceful, so dangerous, and so increasing an evil.'[139] More significantly, a prize-fight was attended by considerable problems of public order. A crowd of thousands, some of them persons of dubious employments, seriously threatened the tranquility of an unprepared locality – 'the established order, and good decorum of society,' complained one writer, 'have been, of late, much disturbed, and nearly set at defiance' by the prevalence of boxing matches;[140] moreover, such gatherings tended to undermine the assurance

[135] Glover, *County of Derby*, i, 262. The newspapers often alluded to the genteel followers of the match.
[136] Kingston-upon-Thames Guildhall, Court of Assembly Book 1834–59, D.I. 4.5, meetings of 29 February and 6 May 1840; *The Times*, 6 March 1840.
[137] *Derby Mercury*, 7 March 1860.
[138] Bedfordshire R.O., Q.S.R. 17, 3 (Epiphany Sessions, 1791).
[139] *Northampton Mercury*, 11 June 1791.
[140] Edward Barry, *A Letter on the Practice of Boxing* (London, 1789), p. 7; cf. a letter of 2 September 1790 from Charles Dundas to Lord Kenyon in *Historical Manuscripts Commission, 14th Report, Appendix, Part IV. The Manuscripts of Lord Kenyon* (London, 1894), pp. 531–2.

and reputation of the local guardians of the peace. Cat-and-mouse contests between the promoters and magistrates were common; matches were often staged near county borders in the hope that, should the magistrates appear, jurisdictional divisions could be more readily exploited. The *Derby Mercury* of 10 August 1842 complained that

> The inhabitants never know any thing of the business until they see the crowds of vagabonds upon the grounds, who forcibly take possession of some field suitable for their purpose, and not only bear down all resistance on the part of the owner, but set at defiance the exertions of the magistrates and peace officers, to stop their lawless proceedings. It has therefore been determined to take a more efficacious plan with them for the future, namely, by instructing the peace officers and others to take particular notice, not only of the parties, and their seconds and bottleholders, but also of the principal ringleaders, who generally consider themselves more respectable, and any other persons on the ground who refuse to assist the peace officers, and afterwards to indict them. By this course the contest with a mob of vagabonds (which really adds to their amusement) will be avoided, and the criminal parties taught that the law, although slow in its march, is sure to overtake them, and will signally punish such outrages wherever perpetrated in defiance of it.

There was no systematic and sustained campaign which was intent on undermining the essential fabric of the traditional holiday calendar. The legitimacy of some sort of festivity, or at least relaxation, at Christmas, Easter, and Whitsuntide was only infrequently brought into question; for the most part they were accepted as justifiable occasions of leisure – they were celebrated in some form by almost everyone, and they were associated with the customary practices of various established institutions (the Church, annual fairs, clubs and friendly societies). Most of the discontent with the traditional holidays was directed at wakes and pleasure fairs, which were open to criticism on a number of grounds: they involved large (sometimes very large) public assemblies and consequently could be difficult for the authorities to control; they were often boisterous and 'licentious'; many of them were exclusively plebeian and only marginally associated with 'respectable' institutions; they were thought by many observers to be thoroughly committed in the crudest of ways to the pursuit of sensual pleasures. One writer suggested that 'few persons are ever to be intrusted to feast. And fewer are to be allowed to meet in numbers together. There is a contagious viciousness in crowds. Though each individual of them, alone and by himself, would act with a religious propriety; yet all together they act with irreligion and folly.'[141] William Somerville claimed that at country wakes 'We see nothing but broken Heads, Bottles flying about, Tables overturn'd, outrageous Drunkenness, and eternal Squabble.'[142]

There are numerous indications from the eighteenth and earlier nine-

[141] John Whitaker, *The History of Manchester* (London, 1775), Book ii, pp. 443–4.
[142] Somerville, *Rural Games*, p. ii.

teenth centuries of this genteel dissatisfaction with parish feasts. In Gloucestershire there were several early attempts to eliminate wakes, and at the second of these, in 1710, the county's Court of Quarter Sessions set out the type of grievance which was to be repeatedly advanced during later generations. The preamble to the order for a general suppression of wakes spoke of how

> it has been Represented to this Court by the ministers and principall Inhabitants of the several Parishes of Coaley Frocester and Nympsfield, That there are yearly held in those Parishes aforesaid as in other places in this County unlawfull Wakes and Revells and other Disorderly meetings upon several Lords Days and which have been continued on for several days of the week following: vizt the Sunday after St Bartholomcws Day at Coaley Palm Sunday at Cowleys Pick and Nympsfield and the Sunday after St. Peters day at Frocester, and on other particular Sundays in other places in this County, which draw great Concourse[s] of People together, to the great Prophanation of the Lords Day in Contempt of her Majesties Gracious Proclamation against Immorality and Prophaneness, where Rioting and Drunkenness, Lewdness and Debauchery and other Immoralities are Committed, which according to the Preamble of the Statute of the 4th of King James the 1st against Drunkenness is the Root and foundation of many other enormous sinnes to the Great Dishonour of God and of our Nation, the overthrow of many good Arts and manual Trades, the Disabling Diverse workmen, and the General Impoverishment of many good Subjects . . .[143]

Similar orders were delivered by the Quarter Sessions in 1718 and 1731, both of which also referred to 'other disorderly Meetings, for Wrestling and Cudgel-Playing for Hats or other Prizes, which are promoted and encouraged by Alehouse-Keepers'.[144] In 1776 the Justices of the Peace for the Bathforum division of Somerset prohibited 'the Custom of Keeping Revels'.[145] The Nottinghamshire Quarter Sessions in 1778 threatened to refuse licences to any publicans who helped to promote wakes: the order complained that on these occasions 'Diverse Riots and Disorderly doings frequently arise by Persons Assembling and Meeting together to be guilty of Excessive Drinking Tippling Gaming or other unlawful Exercises'.[146] In 1796-7 the principal inhabitants of three Lincolnshire communities (Sibsey, Withern, and Morton) announced through the columns of the *Stamford Mercury* that they had determined to discontinue their customary feasts.[147] The notice from Morton argued that country wakes, 'tho' originally intended for religious Meetings, are now quite perverted,

[143] Gloucestershire R.O., Q/SO 3, Easter 1710; see Q/SO 3, Epiphany 1710 for the first of these orders.

[144] Gloucestershire R.O., Q/SO 4, Epiphany 1718, and Q/SO 5, Easter 1731.

[145] *Bath Chronicle*, 23 May 1776, quoted in B. M. Willmott Dobbie, *An English Rural Community: Batheaston with S. Catherine* (Bath, 1969), p. 66.

[146] K. T. Meaby, *Nottinghamshire: Extracts from the County Records of the Eighteenth Century* (Nottingham, 1947), p. 147.

[147] *Stamford Mercury*, 8 July 1796 (Sibsey and Withern) and 23 June 1797 (Morton). I am grateful to Mr Rex Russell for drawing these notices to my attention.

serving chiefly to encourage Drunkenness, the Inlet to Vice and Prophane-ness'; and that since 'the present high Price of Provisions must nearly involve every poor Family in unsurmountable Debts and Difficulties', the ending of the feasts would help to 'keep our Parishioners from such Embarrassments, as well as to check the rapid Growth of Vice and Im-morality'.

The concern for public order and morality was the major source of the opposition to wakes. A Bedfordshire magistrate, for instance, complained that during the feast night at Sharnbrook there was 'an almost riotous assembly of men and women dancing and walking about on the road, clasping each other in a loving manner, all along the turnpike road. He thought this was not conducive to the morals of the public, which was the chief object he should have in view.'[148] This was the sort of complaint which was registered time and time again about many kinds of popular diversion. But there were also several criticisms which were more peculiar to wakes. It was often argued that wakes had seriously degenerated from their original institution as religious occasions, and that as almost exclu-sively profane assemblies their continuance could not be justified. Since they no longer served any significant religious purpose, it would be best (thought some) if their practice were terminated. 'When a thing not only fails to answer the end proposed,' suggested one writer in 1783, 'but operates commonly on the contrary, the sooner it is laid aside or changed the better.'[149] A religious commemoration had become a gathering for licentiousness: 'the Feasting and Sporting got the ascendant of Religion,' complained Henry Bourne, 'and so this Feast of Dedication, degenerated into Drunkenness and Luxury'.[150] Moreover, since wakes normally began on a Sunday, they were liable to disapproval on Sabbatarian grounds. Public sensuality was bad enough, but sensuality on the Lord's Day was completely intolerable. Various efforts were made to restrain these im-pieties, especially the setting up of booths and the sale of drink. In July 1825, for example, the vicar of Bucklebury, Berkshire, noted that he 'Gave instructions to my brother in law to provide that no beer should be sold in private houses nor Booths be erected on the Revel-Sunday, July 31st.'[151] And finally, wakes were thought to involve the common people in financial extravagance, in an improvident expenditure of time and money. A sympathetic commentator was of the opinion that 'the excite-ment lasts too long, and the enjoyment, whatever it may be, is purchased at the sacrifice of too great expense. It is a well-known fact, that many of

---

[148] *Bedfordshire Mercury*, 7 January 1861.

[149] *Gentleman's Magazine*, LIII (1783), part II, 1,004. See also Macaulay, *History of Clay-brook*, p. 128; George Cope, *The Origin, Excellence, and Perversion of Wakes or Parish Feasts* (Hereford, 1816), which was drawn to my attention by Mr Jolyon Hall; Kidd, *Village Wakes*; and John Bowstead, *The Village Wake, or the Feast of the Dedication* (London, 1846).

[150] Bourne, *Antiquitates Vulgares*, p. 228.

[151] Arthur L. Humphreys, *Bucklebury: A Berkshire Parish* (Reading, 1932), p. 369. Cf. *Leeds Intelligencer*, 20 June 1786; *Hull Advertiser*, 4 June and 23 July 1808; *Stamford Mercury*, 20 October 1837; *Derby Mercury*, 1 July 1840; and *Bedfordshire Mercury*, 7 January 1861.

9 Nottingham bear-baiting jug, *c.* 1700

10 *Tavern Interior with Peasants* (1742) by Marcellus Laroon

the poor who have exerted every effort to make this profuse, but short-lived display, have scarcely bread to eat for weeks after. But there is no alternative, if they expect to be received with the same spirit of hospitality by their friends.'[152] Amusement had to be tailored to suit a family's financial capabilities, and the wake, it was thought, was too frequently an occasion when the working man's expenditure became grossly over-extended.

The attacks on other popular holidays were directed mostly against hiring fairs and outright pleasure fairs. In Essex, where pleasure fairs abounded, their suppression was ordered on numerous occasions after the mid-eighteenth century. In 1761–2 two standing orders from Quarter Sessions prohibited a total of twenty-four fairs; during the 1780s and early 1790s several more orders were published against fairs in other parishes.[153] None (or virtually none) of these fairs was a chartered event, and consequently they were regarded by the authorities as 'pretended fairs . . . not warranted by Law'; they were unofficial assemblies, organized only for pleasure and petty business, and they were objected to on the usual grounds – for their 'riots and tumults', their drunkenness, their 'unlawful games and plays', their 'debauching of Servants Apprentices and other unwary people'.[154] (These and other vices were subjected to detailed poetic scrutiny in 1789 by William Sheldrake in his *Picturesque Description of Turton Fair, and its Pernicious Consequences.*) Orders against fairs similar to those in Essex were issued by the Surrey Quarter Sessions in the late 1780s.[155] Although fairs continued to be attacked and sometimes prohibited in particular localities during the first half of the nineteenth century, it seems that their numbers did not significantly decline until later in the century: an Act of 1871 (34 Victoria c.12) provided efficient machinery for the abolition of 'unnecessary' fairs, and during the period 1871–8 its provisions were used to suppress more than 150 fairs.[156]

There appears to have been little active and articulated opposition to hiring fairs prior to the Victorian period. Many of them continued to provide useful service as labour exchanges, and they were still supported by a large number of farmers. It was only in the second half of the century that they came under frequent attack and noticeably declined in importance: several essays were published against them and attempts were made to regulate them more effectively or to substitute other procedures for

---

[152] Hone, *Every-Day Book*, II, col. 55; cf. *Gentleman's Magazine*, LIII (1783), part II, 1,005, and Pilkington, *Derbyshire*, II, 55.

[153] Essex R.O., Q/SBb 225/16 and Q/SO 10, pp. 337–8; Q/SBb 323/52; Q/SO 14, pp. 292–4; Q/SBb 343/26; and *Chelmsford Chronicle*, 26 May 1786 and 8 July 1791.

[154] Essex R.O., Q/SBb 225/16.

[155] Surrey R.O., Acc. 450 (1788); Godschall, *Provincial Police*, p. 111; and Leon Radzinowicz, *A History of English Criminal Law and Its Administration from 1750* (4 vols.; London, 1948–69), III, 491–3.

[156] *Quarterly Review*, XXIV (October 1820), 258; Essex R.O., D/P 263/28/6; *Norfolk Chronicle and Norwich Gazette*, 22 July 1826; Hertfordshire R.O., D/P 121/8/1; and P.R.O., 'Subject Index and Box List to Home Office Papers 1871–1878 (H.O. 45)', pp. 70–7.

hiring labour.[157] They were condemned for the same reasons as pleasure fairs, and particular stress was placed on the mingling of young, inexperienced servants with the older, hardened, and profligate followers of statute meetings (thieves, prostitutes, seducers, adventurers of all sorts) in circumstances which greatly encouraged drunkenness, uproar, and sexual promiscuity. Reformers were particularly concerned about their consequences for innocent maid-servants.

It should be emphasized that in comparison with some of the traditional recreations (such as blood sports), many fairs and parish feasts displayed a considerable staying power. If the area around Stamford was at all representative, it appears that wakes were still being widely celebrated as late as the 1840s; some may already have been suppressed but many certainly survived.[158] There was still a large number of fairs all through the country during the second half of the nineteenth century. Northamptonshire, for instance, had more fairs in the 1850s than it had had a century before.[159] In the countryside fairs continued to serve important marketing functions, and most of them were able to survive as long as they retained some significant economic rationale. This was a point of considerable importance: those fairs, especially the smaller ones, which blended pleasure with business were usually much more resilient than those which were strictly for pleasure; when a fair became economically redundant (and many did during the Victorian period) it was much more liable to attack. The Society for the Suppression of Vice had suggested in 1803 that it would 'be expedient to suppress all Fairs whatever, unless when they are really wanted for the purpose of useful traffic. Such an Act would be extremely beneficial to the morals of the community, without being productive of the smallest inconvenience to the public'.[160] This was a distinction which was widely acknowledged. Unofficial, unchartered fairs, such as those which were suppressed in Essex during the late eighteenth century, could not be defended on any acceptable criteria of economic usefulness. Statute fairs very much fell out of favour after the mid-nineteenth century, partly because by this time, as their hiring services were in many places of depreciating value (at least for employers), they were functioning almost

---

[157] See in particular Greville J. Chester, *Statute Fairs: Their Evils and Their Remedy* (York and London, 1856), and the same author's *Statute Fairs*, a sermon preached in 1858; Nash Stephenson, 'On Statute Fairs: Their Evils and their Remedy', *Transactions of the National Association for the Promotion of Social Science* (1858), pp. 624–31; J. Skinner, *Facts and Opinions Concerning Statute Hirings, Respectfully Addressed to the Landowners, Clergy, Farmers and Tradesmen of the East Riding of Yorkshire* (London, 1861); Kebbel, *Agricultural Labourer*, pp. 118–22 and 131–3; an article on 'Mops' in the *Illustrated London News*, 26 October 1878, p. 398; and Francis G. Heath, *Peasant Life in the West of England* (London, 1880), 68–9.

[158] See above, pp. 17–18, and the *Penny Magazine*, 12 August 1837, pp. 311–12.

[159] Owen, *Fairs* (edns. of 1756 and 1859).

[160] *An Address to the Public from the Society for the Suppression of Vice* (London, 1803), part II, p. 61n. Those pleasure fairs which did in fact prosper during the Victorian period were often the very large events, such as the Nottingham Goose Fair and St Giles's Fair in Oxford. See Sally Alexander, *St Giles's Fair, 1830–1914: Popular Culture and the Industrial Revolution in 19th Century Oxford* (Ruskin College History Workshop pamphlet no. 2, 1970).

entirely as pleasure fairs. A petition of 1875 against the two annual fairs in Sawbridgeworth, Hertfordshire, focused clearly on the central kinds of issues:

> In former, and very different times, the holding of these Fairs might have, as a matter of expediency, been defended on alleged commercial grounds, and for the convenience of the Residents; but now the old order of things has entirely passed away. Even the last lingering shadow of pretence for these Fairs – the Sale of Stock – is rapidly passing away; for, in the opinion of competent judges, the supply of stock is yearly becoming more limited in extent and inferior in quality . . .
>
> But whilst these Fairs are of the smallest possible conceivable worth in a commercial point of view, indefensibly and indisputably they are the prolific seed plots and occasions of the most hideous forms of moral and social evil – drunkenness – whoredom – robbery – idleness and neglect of work . . . [161]

We can see, then, that gatherings which were largely plebeian, and unabashedly devoted to pleasure, enjoyed considerably less security than those in which substantial economic interests were involved – and with time most of these popular events disappeared. However, it should be emphasized that their decline was gradual and relatively gentle; by the mid-nineteenth century it was only moderately advanced. In the long run, in fact, this decline was probably more a consequence of the diminishing role of the countryside in the overall life of the nation, and the rise of a predominantly urban culture, than of the organized attacks of influential opinion. Many changes in rural recreations were a result of a whole set of larger transformations in the nature of rural society. Thomas Hardy, for instance, pointed to the increasing mobility in the countryside as the major reason for the disappearance of many popular traditions: the main change, he thought,

> has been the recent supplanting of the class of stationary cottagers, who carried on the local traditions and humours, by a population of more or less migratory labourers, which has led to a break of continuity in local history, more fatal than any other thing to the preservation of legend, folk-lore, close inter-social relations, and eccentric individualities. For these the indispensable conditions of existence are attachment to the soil of one particular spot by generation after generation. [162]

Moreover, as urban diversions became more accessible to country dwellers, as alternative entertainments became available, the attractiveness and strength of the rural traditions were correspondingly weakened. It was only when the society which supported many of the traditional festivities was fundamentally altered – when the numbers of labouring people in the countryside were declining, when faster communications were breaking down rural insularity, when the countryside was becoming subordinate to the cities, and when the rural proletariat was increasingly assimilating

[161] Hertfordshire R.O., D/P 98/29/6; cf. Harrison, *Drink and the Victorians*, pp. 328–9.
[162] From the preface to *Far From the Madding Crowd*.

many of the urban manners and pastimes – that those diversions which were intrinsically rooted in a country parish, or the environs of a market town, were finally and irreparably dissolved.

It is worth noting, in conclusion, the extent to which many of the attacks on traditional recreations betrayed a pronounced class bias. The reformers' energies were mobilized largely against popular amusements; few were so indelicate as to storm the citadels of genteel pleasure. The critics were able to discriminate nicely between the fashionable diversions of the rich and the less fashionable of the poor – and to act accordingly. Such discrimination was especially noticeable in the movement against animal sports. The R.S.P.C.A., despite disclaimers to the contrary, discreetly disregarded the pleasures of the fashionable world and almost always prosecuted only plebeian sportsmen.[163] The Act of 1835 against cruelty to animals conveniently confined its attention to cattle and domestic animals; it was at pains to exclude from its frame of reference such 'wildlife' as rabbits, deer, and foxes. Henry Alken's *National Sports of Great Britain*, which condemned the baiting of bulls, found it expedient to eulogize field sports and (more remarkably) even to defend cock-fighting and badger-baiting, both of which still retained a select genteel following (the defence here was partly on grounds which were rejected as a justification for bull-baiting – that is, the natural ferocity of the combatants). Fighting cocks, it was ingeniously argued, 'die of that which they love, for it is impossible to make a Cock fight against his will; and as they are in no case, or seldom, permitted to die a natural death, it matters little, in reality of rhyme or reason, at what period, early or late, they may be accommodated with an artificial one'.[164] Richard Martin, a persistent sponsor of bills for the protection of animals during the 1820s, countered the charge of discrimination with the argument that 'Hunting and shooting, in his opinion, were amusements of a totally different character. Many gentlemen who indulged in those recreations had been the foremost to support his bill for preventing cruelty to animals.' 'Those who sported on their own manors, or fished in their own streams,' he suggested, 'were a very different sort of men. He had known men as humane as men could be who followed the sports of the field.'[165]

The flaws in such arguments did not go unnoticed by some contemporaries, especially those who were unimpressed by the general tenor of the evangelical movement. Indeed, there was a considerable awareness of the prejudices and partiality which were involved in the programmes for recreational reform. At the beginning of the century this objection was advanced with particular vigour by William Windham, a vocal opponent of the various legislative attempts to restrain cruelty to animals. His case, which was to be frequently repeated both in and out of Parliament during

---

[163] Brian Harrison, 'Religion and Recreation in Nineteenth-Century England', *Past & Present*, no. 38 (December 1967), 116–18.

[164] Alken, *National Sports*, captions for plate i on cock-fighting, plate ii on bull-baiting, and the plate 'Drawing the Badger'.

[165] *Parliamentary Debates*, New series, x, pp. 133 and 487 (11 and 26 February 1824).

the next several decades, was given public currency through the debate on
the Bull baiting bill of 1800:

> The advocates of this bill . . . proposed to abolish bull-baiting on the
> score of cruelty. It is strange enough that such an argument should
> be employed by a set of persons who have a most vexatious code
> of laws for the protection of their own amusements . . . When
> gentlemen talk of cruelty, I must remind them, that it belongs as
> much to shooting, as to the sport of bull-baiting; nay more so, as it
> frequently happens, that where one bird is shot, a great many others
> go off much wounded . . . And do not gentlemen, for the empty fame
> of being in at the death, frequently goad and spur their horses to
> exertions greatly beyond their strength? . . . The common people
> may ask with justice, why abolish bull-baiting, and protect hunting
> and shooting? What appearance must we make, if we, who have
> every source of amusement open to us, and yet follow these cruel
> sports, become rigid censors of the sports of the poor, and abolish
> them on account of their cruelty, when they are not more cruel than
> our own?[166]

Sidney Smith emphasized the same inconsistency a few years later in
an unflattering assessment of the Society for the Suppression of
Vice:

> The real thing which calls forth the sympathies, and harrows up the
> soul, is to see a number of boisterous artizans baiting a bull, or a
> bear; not a savage hare, or a carnivorous stag, but a poor, innocent,
> timid bear, not pursued by magistrates, and deputy lieutenants, and
> men of education, but by those who must necessarily seek their
> relaxation in noise and tumultuous merriment, by men whose
> feelings are blunted, and whose understanding is wholly devoid of
> refinement . . . A man of ten thousand a year may worry a fox as
> much as he pleases, may encourage the breed of a mischievous
> animal on purpose to worry it; and a poor labourer is carried before
> a magistrate for paying sixpence to see an exhibition of courage
> between a dog and a bear! Any cruelty may be practised to gorge
> the stomachs of the rich, none to enliven the holidays of the poor.
> We venerate those feelings which really protect creatures susceptible
> of pain, and incapable of complaint. But heaven-born pity, now-
> adays, calls for the income tax and the court guide; and ascertains the
> rank and fortune of the tormentor before she weeps for the pain of
> the sufferer.[167]

The one-sidedness of the reformers' concerns was widely recognized, at
least by a substantial body of respectable opinion. 'The *privileged* orders
can be as cruel as they please,' complained a Stamford journal in 1819,
'and few are the mortals who dare say wrong they do; while every evil
action of the lowly is trumpeted forth: the perpetrator is even *named*,

---

[166] *Parliamentary History*, xxxv, p. 207 (18 April 1800); cf. *Cobbett's Parliamentary Debates*,
xiv, p. 990. (12 June 1809).
[167] *Edinburgh Review*, xiii (January 1809), p. 340; cf. *A Letter to a Member of the Society
for the Suppression of Vice* (London, 1804), especially p. 44.

that he may be shunned and despised.'[168] John Drakard's *Stamford News* was at pains to defend the town's bull-running against the outrage of genteel sensibilities (especially as expressed in the *Stamford Mercury*): 'Away, then with this spurious feeling and bastard humanity! which froths and foams at one yearly indulgence of the lower orders, and sympathizes with the daily and destructive enjoyments of the high and the wealthy, or leaves them sanctified and untouched.'[169] Even one of the reform bodies, the Animals' Friend Society (which was much less fashionably supported than the R.S.P.C.A.), showed some awareness of the partiality of the movement which it helped to sustain:

> The lower classes have, as they deserve, been unsparingly censured by every one having the least claim to humanity who has treated on the subject, for bull-baiting, dog-fighting, etc., and even by stag-hunters themselves – while their own equally savage sports are held by them as virtues, and their heartless outrages and treachery to defenceless animals are related by them with all the glee that belongs to brave and generous deeds, with bravado added to their crimes.[170]

Sometimes these objections were simply brushed aside as unworthy of consideration. Another reply was to accept and sanction such discriminations, more or less openly, as an inherent aspect of a hierarchical society. Henry Alken's *National Sports of Great Britain*, for instance, was a candid apologia for the sports of the landed elite. Objections to coursing on the grounds of cruelty were not to be seriously considered: 'The arguments for its high gratification to those who possess leisure and wealth, more especially in land, and for its undisputed conduciveness to health and hilarity, will ever prove decisive.'[171] There was some distress at the general meeting of the R.S.P.C.A. in 1840 when a person stood up and asked 'the noblemen and gentlemen on the platform, who declaimed upon the subject of cruelty to animals, how many hunters had they in their stables, and how many had been ridden to death for their amusement? (Cries of no,no.)'; but the Society's supporters were quick to defend themselves. 'I, for one,' admitted Lord Dudley C. Stuart, 'keep several hunters, and love the pleasures of the chase as sincerely as any man':

> At the same time, my notion is, that as all animals were made for the use of man, there can be no possible harm in making them conducive to our rational enjoyments, as well as employing them for our profit and convenience; but at the same time, I trust, that I never in my life ill-used any animal to promote my pleasure or amusement; (Hear, hear,) and I believe, generally speaking, that in pursuing the sport of hunting, little or no cruelty is practised. No doubt the stern advocate for humanity may object both to hunting and steeple-chasing as unnecessary, and shooting and fishing would of course come within the same rule; but I think these objections to our national sports may be carried too far, and, so long as unnecessary cruelty is avoided, I see no reason to cry them down on the

---

[168] *Fireside Magazine*, i (1819), 48.   [169] *Stamford News*, 19 November 1819.
[170] *Animals' Friend*, no. 6 (1838), 16.
[171] Alken, *National Sports*, caption for the plate 'Coursing-Death of the Hare'.

score of inhumanity; and I believe it is generally admitted, that the sports of the field, if unavoidably attended with a certain degree of suffering on the one hand, produce, on the other hand, many advantages which might fairly be brought forward as a set-off against the alleged cruelty of such practices. (Hear, hear.)[172]

Popular blood sports, however, could not be discovered to offer any such compensating features. Bull-baiting, for instance, was thought to admit of 'no one palliation that may be urged in excuse of some recreations, which though on principles of humanity, cannot be altogether justified; yet not being marked with any of the *peculiar atrocities* of the other, must not be brought into comparison'.[173] Rationalizations for field sports, however, were not always easily sustained, and some writers found it useful to call upon the will of Providence:

> though having no partiality or fondness for the chace in any form, [we are] yet constrained to believe that there is such a provision made for it by an all-wise Providence in the constitution of man, the instinct of hounds, and even in the strategems and fleetness of the hare herself, who may often have a gratification in eluding or out-stripping her pursuers, as to afford some justification of the practice. It has been strongly argued that the great propensity to field sports, which operates on many like an uncontrolled instinct, is a sure indication of the intention of the Deity, not only to permit, but to stimulate to those pursuits. And here, as in all things else, we may discern wisdom and goodness.[174]

'How shall we account for' the fact, queried another advocate of humanity to animals, 'that in every country and every age of the world, the love of the chase has been the distinguishing characteristic of a considerable portion, and far from being the worst portion, of the community?' It must, he concluded, be a legitimate pastime, not to be compared with the atrocities of plebeian diversions.[175]

Other reasons were sometimes advanced in support of a careful differentiation between popular and genteel recreations. It was argued that protection should be given to animals whenever politically possible, that reform should be pursued with due regard for the limits of public tolerance, and that it was not to be expected that everything could be accomplished at once.[176] Some writers allowed that the elegance, excitement, and refinement of certain genteel amusements compensated in part for the cruelty involved.[177] Unlike the popular sports, genteel diversions had been incorporated into a code of sensibility and refined manners. Moreover, while fashionable pleasures were typically private, enjoyed within the confines of a personal estate, the amusements of the people were

[172] *Fourteenth Annual Report of the R.S.P.C.A.* (1840), pp. 40–1 and 45–6.
[173] Barry, *Bull Baiting*, pp. 8–9.
[174] Drummond, *Rights of Animals*, p. 37; cf. pp. 41 and 44.
[175] Youatt, *Humanity to Brutes*, pp. 109–11.
[176] *Parliamentary Debates*, New series, IX, p. 433 (21 May 1823), and X, p. 133 (11 February 1824); Macaulay, *Cruelty to Animals*, pp. 55–7.
[177] Howitt, *Rural Life* (1838 edn), I, 41–2 and 45; Stockdale, *Inhumanity to Animals*, p. 10n.

normally on public display, open to the view of delicate tastes, and consequently they were much more likely to violate the increasingly severe standards of public decorum. 'Open sin' was the principal concern; private vices were not as socially dangerous.[178] The degree of a diversion's publicness significantly conditioned the extent to which there might be a concern for its regulation. 'The Legislature ought to interfere for the protection of animals, wherever public control can be extended,' suggested one writer, 'although it may be deemed impossible to regulate the conduct of individuals in regard to their own property.'[179] Property, as always, was a substantial deterrent to incautious public meddling.

There was as well a pronounced and appreciating general bias against recreations which were public and in favour of domestic pleasures, and such a view was bound to accentuate any established animosities towards popular traditions. The amusements of Christians 'should be rather of a private, than a public and gregarious, kind', opined a contributor to the *Christian Observer* in 1805.[180] 'That the human mind requires recreation, experience proves', admitted an essay of 1827; 'but where the taste is not vitiated, the necessary recreation is more easily and satisfactorily found in domestic privacy, than in the haunts of dissipation and vice, or even in large assemblies of a better character.'[181] Here, then, was a basis for another direct clash of sentiment: while respectability increasingly favoured family relaxation, the traditional pastimes were mostly of a public character, conditioned by their involvement in crowded settings, and hence were out of tune with the newer tastes. The home was a sanctuary and its 'fireside comforts' were the highest rewards. And since these satisfactions were imagined to be accessible to all – 'these best pleasures of our nature the Almighty has put within the reach of the poor no less than the rich', thought Wilberforce[182] – there was no reason to encourage the continuance of more primitive recreational habits. The older usages were incapable of providing genuine pleasure. Happiness, argued William Howitt, 'does not consist in booths and garlands, drums and horns, or in capering around a May-pole. Happiness is a fireside thing. It is a thing of grave and earnest tone; and the deeper and truer it is, the more is it removed from the riot of mere merriment.'[183]

Perhaps the most important basis for the discriminating treatment of recreational practices was the accepted, long-standing distinction between a life of leisure, which was a perquisite of gentility, and a life of onerous and involuntary labour, which was a mark of a plebeian existence. For gentlemen recreation was a natural and legitimate part of their culture; for labouring men it was (or could easily become) a dangerous temptation, a distraction from their primary concerns. 'To be born for no other Purpose than to consume the Fruits of the Earth', wrote Henry Fielding, 'is the

---

[178] Brown, *Fathers of the Victorians*, p. 435; Radzinowicz, *English Criminal Law*, III, 182.
[179] Macaulay, *Cruelty to Animals*, p. 42.
[180] *Christian Observer*, V (1805), 13.
[181] *Observations on Some of the Popular Amusements of this Country, Addressed to the Higher Classes of Society* (London, 1827), p. 21.
[182] *Life of Wilberforce*, II, 449.
[183] Howitt, *Rural Life* (1840 edn), p. 420.

Privilege (if it may be really called a Privilege) of very few. The greater Part of Mankind must sweat hard to produce them, or Society will no longer answer the Purposes for which it was ordained.'[184] Diversion (indeed, often diversion in abundance) was an indulgence which the affluent could readily afford, but the common people had to guard themselves, or be protected, from such potentially destructive practices. This was a distinction which was widely acknowledged. For the working people, said Fielding, 'Time and Money are almost synonymous; and as they have very little of each to spare, it becomes the Legislature, as much as possible, to suppress all Temptations whereby they may be induced too profusely to squander either the one or the other; since all such Profusion must be repaired at the Cost of the Public.'[185] It was entirely proper, then, to treat recreation with due regard for the status of its participants – 'In Diversion, as in many other Particulars, the upper Part of Life is distinguished from the Lower' – and to apply the sort of restraints on popular indulgence which would be quite unnecessary for the upper classes.[186] Labour discipline was not to be directed towards men of property; indeed, for them it was socially meaningless. Social regulations dealt only with the lower classes, and among these classes recreation was found to be especially in need of control from above: 'while these classes ought to be protected and encouraged in the enjoyment of their *innocent* amusements,' reported the Society for the Suppression of Vice, 'surely a greater benefit cannot be conferred upon them, than to deprive them of such amusements as tend to impair their health, to injure their circumstances, to distress their families, and to involve them in vice and misery'.[187] Just as the Game Laws discriminated in favour of the sport of gentlemen, and did so with the approval, or at least general acquiescence, of 'public opinion' – 'Rural diversions certainly constitute a very pleasing and proper amusement for all ranks above the lowest', remarked one essayist[188] – so the attacks on traditional recreation accommodated themselves to the circumstances of social and political power, concentrated their attention on the culture of the multitude, and fashioned their moral protest in a manner which was consistent with the requirements of social discipline.

[184] Henry Fielding, *An Enquiry into the Causes of the late Increase of Robbers* (London, 1751), p. 7.
[185] *Ibid.* pp. 11–12; cf. *Life of Wilberforce*, II, 448–9.
[186] Fielding, *Increase of Robbers*, pp. 10–11 and 22–3.
[187] *Address from the Society for the Suppression of Vice*, part ii, p. 61n.
[188] Vicesimus Knox, *Essays Moral and Literary* (2 vols.; London, 1791), II, 153–4.

8
Social change

In an earlier chapter we emphasized the remarkably conservative sentiments, the paternalistic norms and patterns of behaviour, which are evident in the culture of the first half of the eighteenth century. Many gentlemen, with their respect for antiquity, were favourably disposed to tradition, to ritual and ceremony (especially when the ceremony reinforced their own authority), to robust and manly sports, to festive indulgences (as long as they were not too disorderly or expensive), to old, time-honoured customs; and they were little inclined to meddle with the people's affairs on the grounds of religion or morality. Old-fashioned paternalism included a large dose of tolerance – tolerance, of course, within certain well understood limits – and as J. H. Plumb has recently reminded us, 'Patriarchalism remained a powerful feature in English social attitudes' after the Restoration.[1] A defence of the Book of Sports, published in 1708, was just one expression of this hardy strain of Tory traditionalism, vehemently antipuritan in temper:

> from that time [the death of Charles I] to this, we have been loaded with the pretended Statutes of Reformation; Laws, which if they were to be strictly executed, a Man must not be allow'd to drink a Pot of Ale, or take a Walk in the Fields, or play at Cudgels, or go to the Morrice Dancers, or any such innocent things on the Sabbath Day. But, Thanks be to God, the Awe of these things, which by the Policy of our Puritanical Invaders, was impresssed on the Minds of Our People, begins to wear off again; and were we but once rid of some of our pretended Zealots for good Manners, whose Pretences have still made too much Impression, even in our Days; We might have some Hopes that those Days of Liberty might be restor'd . . . [2]

The puritan outlook, however, was by no means banished. Restoration and eighteenth-century dissent helped to keep alive at least some of the old belief, including its antagonism towards 'idle customs'. 'Lord ever keep me in good and sober Company,' wrote a Lancashire nonconformist in his diary for 26 May 1738, 'and ever give Grace and Strength to watch and guard against mad Frolicks, foolish Sports, unseasonable and dishonourable Diversions, and wicked and sinful Irregularities' (he had been to the races that afternoon).[3] By the middle of the eighteenth century

---

[1] J. H. Plumb, 'Plantation Power', *New York Review of Books*, XIV, no. 4 (26 February 1970), 16.

[2] *A Briefe Defence of the several Declarations of King James the First, and King Charles the First, Concerning Lawful Recreations on Sundays* (n.p., 1708), p. 24.

[3] *Diary of Richard Kay*, p. 23.

Methodism was helping to reinvigorate this tradition of 'ethical rigorism'.[4] We have also stressed the strength and prevalence of those sentiments which favoured a rigorous labour discipline, and those were probably of even greater significance than the tradition of religious austerity (though the two outlooks were often closely related). Many of the commentators on social and economic issues, and others as well, were keenly opposed to the habits of popular leisure; their concern for economic growth allowed slight sympathy for activities not obviously productive. To them what was of doubtful economic value could only be deplored, and theirs was a view which was acquiring appreciating support.

These, in fact, were the two dominant types of social outlook, and both traditions were vigorously alive around the beginning of the eighteenth century; they offered competing standards for assessing social behaviour and they represented opposing models of the desirable society – the one essentially backward-looking, the other energetically 'progressive'. The century after the Restoration can be seen as a period of transition in a specific sense: during these years the two principal traditions existed side by side as the crucial ingredients in a cultural admixture, and it was not until the second half of the eighteenth century that the victory of one tradition, and the disintegration of the other, can be clearly discerned. It is important to appreciate the resilience of the conservative tradition, especially the habit of paternalism, and to recognize its continuing hold on social attitudes, for there is a danger that its prevalence and power may be underestimated: historians are sometimes inclined to pronounce the death of decaying traditions long before their actual expiry.

In the later seventeenth and early eighteenth centuries many men were still intensely suspicious of 'enthusiasm', of pleas for reform, of moral earnestness, and they reserved their favour for moderation, stability, and a cautious worldliness. In contrast to the earlier and later periods, the voice of reform was relatively muted. Sabbatarian sentiments, for instance, appear to have subsided during these years; certainly they were considerably less intense than they had been before 1660, or were to be from the later eighteenth century. Writing of Sunday observance, Edmund Gibson, Bishop of London, opined that

> they who on all other days are confin'd to hard Labour, or are otherwise oblig'd to a close attendance on their worldly Affairs, must be allow'd in some measure to consider this as a Day of Ease and Relaxation from Thought and Labour, as well as a Day of Devotion; provided it be in a way that is innocent and inoffensive, and that the Publick offices of Religion be duly attended.[5]

Although much of the puritan doctrine survived, especially the concern for industriousness, it was partly submerged by the traditionalism of the period; many of the puritan beliefs had been placed very much on the defensive and had come to be regarded as distinctly disreputable. The tide

---

[4] John A. Newton, *Methodism and the Puritans* (Friends of Dr Williams's Library, Eighteenth Lecture, 1964), pp. 16–17.

[5] *The Bishop of London's Pastoral Letter to the People of His Diocese* (London, 1728), p. 46; cf. John Howell, *A Practical Discourse on the Lord's Day* (London, 1704), pp. 223–30.

of reform, which had been so powerful during the first half of the seventeenth century, was checked and contained for three of four generations.
A definite leniency towards popular customs and practices became noticeable,[6] and the measured voices of social criticism were now found to
speak in restrained, nicely modulated tones. One writer, for instance, while
supporting a respectful observance of the Sabbath, suggested that

> Besides times of Rest on the Lords day, which they [Masters] ought,
> and are bound to allow their Servants, they should think of it, and
> allow them sometimes to recreate themselves: The Church hath
> Constituted Holy-days, and though they ought principally to be
> kept, by performing in them Holy and Religious Exercises, yet
> without doubt sports and pastimes at seasonable times may be used
> on these days: And Merciful Masters, if their Servants keep the
> Church duly, and be present at publique Prayers on Holy-days,
> they should allow them Liberty to Recreate themselves on these
> days, to use sports and pastimes.[7]

The recollections of the puritan revolution helped to impress upon many
men's minds the utility of cautiousness, of moderation, and of customary
practices.

The limited influence of 'reformist' views can be explained in part by
the fact that they had not yet conquered the culture of the countryside.
Their main bases of support, the environments in which they flourished,
were the urban and industrial regions. It was in these areas that the concern
for labour discipline was moulded and formulated and from them that
the appeals arose: John Clayton was based in Manchester, William
Temple and Josiah Tucker in the commercial and manufacturing districts
of the West Country; much of the sentiment for reform stemmed from
London. (It is significant that fairs in London were being attacked in the
late seventeenth and early eighteenth centuries, long before they became
matters for serious concern in other parts of the country.)[8] Most of the
social criticism concerning the work force was focused on the manufacturing people and the urban poor, not the agricultural labourers; disciplining the common people was thought to be especially (though not
exclusively) an urban problem. John Houghton, for instance, thought that
'the generality of the poor are very lazy and expensive, especially the
manufacturers, as may be seen in London, Norwich, Manchester, and

---

[6] It appears, for instance, that there was very little official concern during the first quarter
of the eighteenth century for the regulation of public houses or the activities which
they supported. See the Webbs, *History of Liquor Licensing*, pp. 20–1; and R. F. Brether-
ton, 'Country Inns and Alehouses', in Reginald Lennard (ed.), *Englishmen at Rest and
Play: Some Phases of English Leisure 1558–1714* (Oxford, 1931), pp. 175–80 for a
discussion of the lenient licensing policy during the years 1660–1714.

[7] Nicholas Smith, *A Sabbath of Rest to be kept by the Saints* (London, 1675), p. 23.

[8] On the reform efforts in London, see Bahlman, *Moral Revolution, passim*: E. G. Dowdell,
A Hundred Years of Quarter Sessions: The Government of Middlesex from 1660 to 1760
(Cambridge, 1932), pp. 27–33; Radzinowicz, *English Criminal Law*, ii, chap. 1;
Cornelius Walford, *Fairs, Past and Present* (London, 1883), pp. 213–16 and chap. 18;
and Sybil Rosenfeld, *The Theatre of the London Fairs in the 18th Century* (Cambridge,
1960), *passim*.

several other places'.[9] This was where the emphasis was normally placed. 'The Diversion of Cricket may be proper in Holiday-Time, in the Country', thought one writer, 'but upon Days when men ought to be busy, and in the Neighbourhood of a great City, it is not only improper but mischievous in a high Degree.'[10] Rural diversions were much more readily tolerated than their counterparts in the city, especially in London:

> In the Country the Plowman, the Labourer, and the Artificer, are satisfied with their Holydays at Easter, Whitsuntide, and Christmas. At the two former they enjoy their innocent Sports, such as a Cricket-Match, or a Game at Cudgels, or some other laudable Trial of Manhood, to the Improvement of English Courage. At Christmas they partake of the good Cheer of that Season, and return satisfy'd to their Labour: But in this Town [London], Diversions calculated to slacken the Industry of the useful Hands are innumerable: To lessen therefore the Number of these, is the Business of the magistrate.[11]

The concern for discipline, vigorously and repeatedly asserted, was very much a product of urban-industrial society, for it was in these areas (the industrial villages, the textile centres, the metropolis) that contractual relations particularly predominated and paternalist authority was least effectual, that class antagonisms were most acutely developed, that employment was least secure, and that population density was highest; consequently it was here that the problems of social control were most keenly sensed and most closely studied. Adam Smith, with characteristic insight, touched on one of the central issues of social control. 'While he remains in a country village', he said of the labouring man, 'his conduct may be attended to, and he may be obliged to attend to it himself. In this situation . . . he may have what is called a character to lose. But as soon as he comes into a great city, he is sunk in obscurity and darkness. His conduct is observed and attended to by nobody, and he is therefore very likely to neglect it himself, and to abandon himself to every sort of low profligacy and vice.'[12] It was this lack of 'natural' sources of discipline, then, which particularly prompted reformers to concentrate their attention on the problems of urban society.

In agricultural regions the impact of 'reform' was relatively slight. The late seventeenth- early eighteenth-century movement for the reformation of manners, for example, seems to have been concentrated in London and the larger provincial towns; in the countryside it enjoyed only fleeting and usually hesitant support, if any at all.[13] 'Country clergymen, in particular – clergymen interested in the cause of reformation like James Smith of Cambridgeshire or Samuel Wesley of Lincolnshire – felt that reforming societies, although they might serve the cause in cities, were difficult to

[9] John Houghton, A Collection for the Improvement of Husbandry and Trade, ed. Richard Bradley (4 vols.; London, 1727–8), II, 283, from an essay of 16 April 1698.
[10] Gentleman's Magazine, XIII (1743), 486.
[11] Public Advertiser, 2 September 1757.
[12] Cannan (ed.), Wealth of Nations, II, 280.
[13] Bahlman, Moral Revolution, passim; Lennard (ed.), Englishmen at Rest and Play, p. 179.

organize in the country and relatively ineffective.'[14] There are few indications that much was being done in rural areas to curtail Sunday sports,[15] and numerous pieces of evidence suggest that Sunday recreations continued to be practised, and occasionally even condoned. In 1752 the parish of Owston, Lincolnshire, reported: 'The parishioners not very regular, especially the young people as to keeping the Lord's day free from sports and diversions.'[16] It was reputed that Thomas Robinson, rector of Ousby, Cumberland, in the early eighteenth century, was accustomed, 'after Sunday afternoon prayers, to accompany the leading men of his parish to the adjoining ale-house, where each man spent a penny, and only a penny: that done, he set the younger sort to play at foot-ball, (of which he was a great promoter) and other rustical diversions'.[17] A contributor to Hone's *Every-Day Book* recalled that 'When a boy, football was commonly played on a Sunday morning, before church time, in a village in the west of England, and the church-piece was the ground chosen for it.'[18] Many country gentlemen were still sympathetically disposed to established customs and were not inclined to judge them overly nicely on 'moral' grounds; they were concerned to preserve their reputations according to traditional standards, and for the most part they were willing to accede to the conventional expectations concerning the customs of their localities and their own social responsibilities. Toryism remained strong, and it staved off, though only temporarily, the pressures for moral improvement, most of which were city-based. Christopher Hill has pointed to and highlighted this contrast of outlooks:

> After 1660 there is an almost self-conscious anti-Puritanism in the Anglican-dominated countryside. Great propaganda emphasis was laid on the alleged kill-joy activities of the major-generals and Puritans generally during the interregnum . . . As power was monopolized by the great landed magnates and the monied interest, so the lesser gentry found themselves isolated in their little islands of rural sovereignty. They became more and more resentful, nostalgic, Tory. The almost deliberate rural paganism, cakes and ale, hunting and open-air virtues which they cultivated, were contrasted with the book-keeping sordidness and pettifogging plutocracy of London.

[14] Bahlman, *Moral Revolution*, pp. 97–8.
[15] See for instance Whitaker, *Eighteenth-Century English Sunday*, pp. 33–4.
[16] Joan Varley, 'An Archdiaconal Visitation of Stow, 1752', *Reports and Papers of the Lincolnshire Architectural and Archaeological Society*, New Series, III (1948), 160; cf. Jukes (ed.), *Visitation of Thomas Secker, 1738*, pp. 25, 46, 143, and 150.
[17] Hutchinson, *History of Cumberland*, I, 224n.
[18] Hone, *Every-Day Book*, II, col. 374. For other evidence concerning the customary character of Sunday recreation, see Litt, *Wrestliana*, pp. 51–2; *Gentleman's Magazine*, LXXXIX (1819), part I, 110, and XCII (1822), part I, 223; and *Wesleyan Methodist Magazine*, 3rd series, V (1826), 73–4. As late as the early 1830s it was being claimed by one clergyman that some magistrates, 'on the strength of the "Book of Sports", refuse to interfere with games, except such as are unlawful, on the Sunday'. ('Report from the Select Committee on the Observance of the Sabbath Day', *Parliamentary Papers*, 1831–2, VII, p. 430, evidence of J. W. Cunningham, vicar of Harrow, Middlesex.)

The opposing moralities have their apotheosis in the novels of Fielding and Richardson.[19]

By the end of the eighteenth century the opposition to traditional recreation had clearly gained the upper hand. Refinement had triumphed over rusticity: the violence (or semi-violence), the 'vulgarity' and 'coarseness' of many customary sports were no longer so readily accepted; indeed, it was only after the middle of the century that most gentlemen came to regard them as brutal, gross, and uncivilized. 'The country affords almost as strong instances of cruelty, as [the] town,' declared a moralist in 1765, 'for wrestling, single-stick, or even foot-ball, are never considered as diversions by the common people, but as attended with danger, mischief, or blood-shed.'[20] The spirit of Addison, Steele, and their followers was gradually absorbed by the high culture, and popular and genteel tastes became increasingly dissociated from each other. 'Rude jollity and merriment of country feasts and fairs much less frequent now, than formerly', noted an observer in the early nineteenth century of the villages in the Lincolnshire wolds: 'The refinement of manners, and a greater separation between the different ranks of masters and servants, together with the extending influences of sectarian preachers have repressed much of this old hospitality.'[21] Upper and lower class standards for evaluating social behaviour came to have little in common (considerably less, certainly, than they had had around 1700), and the customs which the people continued to honour were increasingly regarded from above as primitive, disorderly, sometimes immoral, and usually at odds with the basic standards of social propriety. In 1777 John Brand was able to speak of 'the present fashionable Contempt of old Customs'.[22]

The disposition towards traditionalism was gradually weakened by the growing concern for 'improvement', a value which had many faces: refinement of manners, 'rational' tastes, the cultivation of moral sensibilities, restraints imposed on some forms of personal indulgence, the streamlining of certain social and economic practices in the interest of greater efficiency. The gentry, clergy, and large farmers became less and less inclined to conform to many of the older expectations concerning the conduct of their relations with the common people. In the third quarter of the eighteenth century, for instance, the rector of Chinnor, Oxfordshire, dispensed with the custom of entertaining his parishioners at the rectory on Easter Monday, though he continued to support the feast at a public house.[23] The paternalistic norms, especially those of tolerance and obligation, were losing force, and there was a waning interest in the kinds of patronage and ceremonial commitments which had previously been widely accepted. The character of this transition in values is suggestively reflected in a scene from Isaac Bickerstaffe's *Love in a Village*

---

[19] Christopher Hill, *Reformation to Industrial Revolution: A Social and Economic History of Britain 1530–1780* (London, 1967), p. 157.

[20] *Village Memoirs: In a Series of Letters Between a Clergyman and his Family in the Country, and his Son in Town* (London, 1765), p. 76. I am indebted to Mr J. D. Walsh for this reference.

[21] Society of Antiquaries, Edward James Willson Collection (Lincoln), XIII, p. 62.

[22] Brand, *Popular Antiquities*, p. 333.   [23] V. C. H. Oxfordshire, VIII (1964), 75.

(1763): Justice Woodcock is a wealthy and fashion-conscious gentleman, Hodge a servant, and Hawthorn a squire of modest means and traditionalist leanings:

> J. Woodcock. [to Hodge] . . . where have you and the rest of those rascals been? But I suppose I need not ask – You must know there is a statute, a fair for hiring servants, held upon my green to-day, we have it usually at this season of the year, and it never fails to put all the folks here-about out of their senses.
>
> Hodge. Lord your honour look out, and see what a nice shew they make yonder; they had got pipers, and fidlers, and were dancing as I com'd along for dear life – I never saw such a mortal throng in our village in all my born days again.
>
> Hawthorn. Why I like this now, this is as it should be.
>
> J. Woodcock. No, no, 'tis a very foolish piece of business; good for nothing but to promote idleness and the getting of bastards: but I shall take measures for preventing it another year, and I doubt whether I am not sufficiently authorized already: For by an act passed Anno undecimo Caroli primi, which impowers a justice of the peace, who is lord of the manor –
>
> Hawthorn. Come, come, never mind the act, let me tell you this is a very proper, a very useful meeting; I want a servant or two myself, I must go see what your market affords; and you shall go, and the girls, my little Lucy and the other young rogue, and we'll make a day on't as well as the rest.
>
> J. Woodcock. I wish, master Hawthorn, I cou'd teach you to be a little more sedate: why won't you take pattern by me, and consider your dignity – Odds heart, I don't wonder you are not a rich man, you laugh too much ever to be rich.[24]

The Hawthorns of the stage and of social reality were decaying figures: with time the points of contact between popular and propertied culture were very much contracted. Robert Bloomfield, for instance, spoke of the 'hated face' of refinement and the heightened sense of social distance between the poor and the prosperous.[25] In 1821 a cottager from Water-beach, Cambridgeshire, was bitterly lamenting those changes which had undermined the former recreational practices: 'Thirty years ago, pride, avarice, and bigotry had not destroyed the social intercourse between the sons and daughters of the farmers, and the sons and daughters of the labourers of our village.'[26] As a result of the decline of hospitality, and the widening gaps between the social classes, some of the traditional recreational supports were withdrawn. Harvest feasts, for example, were in decline, both in favour and practice, during the first half of the nineteenth century. 'The harvest home is a relic of servile customs', opined one observer, 'and in ancient times was considered a part of the reward

[24] Isaac Bickerstaffe, Love in a Village (London, 1763), act i, scene vi.
[25] Bloomfield, Farmer's Boy, pp. 45–9 (from 'Summer', lines 333ff.).
[26] Denson, Peasant's Voice to Landowners, p. 17. Cf. Hutchinson, Northumberland, ii, Appendix, pp. 5–6; and Richard Polwhele (ed.), The Enthusiasm of Methodists and Papists Considered: by Bishop Lavington (London, 1820), p. cxxi (I am grateful to Mr John Rule for this reference).

for customary services. The present mode of hiring labourers and servants has certainly rendered the custom unnecessary; yet it remains for the farmer to consider how far the prospect of the merry-making stimulates the exertions of the workmen.'[27] Around the 1840s at East Burnham, Buckinghamshire, it was said that 'the labouring people entertained an unpleasant feeling towards the farmers, who, as they considered, disregarded their interests . . . Some of the farmers even gave no "harvest supper;" and I am afraid it must be avowed that between these classes no great friendliness subsisted'.[28]

During this period a solid barrier had developed between the culture of gentility and the culture of the people. In Cornwall genteel sympathy for popular diversions had largely disappeared by the early nineteenth century.[29] In most parts of the country aids for traditional pastimes and acquiescence in their practice were no longer so readily obtained. By the mid-nineteenth century in Northamptonshire mumming was much less frequently observed: 'in this age of refinement few only will allow their dwellings to be made the scene of this antic pastime, as the performers enter uninvited, suddenly throwing open the door, and one after the other enact their different parts'.[30] Such forwardness was not to be tolerated, and the financial solicitations which were customarily associated with diversions of this kind were to be resisted rather than reciprocated. 'If instead of giving them money when they call at their doors,' suggested a Derby resident with regard to the Shrovetide customs, 'people would order the police to take them up under the Vagrant Act, as I believe they can, we should soon get rid of the annual nuisance called foot-ball.'[31] Similarly, the practices and processions of Plough Monday came to be regarded as unacceptable impositions and were increasingly met with hostility:

> On the 8th inst. [January 1816] a number of rude persons, calling themselves Plough Bullocks came to the house of the Rev. Mr. Brook of Tutbury, Staffordshire; and, because he refused to encourage their disorderly conduct by giving them money, they immediately proceeded to commit their usual depredations. Mr. Brook, according to the warning given them at the time, summoned the Ringleader before Sir Oswald Mosley, one of his Majesty's Justices of the Peace; who, after a severe but just reprimand, ordered him to pay costs and damages, and the sum of ten shillings to the poor of Tutbury. Weak and ignorant people commonly suppose, that persons calling themselves Plough Bullocks have a right, on a certain day, wantonly to commit depredations upon the premises of those who refuse to give them money: but nothing can

---

[27] Dunkin, *History of Bicester*, p. 270; cf. Hone, *Every-Day Book*, II, cols. 788–9, and *Year Book*, cols. 1,069–70 and 1,172.
[28] *Account of East Burnham*, pp. 44–5.
[29] Rule, 'Labouring Miner in Cornwall', p. 77.
[30] Baker, *Northamptonshire Words*, II, 429; cf. Giles, *History of Bampton*, p. lxv, and William Sandys, *Christmas Carols, Ancient and Modern* (London, 1833), p. cvii.
[31] *Derby Mercury*, 28 February 1844.

be more erroneous, or more reproachful to the laws of the country. The rude persons here referred to, who from year to year infest certain parts of the country, extorting money from the ignorant and unwary, are a great public nuisance; therefore, to suppress such disorderly and outrageous proceedings, we cannot help recommending all persons to withstand their violence, by accusing them to the magistrates. All such legal prosecutions, will obtain the sanction and encouragement, as well as the desired redress, from those in authority; and will assuredly be a public benefit to society.[32]

A letter in the *Derby Mercury* of 9 January 1817 expressed the same point of view: 'The ignorant and unwary imagine that these lawless vagabonds have a legal right to pursue their disgraceful practices; who are so ignorant and infatuated, as to appeal for proof to the custom of the country, and the authority of their Almanacks!'[33]

It should be noted, however, that there were still a number of gentlemen who, for a variety of reasons, continued to support the traditional practices and very much regretted their demise. Recreations continued to be regarded by some gentlemen as useful social tranquillizers: they encouraged cheerfulness, mollified the people's discontents, diverted their attention from political concerns, and sometimes served as occasions of harmless tension-release. They were thought to contribute to the stability of the existing social order; they helped to dampen down conflict and to reinforce sentiments of social well-being. This, for instance, was one of the arguments which William Windham advanced against the early efforts to outlaw bull-baiting.[34] Robert Slaney declared that without recreation, the common people would 'become gloomy, morose, and dissatisfied, and would be ready on every opportunity to break into riot and rebellion'. 'In order that the poorer classes should be happy and contented,' he argued,

---

[32] *Derby Mercury*, 1 February 1816.

[33] See also Howitt, *Rural Life* (1840), pp. 471–2, and *Stamford Mercury*, 26 January 1821, 14 January 1848, 15 January 1858, and 15 January 1864. The *Stamford Mercury* of 10 January 1840 expressed amazement at the degree of public support which was still obtained for the Haxey Hood custom in the relatively unprogressive Isle of Axholme: 'to perpetuate this foolish, wicked, and utterly useless custom, the inhabitants almost to an individual provide for and invite their friends on the most extensive scale: even the farmers and respectable householders encourage it, by giving money or corn to the Boggans (Fools) who go from house to house for the purpose of begging on the two following days.' Such resilience was clearly exceptional. (I am indebted to Mr Rex Russell for some of these Lincolnshire references.)

[34] 'The habits long established among the people', he argued in 1802, 'were the best fitted to resist the schemes of innovation; and it was among the labouring and illiterate part of the people that Jacobinical doctrines had made the smallest progress . . . Out of the whole number of the disaffected, he questioned if a single bull-baiter could be found, or if a single sportsman had distinguished himself in the Corresponding Society . . . The efficient part of the community for labour ought to be encouraged in their exertions, rather by furnishing them with occasional amusements, than by depriving them of one . . . for, if to poverty were to be added a privation of amusements, he knew nothing that could operate more strongly to goad the mind into desperation, and to prepare the poor for that dangerous enthusiasm which was analogous to Jacobinism.' (*Parliamentary History*, xxxvi, pp. 833–4 and 839, debate of 24 May 1802.)

it is not enough that they have adequate wages, and are thereby insured against poverty and sickness in old age. Privation of suffering is not enjoyment: that they may be cheerful at labour, they should have the reasonable hope of relaxation from toil before them, and look to a holiday occasionally for amusement. This is of the utmost consequence, not merely to the poor, but to the security of the great. The main title by which the few who are rich hold possession is, that the many who are not be contented and amused.[35]

Some of the defenders of traditional sports stressed the encouragement they gave to manly discipline and to martial qualities. Sport, it was argued, was the training ground for courage, perseverance, physical vigour, and group loyalty. This was a view which had often been expressed. Athletic sports, thought one writer, 'are an excellent preparation for the military exercises, and render men fit to become defenders of the country'.[36] William Windham claimed of the common people that 'it is not unfair to attribute to their manly amusements much of that valour which is so conspicuous in their martial achievements by sea and land. Courage and humanity seem to grow out of their wholesome exercises.'[37] Similarly, a correspondent who approved of the Derby Shrovetide football match remarked that 'I did not see a blow given, nor hear an oath uttered, and could not help anticipating what the power and spirit of these men would be who strove so hard for such an object, whenever their energy should be called forth in their country's service.'[38]

With the full development of a capitalist society, and the consequent aggravation of class hostilities, men of conservative leanings were inclined to entertain a longing for a social order of patriarchal harmony, the sort of order which some of them associated with community recreations. 'It is an important consideration', wrote one parson, 'whether a great means of promoting good-will between the different ranks of society, has not been wholly lost by suffering the old popular meetings [for sports and pastimes] to fall into disuse . . . Old England once had its joyous holidays, when master met man, no longer as his superior, but as his fellow and brother.'[39] This was the theme of a tract by Lord John Manners, *A Plea for National Holy-Days* (1843): the dominant ideal was that of the organic society, harmoniously structured on paternalist lines.[40] If wakes were to be properly regulated, suggested another observer, 'they have a powerful tendency to do away with the want of fellow-feeling, which now subsists

[35] Slaney, *Rural Expenditure*, pp. 130 and 195–6; cf. pp. 124–8. See also Lord John Manners, *A Plea for National Holy-Days* (London, 1843), p. 19.

[36] Lawrence, *Treatise on Horses*, II, 9. Cf. John Godfrey, *A Treatise Upon the Useful Science of Defence* (London, 1747), dedication; and A. Jones, *The Art of Playing at Skittles: or, the Laws of Nine-Pins displayed* (London, 1773), pp. 9–11.

[37] *Parliamentary History*, XXXV, p. 206, debate of 18 April 1800. Cf. *Pierce Egan's Book of Sports*, p. 11, col. 2, and p. 170, col. 1; and J. C. Reid, *Bucks and Bruisers: Pierce Egan and Regency England* (London, 1971), pp. 12–13, 20, and 134–5.

[38] *Derby Mercury*, 9 February 1815.

[39] J. A. Giles, *History of Witney* (London, 1852), p. 57.

[40] See also *A Letter to Lord John Manners, M.P., on His Late Plea for National Holy-Days, by a Minister of the Holy Catholic Church* (London, 1843).

among the different degrees of men amongst us, and to bind all classes of
the people together in one bond of Christian sympathy and love'.[41]

But these had become very much minority concerns well before the
mid-nineteenth century. With the exception of some traditional squires,
nostalgic Tories, gentlemen of pleasure, and of course many of the common
people themselves, the decline of 'rude diversions' and of 'vulgar games'
was generally applauded. It was reported in 1848, for example, that 'the
silly pagan custom, happily sinking into desuetude, of men's parading
the streets dressed in colored rags and white external petticoats, was
practised at Louth by half a dozen money-hunters on Monday last (Plough
Monday)',[42] and this was the kind of 'progressive' view which was most
often heard and most widely supported, at least among the people who
counted – people of the middle class, evangelicals, the moulders of public
opinion, and (increasingly) members of the landowning class. For the
most part popular diversions were no longer sanctioned, and all sorts of
customary practice were being subjected to close examination. 'Ancient
customs are very well in their way . . . but some are indeed more honoured
in the breach than in the observance', as one source mildly put it.[43] 'I
know of nothing more detracting to the respectability of our town',
wrote an inhabitant of Derby, 'than the beastly and disgusting exhibition,
absurdly called the "Foot-ball play" . . . This relic of barbarism, for it
deserves not a better name, is wholly inconsistent with the intelligence and
the spirit of improvement which now characterize the people of Derby.'[44]
This was a typical outlook, only expressed here with particular vigour.
'Seen at hand,' confessed William Howitt, 'there is a vulgarity in most
popular customs that offends invariably our present tastes.'[45]

Around the end of the eighteenth century an aggressive moral earnestness
re-emerged in public life, sweeping aside much of the complacency which
remained and galvanizing men for the task of moral reform. 'Is it not a
palpable truth,' asked Henry Zouch in 1786, 'that a spirit of unbounded
licentiousness is gone forth, and every where pervades the land?'[46] 'Moral'
considerations rose to the forefront in public debate, imposing increasingly
rigorous criteria for the assessment of every form of social behaviour.
Moral values were more vigorously injected into play activities, and it
came to be assumed (as one historian has said) that 'if recreation was
permissible at all, it must be "rational" and must prepare mind and body
for work, instead of being an end in itself '.[47] 'Rational amusement' became a Victorian cliché, an expression of approval only for those pleasures
which were patently moral and improving in intent. The new, more militant
morality came to be widely accepted and powerfully promoted, and its

[41] Bowstead, Village Wake, p. 9.   [42] Stamford Mercury, 14 January 1848.
[43] Stamford Mercury, 15 January 1864.
[44] Derby and Chesterfield Reporter, 9 February 1844.
[45] Howitt, Rural Life (1838), II, 151.   [46] Zouch, Public Police, p. 16.
[47] 'Work and Leisure in Industrial Society: Conference Report', Past & Present, no. 30
    (April 1965), 101, comment of B. H. Harrison. For a general statement concerning some
    of the aspects and implications of 'rational amusement', see the comments of Baptist
    W. Noel in 'Minutes of the Committee of Council on Education', Parliamentary Papers,
    1841, xx, p. 172.

most zealous advocates were energetic and persevering in the cause of
reform. One such activist was Denys Rolle, Esq., of Devon, whose
obituary in 1797 pointed out that

> As a magistrate, he was remarkably attentive to the morals of the
> people within his district, and successively laboured, though with
> great and long opposition, in suppressing village-alehouses, cock-
> fighting, and bull-baiting. Torrington, near which his seat stands,
> was a place much disgraced with these worse than savage diversions,
> and Mr Rolle took extraordinary pains to correct the evil. For this
> evil he not only exerted his authority, as a magistrate, with great zeal
> and impartiality, but circulated large impressions of a pamphlet,
> written by himself, against such cruel amusements. In 1789 he printed
> an address to the nobility and gentry, circulated privately, calling
> for their concurrence in the great object which he had in view, of
> parochial reformation.[48]

A closer regulation of popular behaviour, an improvement in the
common people's tastes and morals, a reform of their habitual vices,
the instilling in them of discipline and orderliness: these were some of the
principal objectives of the movement for the reformation of manners
which arose in the later 1780s and matured during the following half
century. By the early years of Victoria's reign there must have been few
localities which were not experiencing the efforts of parson or squire,
employer or chapel, philanthropic lady or temperance reformer, Bible
society or charitable foundation, to civilize the labouring people and to
enlighten them as to their real interests. A memorandum of a Sunday
School teacher in Fulletby, Lincolnshire, in 1846 is just one illustration of
a movement which had penetrated virtually all corners of the land, though
not always without opposition; before the Sunday school was established
(around 1826), he said,

> the sabbath day in our village was awfully desecrated. The young
> men and youths, and some of the married men too, usually spent
> the chief part of the day in playing games of chance, football, nur-
> spell, etc. by which the rising generation were allured to sabbath-
> breaking; and were brought under the demoralizing influence of
> wicked pursuits, and evil company.

Under the counteracting influence of the Sunday School a change
for the better soon began to manifest itself; and though there was
still much sabbath-breaking and immorality among our youth, to
lament over, gambling on the Sabbath day was almost abolished until
the present year, when it has been revived by the farm servants in
the village; a set of raw, thoughtless, youths who have never had the
moral training of a Sunday School.

The revival of these pastimes on the Sabbath has already had its

---

[48] *Gentleman's Magazine*, LXVII (1797), part II, 1,125. See also the interesting account of
  genteel doubts about the staging of a popular drama in the *Monthly Magazine*, VI
  (1798), 9–10; and E. P. Thompson, *Education and Experience* (Leeds U.P., Fifth
  Mansbridge Memorial Lecture, 1968), pp. 9–14, which includes a lengthy extract from
  this source.

influence upon our Sunday School; and has given me considerable pain, and not a little trouble. Sometimes a few of the elder boys will come in late – hurried – and confused, and on inquiring the cause I have ascertained that a game at football was being played somewhere in the parish, and thus some have been tempted to impinge upon the hours allotted to school, and others who ought to be present to play trauant. The evil is further manifested by their inattention; their thoughts are so full of play that for the rest of the time it is difficult to engage their attention, or to prevent them from whispering to each other; and on leaving school they have eagerly ran off to the forbidden pastime, and I have only mourned to see the seed I have been attempting to sow fall by the way side, to be trodden under-foot, or devoured by the fowls of the air.[49]

'A mighty revolution has taken place in the sports and pastimes of the common people', wrote William Howitt at the beginning of Victoria's reign.[50] During the previous century the character of popular leisure had been very substantially overhauled, and most of these remarkable changes had occurred, or at least been significantly accelerated, since about the 1780s. The recreational culture of the Cornish miners, for example, was very noticeably eroded during the late eighteenth and early nineteenth centuries.[51] Virtually all contemporaries were in agreement concerning the basic facts of this trend, even when their assessments differed sharply. 'The few remnants of our old Sports and Pastimes are rapidly disappearing,' observed an Oxfordshire parson, 'and this is, in my opinion, a change much to be lamented.'[52] Football was said by a writer in 1823 to be 'an exercise which has dwindled down to nothing, compared to the estimation in which it was formerly held'.[53] 'In my own recollection,' said Howitt, 'the appearance of morris-dancers, guisers, plough-bullocks, and Christmas carollers, has become more and more rare, and to find them we must go into the retired hamlets of Staffordshire, and the dales of Yorkshire and Lancashire.'[54]

The decline of popular recreation, it is clear, was intimately associated with the gradual breakdown of what we now call 'traditional society'. With the rise of a market economy, and the accompanying development of new normative standards and material conditions for the conduct of social relations, the foundations of many traditional practices were relentlessly swept away, leaving a vacuum which would be only gradually re-occupied, and then of necessity by novel or radically revamped forms of diversion. Traditional recreation was rooted in a social system which was

[49] Lincolnshire R.O., 'Fulletby Sunday School, The Teacher's Diary 1846', Winn. 1/2, pp. 2–3.
[50] Howitt, *Rural Life* (1840), p. 515.
[51] Rule, 'Labouring Miner in Cornwall', pp. 76–80.
[52] Giles, *History of Witney*, p. 57; cf. Joseph Kay, *The Social Condition and Education of the People in England and Europe* (2 vols.; London, 1850), I, 231.
[53] Litt, *Wrestliana*, p. 51; cf. Frederick Gale, *Modern English Sports: Their Use and their Abuse* (London, 1885), p. 49.
[54] Howitt, *Rural Life* (1840), p. 422.

predominantly agrarian, strongly parochial in its orientations, marked by a deep sense of corporate identity; it could not be comfortably absorbed into a society which was urban-centred, governed by contractual relations, biased towards individualism, increasingly moulding its culture in a manner appropriate to the requirements of industrial production. In the new world of congested cities, factory discipline, and free enterprise, recreational life had to be reconstructed – shaped to accord with the novel conditions of non-agrarian, capitalistic society – and the reconstruction was only gradually accomplished over a period of several generations. One indication of the very limited supply of alternative (and attractive) forms of diversion during much of the nineteenth century is the overwhelming importance of the public house as a recreational centre for the common people. 'In England,' thought Joseph Kay, 'it may be said that the poor, have now no relaxation, but the alehouse or the gin palace.'[55] Although this was an exaggeration, it was an understandable one. 'At present,' remarked Robert Slaney in 1833, 'the poor workman in the large manufacturing town, was actually forced into the public house, there being no other place for him to amuse himself in.'[56] And by this time conditions in the countryside were often not much different. In the short run, then, in this period of exceptionally acute social change, the dislocation of recreational life was keenly felt and only marginally alleviated. The low point of this particular process of social depression was roughly coincident with the second quarter of the nineteenth century: much of the traditional culture had disintegrated, and the new possibilities were only beginning to emerge. The reshaping of popular leisure was largely a phenomenon of the period after 1850.

[55] Kay, *Social Condition*, I, 231.
[56] *Parliamentary Debates*, 3rd series, xv, p. 1,054, debate of 21 February 1833.

Appendix

THE REFORM MOVEMENT AGAINST CRUELTY
TO ANIMALS

The Society for the Suppression of Vice (founded in 1802) was incidentally concerned with attacking cruelty to animals, and in 1809 a Society for the Suppression of Wanton Cruelty to Animals was formed in Liverpool;[1] however, it was only in the second quarter of the century that the cause of humanity to animals came to be represented by a distinctive and significant reform movement. The formation of the Society for the Prevention of Cruelty to Animals in 1824, which was to become the dominant society, along with the South Staffordshire Association for the Suppression of Bull-baiting, initiated the movement, though its first decade was very much one of insecurity, disorder, and internal dissension.[2] The R.S.P.C.A. was in frequent financial difficulties; its concentration on the prosecution of offenders and its use of paid informers were under attack from another society, the Association for Promoting Rational Humanity Towards the Animal Creation (organized by a group of secessionists from the R.S.P.C.A.), which enjoyed a brief existence from 1830 or 1831 until 1833; and in 1832 one of the R.S.P.C.A.'s prominent members, Lewis Gompertz, left the organization after a quarrel with his associates and set up his own group, the Animals' Friend Society for the Prevention of Cruelty to Animals.[3] The societies enjoyed only partial public favour, for they were thought by many observers to be guilty of meddlesome and fanatical behaviour. The movement was also unsettled by the activities of fraudulent (or at least dubious) societies, whose promoters' main interest

[1] Brown, *Fathers of the Victorians*, pp. 407–8; Maurice J. Quinlan, *Victorian Prelude: A History of English Manners 1700–1830* (New York, 1941; repr. 1965), p. 206; Arthur W. Moss, *Valiant Crusade: The History of the R.S.P.C.A.* (London, 1961), pp. 20–1 and plate following p. 52.

[2] The main sources for the early history of the R.S.P.C.A., all of which are held in the Society's London offices, are the following: MS Minute Book for 1824–32; MS Minute Books nos. 1–4 for 1832–42; and the printed *Annual Reports* for 1832–43. I am indebted to the Society for permission to consult its early records and to several of its officers, especially Mr T. Richardson, for their personal attentiveness. Further evidence on the Society may be found in Lewis Gompertz, *Fragments in Defence of Animals* (London, 1852), pp. 173–80 and 273–7. On the Staffordshire society see Frederick W. Hackwood, *A History of West Bromwich* (Birmingham, 1895), p. 115, and John F. Ede, *History of Wednesbury* (Wednesbury, 1962), p. 155.

[3] The evidence relating to the Association is to be found in the *Voice of Humanity*, 3 vols., 1830–3; see also the long article on 'The Voice of Humanity' in the *Bristol Mercury*, 20 March 1832. The establishment of the Association itself seems to have succeeded the founding of the journal; during its first year the *Voice of Humanity* was sympathetically disposed towards the R.S.P.C.A. For details on the Animals' Friend Society, see the *Animals' Friend*, nos. 1–9, 1833–41; and Gompertz, *Defence of Animals*.

was the financial return forthcoming from zealous and gullible animal lovers.[4]

The R.S.P.C.A. began to establish itself more securely after the early 1830s: by 1835 it had an energetic and full-time secretary; in 1836 a timely legacy of £1,000 allowed it to consolidate its position and expand its programme (and in particular to intensify its campaign against the Stamford bull-running); and with time its supporters grew in numbers and its income became more substantial, especially after royal patronage was granted in 1840. Thereafter it enjoyed relative security. Faced with such a prospering competitor – which was accused, and not unjustly, with paying 'extreme and intrusive adulation . . . to nobility and rank'[5] – the Animals' Friend Society quickly collapsed, and by the mid-1840s it was no longer issuing any publications or otherwise exercising influence.

Blood sports occupied only a portion, and not the major portion, of the societies' energies. The societies were, however, partly responsible for some of the developments discussed in Chapter 7. Both the R.S.P.C.A. and the Animals' Friend Society applied pressure in favour of an effective law on blood sports, and their influence may have had some weight in the enactment of the 1835 Cruelty to Animals Act;[6] the R.S.P.C.A. was a major force behind the suppression of the Stamford bull-running and in the early 1840s it was active in prosecuting cock-fighters; and the Animals' Friend Society was actively involved in the elimination of bull-baiting from the West Midlands. But on the whole it would seem that they played only a secondary role in the decline of blood sports (and especially bull-baiting), for by the time they were actively established only the remnants of these diversions still existed, and though pressure and publicity from London may have hastened their final demise, in the places where they did survive local hostility and intervention was probably of equal, if not greater, importance.

[4] See for instance the *15th Annual Report of the R.S.P.C.A.* (1841), p. 183; and Gompertz, *Defence of Animals*, pp. 177–8. One of these questionable characters was a man named Charles Wheeler, who served briefly as an inspector for the R.S.P.C.A. during its first few years; later he appeared periodically in various incidents connected with the reform movement, on most occasions in an incriminating light: soliciting money under false pretences, misrepresenting one of the other societies, collecting funds for imaginary projects. In the 1830s Wheeler was running a concern known as the Ladies Society for the Suppression of Cruelty to Animals. (*Voice of Humanity*, III (1832–3), 116; *Animals' Friend*, no. 1 (1833), 9; and *Wolverhampton Chronicle*, 3 August 1836.)

[5] Gompertz, *Defence of Animals*, p. 276.

[6] *Ibid.* p. 277.

Select Bibliography

A NOTE ON THE PRIMARY SOURCES

Although there are no categories of manuscript material which are of central importance, one is sometimes able to uncover useful references with the aid of suitable subject indexes. Most of these sources are to be found in the County Record Offices of England, and I visited about a score of these local archives in the course of my research. Recreational activities which attracted the notice of the central authorities can sometimes be investigated in the Public Record Office. The bulk of the primary material, however, has been found in various printed sources. This material falls into five main categories: (1) tracts, pamphlets, essays, sermons, and books which bear on recreational topics; (2) local studies; (3) diaries, journals, memoirs, autobiographies, poetry, and other literary sources; (4) Parliamentary papers; and (5) newspapers and periodicals.

The following listing provides a selective bibliography for the first four of these classes of material. Sources referred to in the text which include only a brief reference to one of our topics have not been listed unless they were acknowledged more than once; many of the local studies, in particular, fall into this category. At the same time some titles which do not appear in the notes are to be found in the bibliography if they relate directly to our general subject. Newspapers and periodicals have been widely sampled. For the eighteenth century the most important of these publications were the *Northampton Mercury*, the *Ipswich Journal*, the *Gentleman's Magazine*, and the *London Magazine*. All of the Stamford papers were consulted for references to the bull-running, the *Stamford Mercury* being the most valuable. For the first half of the nineteenth century particular attention was paid to the Derbyshire press (especially the *Derby Mercury*), *Aris's Birmingham Gazette*, the *Animals' Friend*, and the *Voice of Humanity*. The great majority of the printed sources were consulted in the British Museum, the Bodleian Library, or the Goldsmiths' Library, University of London. Work on local materials was much facilitated by the resources of the Society of Antiquaries.

PRIMARY SOURCES

MANUSCRIPT SOURCES

Bodleian Library
    'Diary of Rev. James Newton of Nuneham Courtenay, Oxon, 1761–62.' MS Eng. misc.
      e. 251.
British Museum
    'Diary of Rev. William Cole.' Add. MS 5835.
    'Diary of Rev. Abraham Maddock, 1765–1771.' Add. MS 40,653.
Royal Society for the Prevention of Cruelty to Animals, 105 Jermyn Street, London,
    S.W.1.
    Minute Book for 1824–32. 1 vol.
    Minute Books nos. 1–4 for 1832–42. 4 vols.
Stamford Town Hall
    Phillips Collection, no. 183. A book of cuttings and miscellaneous notes on the Stamford bull-running.

PRINTED SOURCES

Tracts, pamphlets, essays, sermons, and books (general)

The Genuine Account of the Life and Trial of Eugene Aram, for the Murder of Daniel Clark. London, 1759. Includes an essay on 'The Melsupper, and Shouting the Churn'.

Adams, William. *The Duties of Industry, Frugality and Sobriety. A Sermon Preached before a Society of Tradesmen and Artificers, in the Parish Church of St. Chad, Salop, on Easter-Monday, 1766.* 3rd edn, Shrewsbury, 1770.

An Address to the Public from the Society for the Suppression of Vice. London, 1803.

Alken, Henry. *The National Sports of Great Britain.* London, 1821.

Aspin, Jehoshaphat. *Ancient Customs, Sports, and Pastimes of the English.* London, 1832.

Aubrey, John. *Remaines of Gentilisme and Judaisme.* Edited and annotated by James Britten. London, 1881; repr. 1967.

Barry, Edward, *Bull Baiting! A Sermon on Barbarity to God's Dumb Creation, Preached in the Parish Church of Wokingham, Berkshire, on Sunday the 20th of December, 1801.* Reading, n.d.

A Letter on the Practice of Boxing, Addressed to the King, Lords, and Commons. London, 1789.

Baxter, Richard. *A Christian Directory.* 2nd edn, London, 1678.

Blackhall, Ofspring. *The Lawfulness and the Right Manner of Keeping Christmas and other Festivals: A Sermon Preach'd at the Parish-Church of St Dunstan in the West, upon Christmas-Day, 1704.* 2nd edn, London, 1707.

Blount, Thomas. *Fragmenta Antiquitatis. Antient Tenures of Land, and Jocular Customs of some Mannors.* London, 1679.

Booker, Luke. 'On Humanity to the Brute Creation', in his *Sermons on Various Subjects.* Dudley, 1793.

Bourne, Henry. *Antiquitates Vulgares; or, the Antiquities of the Common People.* Newcastle, 1725.

Bowstead, John. *The Village Wake, or the Feast of the Dedication: Its Religious Observance a Bond of Union Between the Higher and Lower Classes.* London, 1846.

Brady, John. *Clavis Calendaria; or, a Compendious Analysis of the Calendar.* 2 vols.; London, 1812.

Brand, John. *Observations on Popular Antiquities.* Newcastle upon Tyne, 1777. Revised edn by Henry Ellis. 2 vols.; London, 1813.

Bridges, J. *A Book of Fairs, or, A Guide to West-Country Travellers.* n.p., n.d.

Burder, George. *Lawful Amusements; A Sermon, Preached at the Thursday-Evening Lecture Fetter-Lane, January 10, 1805.* 2nd edn, London, 1805.

Caraccioli, Charles. *An Historical Account of Sturbridge, Bury, and the Most Famous Fairs in Europe and America.* Cambridge, 1773.

Chadwick, Edwin. *Report on the Sanitary Condition of the Labouring Population of Great Britain, 1842.* Edited by M. W. Flinn. Edinburgh, 1965.

Chamberlayne, Edward. *Angliae Notitia, or the Present State of England.* London, 1669 (and numerous later edns).

Chester, Greville J. *Statute Fairs: Their Evils and Their Remedy.* York and London, 1856.

Statute Fairs. A Sermon Preached At the Parish Churches of Farndish and Puddington, Beds. London, 1858.

The Young Man at Rest and at Play. A Plain Sermon, Preached to Young Men in 1859, at the Parish Church of St Jude, Moorfields, Sheffield. London and Sheffield, 1860.

Clayton, John. *Friendly Advice to the Poor.* Manchester, 1755.

Clemency to Brutes; The Substance of two Sermons Preached on a Shrove-Sunday. London, 1761.

Close, Francis. *The Evil Consequences of Attending the Race Course Exposed, in a Sermon, Preached in the Parish Church of Cheltenham, on Sunday Morning, June 17th, 1827.* 2nd edn, Cheltenham, 1827.

Considerations on Taxes, as They are Supposed to Affect the Price of Labour in our Manufactures. London, 1765.

Cope, George. *The Origin, Excellence, and Perversion of Wakes or Parish Feasts.* Hereford, 1816.

The Country Clergyman's Shrovetide Gift to His Parishioners. 3rd edn, Sherborne, n.d.

Crowe, Henry. *Animadversions on Cruelty to the Brute Creation, Addressed Chiefly to the Lower Classes.* Bath, 1825.

A Briefe Defence of the Several Declarations of King James the First, and King Charles the First, Concerning Lawful Recreations on Sundays. n.p., 1708.

Denson, John. *A Peasant's Voice to Landowners, on the Best Means of Benefiting Agricultural Labourers, and of Reducing Poor's Rates.* Cambridge, 1830.

Dillon, R. C. *A Sermon on the Evils of Fairs in General and of Bartholomew Fair in Particular.* London, 1830.

A Discourse Concerning the Lawfulness and Right Manner of Keeping Christmas, and other Christian Holy-Days, by Way of Question and Answer. Intended for the Use of a Charity-School. London, 1708.

A Dissuasive from Sabbath-Breaking; Deliver'd in a Sermon on April the 22nd, 1723. Cambridge, 1735.

Drummond, William H. *The Rights of Animals, and Man's Obligation to Treat them with Humanity.* London, 1838.

Dymond, Jonathon, *Essays on the Principles of Morality, and on the Private and Political Rights and Obligations of Mankind.* 2 vols.; London, 1829.

Edwards, H. *A Collection of Old English Customs, and Curious Bequests and Charities, Extracted from the Reports Made by the Commissioners for Enquiring into Charities in England and Wales.* London, 1842.

Egan, Pierce. *Pierce Egan's Book of Sports and Mirror of Life.* London, 1832.

An Essay on Trade and Commerce. London, 1770.

Fetherston, Christopher. *A Dialogue agaynst light, lewde, and lascivious dauncing.* London, 1582.

Fielding, Henry. *An Enquiry into the Causes of the late Increase of Robbers.* London, 1751. *A Proposal for Making an Effectual Provision for the Poor.* London, 1753.

Fletcher, John. *An Appeal to Matter of Fact and Common Sense.* Bristol, 1772.

Godfrey, John. *A Treatise upon the Useful Science of Defence, Connecting the Small and Back-Sword, and Shewing the Affinity between Them.* London, 1747.

Godschall, William M. *A General Plan of Parochial and Provincial Police.* London, 1787.

Gompertz, Lewis. *Fragments in Defence of Animals.* London, 1852.

Granger, James. *An Apology for the Brute Creation, or Abuse of Animals censured.* London, 1772.

Hall, Thomas. *Funebria Florae, The Downfall of May-Games.* 3rd edn, London, 1661.

Hanway, Jonas. *Virtue in humble life.* 2 vols.; London, 1774.

Henslow, J. S. *Suggestions Towards an Enquiry into the Present Condition of the Labouring Population of Suffolk.* Hadleigh, 1844.

[Hill, Sir Richard.] *A Letter to the Right Hon. William Windham, on his Late Opposition to the Bill to Prevent Bull-Baiting.* 2nd edn, London, n.d.

Hone, William. *The Every-Day Book.* 2 vols.; London, 1825–7.
   The Table Book. 2 vols.; London, 1827–8.
   The Year Book. London, 1832.

Houghton, John. *A Collection of Letters for the Improvement of Husbandry and Trade.* 2 vols.; London, 1681–3.

Howitt, William. *The Rural Life of England.* 2 vols.; London, 1838. 2nd edn, London, (1 vol.), 1840.

Jenyns, Soame. 'On Cruelty to Inferior Animals', in his *Disquisitions on Several Subjects.* London, 1782.

Jewitt, Llewellyn. 'On Ancient Customs and Sports of the County of Derby', *Journal of the British Archaeological Association,* VII (1852), 199–210.
   'On Ancient Customs and Sports of the County of Nottingham', *Journal of the British Archaeological Association,* VIII (1853), 229–40.

Jones, A. *The Art of Playing at Skittles: or, the Laws of Nine-Pins Displayed.* London, 1773.

Jukes, H. A. Lloyd (ed.). *Articles of Enquiry Addressed to the Clergy of the Diocese of Oxford at the Primary Visitation of Dr Thomas Secker, 1738.* Oxfordshire Record Society, XXXVIII, 1957.

Kebbel, T. E. *The Agricultural Labourer.* London, 1870.

Kethe, William. *A Sermon made at Blanford Forum, in the Countie of Dorset.* London, 1571.

Kidd, William J. *Village Wakes; Their Origin, Design and Abuse. A Sermon Preached in the Parochial Chapel of Didsbury, on Sunday Afternoon, August 1, 1841*. Manchester, 1841.

Knox, Vicesimus. 'On the Amusements of Sunday', in his *Essays Moral and Literary*. 2 vols.; 12th edn, London, 1791.

Lawrence, John. *A Philosophical and Practical Treatise on Horses, and on the Moral Duties of Man Towards the Brute Creation*. 2 vols.; London, 1796–8.

A Letter to Lord John Manners, M.P., on his Plea for National Holy-Days, by a Minister of the Holy Catholic Church. London, 1843.

A Letter to the Rev. George Burder, Occasioned by his Sermon on Lawful Amusements. London, 1805.

Litt, W. *Wrestliana; or, An Historical Account of Ancient and Modern Wrestling*. Whitehaven, 1823.

Lovell, Thomas. *A Dialogue between Custom and Veritie concerning the use and abuse of Dauncing and Minstrelsie*. London, n.d.

Macaulay, James. *Essay on Cruelty to Animals*. Edinburgh, 1839.

Mandeville, Bernard. *The Fable of the Bees*. Edited by Phillip Harth. Penguin edn, 1970.

Manners, Lord John. *A Plea for National Holy-Days*. London, 1843.

Mayo, Richard. *A Present for Servants, From Their Ministers, Masters, and Other Friends, Especially in Country Parishes*. London, 1693.

Moore, Thomas. *The Sin and Folly of Cruelty to Brute Animals: A Sermon*. Birmingham, 1810.

Northbrooke, John. *Spiritus est vicarius Christi in terra. A Treatise wherein Dauncing, Vaine plaies or Enterludes with other idle pastimes, etc. commonly used on the Sabboth day, are reprooved*. London, 1597.

Observations on some of the Popular Amusements of this Country, Addressed to the Higher Classes of Society. London, 1827.

Ogilby, John, and William Morgan. *The Traveller's Pocket-Book*. London, 1759 (and numerous later edns).

Oliphant, George H. H. *The Law Concerning Horses, Racing, Wagers and Gaming*. London, 1847.

Oswald, John. *The Cry of Nature; or, An Appeal to Mercy and to Justice, on Behalf of the Persecuted Animals*. London, 1791.

Owen, William. *An Authentic Account . . . of all the Fairs in England and Wales*. London, 1756 (and numerous later edns).

Parkyns, Sir Thomas. *The Inn-Play: or, Cornish-Hugg Wrestler*. 3rd edn, London, 1727.

Pegge, Samuel. 'The Bull-running, at Tutbury, in Staffordshire, considered', *Archaeologia*, II (1773).

Perkins, William. *William Perkins, 1558–1602: English Puritanist. His Pioneer Works on Casuistry: 'A Discourse of Conscience' and 'The Whole Treatise of Cases of Conscience'*. Edited by Thomas F. Merrill. Nieuwkoop, 1966.

A Present for a Servant-Maid: or, The Sure Means of Gaining Love and Esteem. London, 1743.

Primatt, Humphry. *A Dissertation on the Duty of Mercy and Sin of Cruelty to Brute Animals*. London, 1776.

Reflections on Various Subjects Relating to Arts and Commerce. London, 1752.

A Report of the Proceedings at the Annual Meeting of the Association for Promoting Rational Humanity Towards the Animal Creation, Held at Exeter Hall, May 23, 1832. London, 1832.

Roberts, Hugh. *The Day of Hearing*. Oxford, 1600.

Roberts, Humphrey. *An earnest Complaint of divers vain, wicked and abused Exercises, practised on the Saboth day*. London, 1572.

Sandys, William. *Christmas Carols, Ancient and Modern*. London, 1833.

A Sermon Preached to a Large Congregation in the Country, on Old Christmas-Day. London, 1753.

The Servants Calling; With some Advice to the Apprentice. London, 1725.

Skinner, J. *Facts and Opinions Concerning Statute Hirings, Respectfully Addressed to the Landowners, Clergy, Farmers and Tradesmen of the East Riding of Yorkshire*. London, 1861.

Slaney, Robert, A. *Essay on the Beneficial Direction of Rural Expenditure*. London, 1824.

Smith, Abraham. *A Scriptural and Moral Catechism, Designed Chiefly to Lead the Minds of the Rising Generation to the Love and Practice of Mercy, and to Expose the Horrid Nature and Exceeding Sinfulness of Cruelty to the Dumb Creation.* Birmingham, 1833.

Smith, Adam. *An Inquiry into the Nature and Causes of the Wealth of Nations.* Edited by Edwin Cannan. 2 vols.; London, 1950.

Smith, Nicholas. *A Sabbath of Rest to be Kept by the Saints here: or, A Treatise of the Sabbath.* London, 1675.

[Smith, Sidney.] 'Proceedings of the Society for the Suppression of Vice', *Edinburgh Review*, XIII (January 1809), 333–43.

Stephenson, Nash. 'On Statute Fairs: Their Evils and their Remedy', *Transactions of the National Association for the Promotion of Social Science* (1858), pp. 624–31.

Stevenson, Matthew. *The Twelve Moneths; or, A Pleasant and Profitable Discourse of every Action, whether of Labour or Recreation, Proper to each Particular Moneth.* London, 1661.

Stockdale, Percival. *A Remonstrance Against Inhumanity to Animals; and Particularly Against the Savage Practice of Bull-Baiting.* Alnwick, 1802.

Stockwood, John. *A Sermon Preached at Paules Cross on Barthelmew day, being the 24 of August 1578.* London, n.d.

Stot, Joseph. *A Sequel to the Friendly Advice to the Poor of the Town of Manchester.* Manchester, 1756.

Strutt, Joseph. *Glig-Gamena Angel-Deod; or, the Sports and Pastimes of the People of England.* London, 1801.

Stubbes, Phillip. *Phillip Stubbes's Anatomy of the Abuses in England in Shakespere's Youth, A.D. 1583.* Edited by Frederick J. Furnivall. 2 parts; London, 1877–9.

[Temple, William.] *A Vindication of Commerce and the Arts.* London, 1758.

Townsend, Joseph. *A Dissertation on the Poor Laws.* Berkeley and Los Angeles, 1971.

Tucker, Josiah. *An Earnest and Affectionate Address to the Common People of England, Concerning their Usual Recreations on Shrove Tuesday.* London, n.d. Probably published c. 1752–3.

'Instructions for Travellers' (1757), in *Josiah Tucker: A Selection from his Economic and Political Writings.* Edited by Robert L. Schuyler. New York, 1931.

Six Sermons on Important Subjects. Bristol, 1772.

Wilberforce, Robert Isaac, and Samuel Wilberforce. *The Life of William Wilberforce.* 5 vols.; London, 1838.

Winks, J. F. *The Bull Running at Stamford, a Transgression of the Divine Laws, and a Subject of Christian Grief; Being the Substance of a Sermon Delivered in the General Baptist Meeting-House, Stamford, on Lord's Day Evening, Nov. 15, 1829.* London, n.d.

Wood, James. *An Address to the Members of the Methodist Societies, on Several Interesting Subjects.* London, 1799.

Youatt, William. *The Obligation and Extent of Humanity to Brutes, Principally Considered with Reference to the Domesticated Animals.* London, 1839.

Young, Thomas. *An Essay on Humanity to Animals.* London, 1798.

Zouch, Henry. *Hints Respecting the Public Police.* London, 1786.

Local studies

Some Account of the Hamlet of East Burnham, Co. Bucks., by a Late Resident. London, 1858.

Baker, Anne Elizabeth. *Glossary of Northamptonshire Words and Phrases.* 2 vols.; London, 1854.

Barton, B. T. *History of the Borough of Bury and Neighbourhood.* Bury, 1874.

Bedell, E. W. *An Account of Hornsea, in Holderness, in the East-Riding of Yorkshire.* Hull, 1848.

Blakeborough, Richard. *Wit, Character, Folklore and Customs of the North Riding of Yorkshire.* 2nd edn, Salturn-by-the-Sea, 1911.

Borlase, William. *The Natural History of Cornwall.* Oxford, 1758.

Bridges, John. *The History and Antiquities of Northamptonshire.* Compiled by Peter Whalley. 2 vols.; Oxford, 1791.

Burne, Charlotte S. (ed.), *Shropshire Folk-lore: A Sheaf of Gleanings.* London, 1883.

Burton, George. *Chronology of Stamford.* Stamford, 1846.

Burton, George H. (ed.). *Old Lincolnshire, A Pictorial Quarterly Magazine*. Stamford, 1883–5.

Clarkson, Christopher. *The History and Antiquities of Richmond in the County of York*. 2nd edn, Richmond, 1821.

Cole, John. *The History and Antiquities of Weston Favell*. Scarborough, 1827.

Collections Towards a Parochial History of Berkshire. Printed by John Nichols. London, 1783. Included in vol. IV of Nichols's *Bibliotheca Topographica Britannica*. 10 vols.; London, 1780–98.

Couch, Thomas Q. (ed.). *The History of Polperro, by the late Jonathon Couch*. Truro, 1871.

Dawson, W. Harbutt. *History of Skipton*. London, 1882.

Drakard, John. *The History of Stamford*. Stamford, 1822.

Dunkin, John. *The History and Antiquities of Bicester*. London, 1816.

Farey, John. *General View of the Agriculture of Derbyshire*. 3 vols.; London, 1811–17.

Forby, Robert. *The Vocabulary of East Anglia*. 2 vols.; London, 1830.

Gibbs, Robert. *A History of Aylesbury*. Aylesbury, 1885.

Giles, J. A. *History of the Parish and Town of Bampton*. Oxford, 1847.

History of Witney. London, 1852.

Glover, Stephen. *The History and Gazetteer of the County of Derby*. 2 vols.; Derby, 1831.

Housman, John. *A Topographical Description of Cumberland, Westmoreland, Lancashire, and a Part of the West Riding of Yorkshire*. Carlisle, 1800.

Hutchinson, William. *A View of Northumberland*. 2 vols.; Newcastle, 1778.

The History of the County of Cumberland. 2 vols.; Carlisle, 1794.

Jones, John. *The History and Antiquities of Harewood, in the County of York*. London, 1859.

Kennet, White. *Parochial Antiquities Attempted in the History of Ambrosden, Burcester, and other Adjacent Parts in the Counties of Oxford and Bucks*. Oxford, 1695.

Latimer, John. *The Annals of Bristol in the Nineteenth Century*. Bristol, 1887.

Lawson, Joseph. *Letters to the Young on Progress in Pudsey during the Last Sixty Years*. Stanninglen, 1887.

Lucas, John. *John Lucas's History of Warton Parish*. Edited by J. R. Ford and J. A. Fuller-Maitland. London, 1931.

Macaulay, Aulay. *The History and Antiquities of Claybrook, in the County of Leicester*. London, 1791.

MacKinnon, John. *John MacKinnon's Account of Messingham in the County of Lincoln*. Edited by Edward Peacock. Hertford, 1881.

Marshall, William. *The Rural Economy of Norfolk*. 2 vols.; London, 1787.

The Rural Economy of Yorkshire. 2 vols.; London, 1788.

The Rural Economy of the Midland Counties. 2 vols.; London, 1790.

Mastin, John. *The History and Antiquities of Naseby*. Cambridge, 1792.

Moor, Edward. *Suffolk Words and Phrases*. London, 1823.

Mosley, Sir Oswald. *History of the Castle, Priory, and Town of Tutbury*. London, 1832.

Oliver, George. *The History and Antiquities of the Town and Minster of Beverley, in the County of York*. Beverley, 1829.

Pilkington, James. *A View of the Present State of Derbyshire*. 2 vols.; London, 1789.

Pitt, William. *A General View of the Agriculture of the County of Leicester*. London, 1809.

Plot, Robert. *The Natural History of Staffordshire*. Oxford, 1686.

Rudder, Samuel. *A New History of Gloucestershire*. Cirencester, 1779.

Shaw, Stebbing. *The History and Antiquities of Staffordshire*. 2 vols.; London, 1798–1801.

Tate, George. *The History of the Borough, Castle, and Barony of Alnwick*. 2 vols.; Alnwick, 1866–9.

Throsby, John. *Select Views in Leicestershire*. 2 vols.; London, 1790.

Whellan, William. *The History and Topography and the Counties of Cumberland and Westmoreland*. Pontefract, 1860.

Willis, Browne. *The History and Antiquities of the Town, Hundred, and Deanery of Buckingham*. London, 1755.

Young, George. *A History of Whitby*. 2 vols.; Whitby, 1817.

Diaries, journals, memoirs, autobiographies, poetry, and other literary sources

Bamford, Samuel. *The Autobiography of Samuel Bamford*, vol. I: *Early Days*. Edited by W. H. Chaloner. London, 1967.

Barnes, William. *The Poems of William Barnes.* Edited by Bernard Jones. 2 vols.; London, 1962.

Bee, Jacob. 'Diary of Jacob Bee of Durham', in *Six North Country Diaries.* Publications of the Surtees Society, cxviii, 1910.

Bloomfield, Robert. *The Farmer's Boy; A Rural Poem.* 4th edn, London, 1801.

Blundell, Nicholas. *The Great Diurnal of Nicholas Blundell of Little Crosby, Lancashire.* Edited by J. J. Bagley. Transcribed and annotated by Frank Tyrer. 2 vols.; Record Society of Lancashire and Cheshire, 1968–70.

Byng, John. *The Torrington Diaries, Containing the Tours through England and Wales of the Hon. John Byng (Later Fifth Viscount Torrington) between the Years 1781 and 1794.* Edited by C. B. Andrews. 4 vols.; London, 1934–8.

Calverley, Sir Walter. 'Memorandum Book of Sir Walter Calverley, Bart.', in *Yorkshire Diaries and Autobiographies in the Seventeenth and Eighteenth Centuries.* Publications of the Surtees Society, lxxvii, 1886.

Chicken, Edward. *The Collier's Wedding. A Poem.* 2nd. edn, London, 1764.

Clare, John. *The Village Minstrel.* London, 1821.

    The Shepherd's Calendar. Edited by Eric Robinson and Geoffrey Summerfield. London, 1964.

    Clare: Selected Poems and Prose. Edited by Eric Robinson and Geoffrey Summerfield. London, 1966.

Cole, William. *The Blecheley Diary of the Rev. William Cole 1765–67.* Edited by F. G. Stokes. London, 1931.

Defoe, Daniel. *A Tour through the Whole Island of Great Britain.* 2 vols.; London, Everyman edn, 1962.

Duck, Stephen. 'The Thresher's Labour', in his *Poems on Several Subjects.* London, 1730.

Gay, John. *The Shepherd's Week. In Six Pastorals.* London, 1714.

Greene, Joseph. *Correspondence of the Reverend Joseph Greene 1712–1790.* Edited by Levi Fox. London, 1965.

Heywood, Oliver. *The Rev. Oliver Heywood, B.A., 1630–1702; His Autobiography, Diaries, Anecdotes and Event Books.* Edited by J. H. Turner. 4 vols.; Brighouse and Bingley, 1881–5.

Hilman, Daniel. *Tusser Redivivus: Being Part of Mr Thomas Tusser's Five Hundred Points of Husbandry.* London, 1710.

Isham, Thomas. *The Journal of Thomas Isham, of Lamport, in the County of Northampton, 1671–1673.* Edited by Walter Rye. Norwich, 1875.

Kay, Richard. *The Diary of Richard Kay, 1716–1751, of Baldingstone, near Bury: A Lancashire Doctor.* Edited by W. Brockbank and F. Kenworthy. Publications of the Chetham Society, 3rd series, xvi, 1968.

Marshall, Sybil. *Fenland Chronicle.* Cambridge, 1967.

Misson, Henri. *M. Misson's Memoirs and Observations in His Travels over England, with some Account of Scotland and Ireland.* Edited by John Ozell. London, 1719.

Mitford, Mary Russell. *Our Village: Sketches of Rural Character and Scenery.* 5 vols.; London, 1824–32.

Morris, Claver. *The Diary of a West Country Physician 1684–1726.* Edited by Edmund Hobhouse. London, 1934.

Neville, Sylas. *The Diary of Sylas Neville 1767–1788.* Edited by Basil Cozens-Hardy. Oxford, 1950.

Pepys, Samuel. *The Diary of Samuel Pepys.* Edited by Henry B. Wheatley. 8 vols.; London, 1904–5.

Pryme, Abraham de la. *The Diary of Abraham de la Pryme.* Edited by Charles Jackson. Publications of the Surtees Society, liv, 1870.

Purefoy, Henry, and Elizabeth Purefoy. *Purefoy Letters 1735–1753.* Edited by G. Eland. London, 1931.

Saussure, César de. *A Foreign View of England in the Reigns of George I and George II: The Letters of Monsieur César de Saussure to his Family.* Edited by Madame van Muyden. London, 1902.

Sheldrake, William. *A Picturesque Description of Turton Fair, and its Pernicious Consequences. A Poem.* London, 1789.

Smith, William. B. S. Trinder, 'The Memoir of William Smith', *Shropshire Archaeological Society Transactions*, LVIII, part ii (1966), 178–85.

Somerville, William. *Hobbinol, or the Rural Games. A Burlesque Poem, in Blank Verse.* London, 1740.

Spershott, James. *The Memoirs of James Spershott.* Edited by Francis W. Steer. Chichester Papers, no. 30, 1962.

Uffenbach, Zacharias Conrad von. *London in 1710, From the Travels of Zacharias Conrad von Uffenbach.* Edited and translated by W. H. Quarrell and Margaret Mare. London, 1934.

Withers, J. R. 'My Native Village', in *Poems Upon Various Subjects.* 3 vols.; Cambridge and London, 1856–61.

Woodforde, James. *The Diary of a Country Parson: The Reverend James Woodforde.* Edited by John Beresford. 5 vols.; Oxford, 1924–31.

Parliamentary papers

Parliamentary Debates. 1780–1838.

'Report from the Committee on the "Bill to consolidate and amend several Laws relating to the cruel and improper Treatment of Animals . . . "' *Parliamentary Papers*, 1831–2, v.

'Report from the Select Committee on the Observance of the Sabbath Day'. *Parliamentary Papers*, 1831–2, VII.

'Report from the Select Committee on Public Walks'. *Parliamentary Papers*, 1833, xv.

'Report from the Select Committee on the Health of Towns'. *Parliamentary Papers*, 1840, XI.

'Report from the Select Committee on Commons' Inclosure'. *Parliamentary Papers*, 1844, v.

'First Report of the Commissioners for Inquiring into the State of Large Towns and Populous Districts'. *Parliamentary Papers*, 1844, XVII.

'Second Report of the Commissioners for Inquiring into the State of Large Towns and Populous Districts'. *Parliamentary Papers*, 1845, XVIII.

SECONDARY SOURCES

BOOKS

Alexander, Sally. *St Giles's Fair, 1830–1914: Popular Culture and the Industrial Revolution in 19th century Oxford.* Ruskin College History Workshop pamphlet no. 2, 1970.

Bahlman, Dudley W. R. *The Moral Revolution of 1688.* New Haven, Conn., 1957.

Bakhtin, Mikhail. *Rabelais and His World.* Cambridge, Mass., 1968.

Bowen, Rowland. *Cricket: A History of its Growth and Development throughout the World.* London, 1970.

Brailsford, Dennis. *Sport and Society: Elizabeth to Anne.* London and Toronto, 1969.

Brown, A. F. J. *English History from Essex Sources 1750–1900.* Chelmsford, 1952.

Brown, Ford K. *Fathers of the Victorians: The Age of Wilberforce.* Cambridge, 1961.

Buckley, George B. *Fresh Light on 18th Century Cricket: A Collection of 1,000 New Cricket Notices from 1697 to 1800.* Birmingham, 1935.

Fresh Light on Pre-Victorian Cricket: A Collection of New Cricket Notices from 1709 to 1837. Birmingham, 1937.

Burton, Alfred. *Rush-Bearing.* Manchester, 1891.

Caillois, Roger. *Man, Play, and Games.* London, 1962.

Coser, Lewis A. *The Functions of Social Conflict.* London, 1956.

Cox, Robert. *The Literature of the Sabbath Question.* 2 vols.; Edinburgh, 1865.

Dorson, Richard M. *The British Folklorists: A History.* Chicago, 1968.

Douch, H. L. *Old Cornish Inns, and their Place in the Social History of the County.* Truro, 1966.

Dumazedier, Joffre. *Toward a Society of Leisure.* New York, 1967.

Dunning, Eric (ed.). *The Sociology of Sport: A Selection of Readings.* London, 1971.

Fuller, Margaret D. *West Country Friendly Societies.* Reading, 1964.

Furniss, Edgar S. *The Position of the Laborer in a System of Nationalism: A Study in the Labor Theories of the later English Mercantilists*. New York, 1920; repr. 1965.

Goffman, Erving. *Encounters: Two Studies in the Sociology of Interaction*. Indianapolis and New York, 1961.

— *Behavior in Public Places: Notes on the Social Organization of Gatherings*. New York, 1963.

Govett, L. A. *The King's Book of Sports*. London, 1890.

Hackwood, Frederick W. *Old English Sports*. London, 1907.

Hammond, J. L., and Barbara Hammond. *The Age of the Chartists 1832–1854: A Study of Discontent*. London, 1930.

Harrison, Brian. *Drink and the Victorians: The Temperance Question in England 1815–1872*. London, 1971.

— and Barrie Trinder. *Drink and Sobriety in an Early Victorian Town: Banbury 1830–1860*. English Historical Review Supplement 4, 1969.

Hart, A. Tindal. *Country Counting House: The Story of Two Eighteenth-Century Clerical Account Books*. London, 1962.

Hill, Christopher. *Society and Puritanism in Pre-Revolutionary England*. London, 1964.

Hole, Christina. *English Sports and Pastimes*. London, 1949.

Huizinga, J. *Homo Ludens: A Study of the Play-Element in Culture*. London, 1949.

Hunt, C. J. *The Lead Miners of the Northern Pennines in the Eighteenth and Nineteenth Centuries*. Manchester, 1970.

Hunter, Sir Robert. *The Preservation of Open Spaces, and of Footpaths and other Rights of Way*. London, 1902.

Jaeger, Muriel. *Before Victoria: Changing Standards and Behaviour 1787–1837*. Penguin edn, 1967.

Lennard, Reginald (ed.). *Englishmen at Rest and Play: Some Phases of English Leisure 1558–1714*. Oxford, 1931.

Loftis, John. *Comedy and Society from Congreve to Fielding*. Stanford, 1959.

Magoun, Francis P., Jr. *History of Football from the Beginnings to 1871*. Bochum-Langendreer, 1938.

Marples, Morris. *A History of Football*. London, 1954.

Merton, Robert K. *On Theoretical Sociology: Five Essays, Old and New*. New York, 1967.

Mingay, G. E. *English Landed Society in the Eighteenth Century*. London and Toronto, 1963.

Pimlott, J. A. R. *Recreations*. London, 1968. In the series *A Visual History of Modern Britain*, edited by Jack Simmons.

Pollard, Sidney. *The Genesis of Modern Management*. London, 1965.

Porter, Enid. *Cambridgeshire Customs and Folklore*. London, 1969.

Quinlan, Maurice J. *Victorian Prelude: A History of English Manners 1700–1830*. New York, 1941; repr. 1965.

Radzinowicz, Leon. *A History of English Criminal Law and its Administration from 1750*. 4 vols.; London, 1948–69.

Reid, J. C. *Bucks and Bruisers: Pierce Egan and Regency England*. London, 1971.

Rosenfeld, Sybil. *The Theatre of the London Fairs in the 18th Century*. Cambridge, 1960.

Thomas, Keith. *Religion and the Decline of Magic*. London, 1971.

Thompson, E. P. *The Making of the English Working Class*. Penguin edn, 1968.

Walford, Cornelius. *Fairs, Past and Present*. London, 1883.

Walzer, Michael. *The Revolution of the Saints: A Study in the Origins of Radical Politics*. Cambridge, Mass., 1965.

Webb, Sidney, and Beatrice Webb. *The History of Liquor Licensing in England, Principally from 1700 to 1830*. London, 1903.

Whistler, Laurence. *The English Festivals*. London, 1947.

Whitaker, W. B. *The Eighteenth-Century English Sunday: A Study of Sunday Observance from 1677 to 1837*. London, 1940.

Whitfield, Christopher (ed.). *Robert Dover and the Cotswold Games: Annalia Dubrensia*. London, 1962.

Wiles, R. M. *Freshest Advices: Early Provincial Newspapers in England*. Columbus, Ohio, 1965.

Wright, A. R. *British Calendar Customs*. Edited by T. E. Lones. 3 vols.; London, 1936–40.

ESSAYS AND ARTICLES

Barnes, Thomas G. 'County Politics and a Puritan Cause Célèbre: Somerset Churchales, 1633'. *Transactions of the Royal Historical Society*, 5th series, IX (1959), 103–22.

Briffault, Robert. 'Festivals'. *Encyclopaedia of the Social Sciences*, VI, 198–200.

Coats, A. W. 'Changing Attitudes to Labour in the Mid-Eighteenth Century'. *Economic History Review*, 2nd series, XI (1958–9), 35–51.

Craven, Ida. 'Public Amusements'. *Encyclopaedia of the Social Sciences*, II, 39–46.

Cuming, E. D. 'Sports and Games', in *Johnson's England*, edited by A. S. Turberville. 2 vols.; Oxford, 1933.

Davidson, Thomas. 'Plough Rituals in England and Scotland'. *Agricultural History Review*, VII (1959), 27–37.

Dumazedier, Joffre. 'Leisure'. *International Encyclopaedia of the Social Sciences*, IX, 248–53.

Dunning, E. G. 'The Evolution of Football'. *New Society*, 30 April 1964.

Elias, Norbert, and Eric Dunning. 'Dynamics of Group Sports with Special Reference to Football'. *British Journal of Sociology*, XVII (1966), 388–402.

Giddens, A. 'Notes on the Concepts of Play and Leisure'. *Sociological Review*, New series, XII (1964), 73–89.

Harrison, Brian. 'Religion and Recreation in Nineteenth-Century England'. *Past & Present*, no. 38 (December 1967), 98–125.

Ketton-Cremer, R. W. 'Camping – a forgotten Norfolk Game'. *Norfolk Archaeology*, XXIV (1932), 88–92.

Leach, E. R. 'Two Essays Concerning the Symbolic Representation of Time', in his *Rethinking Anthropology*. London, 1961.

McKendrick, Neil. 'Josiah Wedgwood and Factory Discipline'. *Historical Journal*, IV (1961), 30–55.

Manning, Percy. 'Sport and Pastime in Stuart Oxford'. *Oxford Historical Society*, LXXV (1923), 83–125.

Owst, G. R. 'The People's Sunday Amusements in the Preaching of Mediaeval England'. *Holborn Review*, N.S. XVII (January 1926), 32–45.

Phythian-Adams, Charles. 'Ceremony and the citizen: The communal year at Coventry', in Peter Clark and Paul Slack (eds.), *Crisis and order in English towns 1500–1700: Essays in urban history*. London, 1972.

Pollard, Sidney. 'Factory Discipline in the Industrial Revolution'. *Economic History Review*, 2nd series, XVI (1963–4), 254–71.

Redlich, Fritz. 'Leisure-Time Activities: A Historical, Sociological, and Economic Analysis'. *Explorations in Entrepreneurial History*, 2nd series, III (Autumn 1965), 3–24.

Thomas, Keith. 'Work and Leisure in Pre-Industrial Society'. *Past & Present*, no. 29 (December 1964), 50–62.

Thompson, E. P. 'Time, Work-Discipline, and Industrial Capitalism'. *Past & Present*, no. 38 (December 1967), 56–97.

Wiles, R. M. 'Crowd-Pleasing Spectacles in Eighteenth-Century England'. *Journal of Popular Culture*, I (Autumn 1967), 90–105.

'Work and Leisure in Industrial Society: Conference Report'. *Past & Present*, no. 30 (April 1965), 96–103.

THESES

Allan, Kenneth. 'The Recreations and Amusements of the Industrial Working Class, in the Second Quarter of the Nineteenth Century, with Special Reference to Lancashire'. Unpubl. M.A. thesis, University of Manchester, 1947.

Dunning, E. G. 'Early Stages in the Development of Football as an Organized Game'. Unpubl. M.A. thesis, University of Leicester, 1961.

Ellis, George Mark. 'The Evangelicals and the Sunday Question, 1830–1860: Organized Sabbatarianism as an Aspect of the Evangelical Movement'. Unpubl. Ph.D. thesis, Harvard University, 1951.

Harrison, Brian H. 'The Temperance Question in England: 1828–1869'. Unpubl. D.Phil. thesis, Oxford University, 1965.

Rule, John Graham. 'The Labouring Miner in Cornwall c.1740–1870: A Study in Social History'. Unpubl. Ph.D. thesis, University of Warwick, 1971.

Smith, Morris Brooke. 'The Growth and Development of Popular Entertainment and Pastimes in the Lancashire Cotton Towns 1830–1870'. Unpubl. M.Litt. thesis, University of Lancaster, 1970.

Stigant, E. P. 'Methodism and the Working Class, 1760–1821: A Study in Social and Political Conflict'. Unpubl. M.A. thesis, University of Keele, 1968.

Index